List of Illustrations

Figure	Caption	Page
1-1	Why another EMDR protocol?	1
1-2	Standard EMDR therapy	2
1-3	Conference room (dissociative table)	6
2-1	Attuned mother-child relationship is the basis of healthy self	9
2-2	Panksepp's affective brain processing	11
2-3	Pankseppian affective brain processing levels in baby	12
2-4	Right hemisphere holds unprocessed trauma, emotions, somatic sensation, implicit memory, attachment relationships	13
2-5	Emotional and somatic flashbacks are nuances of memory wafting from implicit memory, like vapors leaking up from King Tut's tomb	15
2-6	Nightmares are evidence of the brain's failed attempt to process disturbing memories in REM sleep	16
3-1	Unprocessed and unintegrated traumatic experience held in disparate sequestered neural networks or ego states/alter personalities frozen at the time of trauma	20
3-2	Once processed in temporal sequence, networks can be linked and integrated and missed developmental milestones achieved	20
4-1	As in house painting, preparation is everything and makes the work go easier and faster	23
4-2	When the processing capacity is too small for the volume of material to process, the EMDR therapy can't complete normally	24
4-3	When the processing capacity is greater than the volume of material to process, the EMDR therapy can complete normally	25
5-1	ISST&D Treatment Guidelines—3rd edition addressed the safe use of EMDR therapy in complex cases	27
5-2	For highly dissociative clients, much more preparation is likely needed prior to temporal integration	28
5-3	The child introjects the point of view of the perpetrator, the locus of identification with the aggressor	29
5-4	A keystone intervention to stabilize clients is to work with perpetrator introject parts of self, to reduce loyalty to the aggressor.	31
5-5	Before attempting temporal integration, in cases of DID, appreciation, orientation, and consent of the "honchos" is extremely important.	32
5-6	Looking at something "over there," adds objectivity, which brings neocortical resources to bear	33

5-7	De-conflictualizing the relationship between self-states increases inner peace and stability, making energy and resources available	34
5-8	The client's sympathetic nervous system can be activated by slow motion fight or flight responses, with careful resistance where appropriate for complex cases—here the resistance requires no touch	35
5-9	Cooperative alters will quickly stand aside, but ego state maneuvers will be needed to enlist the cooperation of the fierce protective parts who came into existence early in life to protect the same small child by identifying with the aggressor	37
6-1	Tactical maneuvers needed in preparation for temporal integration	39
6-2	Targeting in standard EMDR therapy aims at the elements of trauma held in explicit memory: picture, cognition, emotion and body sensation	40
6-3	Targeting in the early trauma approach, by time frame, from the beginning	41
6-4	Because there are no cognitions in implicit memory, we capture them as they emerge during processing of implicit memory	42
7-1	Containment imagery helps fractionate the target to titrate intensity	45
7-2	Having one alter "looking through the eyes" at a time also fractionates the work in complex trauma/dissociation	46
7-3	It's important to keep the level of activation within the optimal arousal window, neither hyper nor hypo aroused (Siegel, 1999).	47
7-4	With practice, the client can use an imaginal rheostat to down-regulate emotion	47
7-5	When containment strategies are well practiced, the client can do the work and remain in the optimal arousal zone, not too hot (sympathetic arousal), not too cold (dorsal vagal shutdown), but just right (Paulsen calls this Porges porridge theory).	48
7-6	Memories can be fractionated by many dimensions including by alter/ego state, BASK channel, time fragment or other ways.	49
7-7	As in beadwork, temporal integration is detailed and nuanced, requiring a "clear desktop" free of distractions in the client's mind	50
7-8	Containment strategies will be helpful in closing down incomplete sessions or sessions where ego state work has touched on traumatic memories	51
8-1	Learning to evoke a felt sense of safety or "safe state"	55
8-2	The therapeutic relationship itself may activate the client's ventral vagal nervous system, especially if, gently, over time, they share life-enhancing experiences, so the client learns ways to stay in the window of tolerance.	58
8-3	Usually, even those without a formal religious frame of reference or spiritual understanding can activate their ventral vagal nervous system in nature	59
8-4	Highly dissociative people feel as if they have no body	62
8-5	"Whose hand is that?" can orient parts to the body they actually live in	63

9-1	Affect regulation, health and resilience is learned in the reliable presence of mother in the moment-to-moment attunement	69
9-2	Chronic opioid activation may manifest as "Raggedy Ann eyes" or that far away "spaced out" look	70
9-3	SHAME is a deep brain function, a switching off of the neocortex at the circuit breaker, when it's necessary to forsake one's own point of view to adopt the other's	70
9-4	The Pankseppian three levels of affective processing in the brain	72
9-5	The affective circuits are integrated at the periaqueductal gray	73
9-6	The SEEKing circuit is the mother of all circuits according to Panksepp (1998)	74
9-7	When SEEKing is suppressed, life is suppressed	76
9-8	Conditioned responses at the time of trauma can wire together circuits that are otherwise unrelated, in over-coupled responses	77
9-9	The PLAY circuit activates more of the brain than any other circuit	78
9-10	The PANIC and CARE circuits are evolutionary bookends, mother and child, the chicken and egg	78
9-11	The CARE circuit is typically stronger in the female, but not always	80
9-12	Some children are parentified to meet the unmet dependency needs of their parents, which causes life-long symptoms in the child	81
9-13	The FEAR circuit, involved in flight, and in surrender, is a defensive circuit. Adrenalin is stimulated in sympathetic arousal, and if flight, or fight, is not possible, then surrender and dorsal vagal shutdown is the remaining path	82
9-14	The RAGE circuit is a defensive circuit, powered by adrenalin, which activates the sympathetic nervous system response to prepare us for fight	82
10-1	The brain's capacity for visualization allows us to create repair, in imagination, that provides the biochemical "marinade" that the brain has waited for all these years	85
10-2	Imagination is a uniquely human function of the neo-mammalian brain. Visualizing what is needed to have a different outcome enables the client to obtain a biochemical wash of the "marinade" of what they want on their own terms	86
10-3	In the resetting-the-circuits process, the client's neocortical capacity is utilized to look at each emotion with objectivity, and without the subjective felt sense; this enables the circuit to process without an affective load on it, the same way an electrician turns off the circuit breaker before tinkering with electrical circuits	89
11-1	Resetting the Pankseppian hardwired affective circuits so the emotional information can freely flow through them during processing	91
11-2	Typically after circuit resetting, the client feels more calm, though an exception might be when feeling calm is startling; it's important for the therapist to keep the client in objectivity, lest subjectivity evoke premature trauma processing	94

11-3	Once the circuits are available for information without reactivity, the client can better sit in the felt sense of the body and emotion during trauma processing, later in the work	96
11-4	When the circuits are not horizontally integrated in the attachment period, state-dependent learning accumulates vertically in columns, which manifest as alter personalities	97
11-5	In the Pankseppian formulation, the first affective processing level is the hardwired subcortical circuits, the second affective processing level is object-relations learning and relationship templates, including introjection, and the third affective processing level is the neo-cortical, which includes all other affective learning	99
11-6	When the client is locked into toxic shame, the solution might be the objectivity interweave, "let's imagine someone you don't know, in Pocatello, in a similar situation"	102
11-7	When presented with a similar situation viewed with objectivity, instead of the shame held in subjectivity, the client can often see that the child is always innocent	103
11-8	After resetting the circuits, the client will still experience emotional variations, but the baseline or "idle" will be lower, in most cases	104
11-9	The hardest part of resetting the circuits, for many, is to look at each emotion with objectivity, and not slide in to subjectivity; the therapist advises the client to hang on to the birch tree on the river bank, and watch the river flow by, without sliding in	105
11-10	The client views each emotion with objectivity, and without the felt subjective sense of the emotion, processing with bilateral stimulation until the image becomes positive or neutral and/or stops changing	108
11-11	For highly dissociative clients, it may be necessary to reset the safety systems for fight, flight, freeze and connect, before resetting the individual emotional circuits, to increase client comfort with the amygdala alarm system and with their nervous system overall	109
11-12	When babies don't have help down-regulating their emotions, they have no choice but to "clip their dashboard wires" and dissociate their experience; this is like switching off the circuit at the circuit breaker	114
12-1	In temporal integration, the trauma from the earliest years is cleared by reviewing it by time frame from the beginning of the life time line	122
12-2	When the target is too large for the client's capacity, it's like trying to three-hole punch too many pages at a time, gumming up the works; instead, we right-size the target by fractionating within the client's capacity	123
12-3	When trauma is cleared in sequential time segments from the beginning, integration occurs bottom up	124
12-4	Temporal integration works directly on the deeper structures of the brain's affective processing, including the secondary affective processing level, reconfiguring object relations, in conjunction with ego state therapy, somatic therapy and EMDR therapy	125

12-5	The standard protocol when applied to implicitly held trauma from infancy can produce overwhelm, if the work isn't paced and targets are large or undefined	125
12-6	One of the key benefits of the early trauma approach is that it is systematic and targeting can be titrated to prevent overwhelm	126
12-7	Processing very early trauma by sequential time segment is like hole punching a few pages at a time instead of fifty, which gums up the works	127
12-8	When infants are exposed to high levels of stress early in life, they can be primed for chronic high levels of arousal, dissociation, and endogenous opioids	130
12-9	When working in implicit memory, maintaining dual-attention awareness of the "then" and the "now" is challenging because there is no picture or narrative as there would be when processing an explicit memory; traumatic transference or reenactments emerge in the relationship field to tell the untold story	131
12-10	The therapist's mirror neurons and clinical intuition can apperceive information in the energy/ relationship field to hear the story in the non-verbals	132
12-11	Very commonly, people think their present mood is from present matters, but often, it's really from unprocessed memories, leaking up from implicit memory and wrongly associated with a current trigger	133
12-12	As first the therapist and then the client hear the baby's unspoken story through the non-verbals, the symptoms, which are shrines to that story, remit; this is the "catch and release program."	133
13-1	The primary task is for the therapist to hear the story as it's told in the non-verbals, for the first time ever, so the symptoms can finally remit	135
13-2	EMDR therapy targeting in the early trauma approach involves selecting time segments of the right size or "bite size" and digestible by the client's capacity to process	140
13-3	Because the target memory is implicitly held without narrative or picture, the negative and positive cognitions are captured as they emerge in the processing	142
13-4	Six p-p-pearls that characterize good positive cognitions	143
13-5	Tiny shoes, wordlessly presented, will confront the client with the truth that s/he was an innocent child	145
13-6	All-points bulletin to the far corners of the self-system	146
13-7	Imaginal repair with DAS/BLS	147
13-8	Orienting to present circumstances	150
14-1	Expect the unexpected	151
14-2	Every session using ego state maneuvers must include a closure procedure	153
14-3	Tulips coming together bottom up	154
14-4	Lavishly providing what the brain has been waiting for all these years	156
14-5	All I need is a dry crust of bread.	157

14-6	The emergence of a headache is a signal of approach avoidance or a conflicted self; usually the remedy is to address the "honchos", often perpetrator introjects, which keep the perpetrator's secrets for survival	160
14-7	We ask the older parts of self to hold apart their memories until the time is right, but we will take the theme and see if it applies to baby's story	161
14-8	Doing EMDR therapy without permission from the "honchos" that guard the core of self, the baby, is inviting trouble and decompensation; however, when asked if the therapist can help the baby, the honchos will often stand aside	162
14-9	It is key for the therapist to get the introjects on board with the work before and during processing to reduce resistance, especially loyalty to the aggressor	163
14-10	Adding ego energy by speaking directly to a part adds a spotlight of focus and energy to the aspect in question, a powerful tool in the therapeutic armamentarium	167
14-11	"Imagine a family we don't know, not your family, in Pocatello," for neocortical objectivity	168
14-12	The therapist should use somatic micro-movements for DID clients cautiously and only after obtaining agreement from the honchos for client empowerment	169
14-13	Somatic micro-movements can allow thwarted sympathetic arousal (fight/flight) to be released, facilitated with attenuated resistance, where appropriate	170
14-14	Clients often stop micro-movements prematurely, but the release generally occurs with full extension, and a time of holding the full power position	171
14-15	For many highly dissociative clients, touch is clinically contraindicated; but a therapist can sit on a footstool for resistance, so the client can push with the feet, when able to tolerate the felt sense of sympathetic arousal (after the introjects are on board)	171
14-16	When stuck, the therapist asks the older alters what she is missing in hearing baby's story	173
14-17	Review, release and repair, review, release, repair, review, release, repair	174
14-18	Tucking in alters who processed or helped includes appreciating them and acknowledging that work is progressing even when incomplete	175
14-19	The therapist avoids "bossing around" the honchos/perpetrator introjects, but kindly points out that there is a ranger station on the horizon and a comfortable cot and binoculars, in case they are weary from their burden	176
15-1	Baby was alone in a world with no people. Once we hear the story, with resonant attunement, the symptoms will remit. This time baby is not alone.	182
B-1	ISST&D Treatment Guidelines caution against long sessions except, rarely, for special procedures	194
B-2	To orient to body, ask a part to peek through the eyes, and say, "whose hands are those? The girls? Or the mother's?"	195
C-1	Clients typically experience perpetrator introjects as "monstrous," though they may not appear in the mind's eye as a monster, per se	197

Acknowledgements

Katie O'Shea, M.S. — This work memorializes and expands on the contributions of Katie O'Shea, who developed the original four steps of the early trauma approach. She brought the method to my attention in 2005 because of my work with ego states and dissociation, and invited me to contribute to the application of the early trauma approach on the more complex cases.

I have attempted to note in the text those places where her language is used and where mine is used. If there are omissions they are inadvertent, and if there is an ambiguity about the origin of a particular recommended language for one of the four original steps, the reader can assume that the language is Katie's unless I have indicated otherwise. The language for use with complex trauma is mine, as are the ego state and somatic language, where offered, and any theoretical postulates not otherwise attributed. Future work will reflect the full degree to which my own work has evolved to incorporate somatic and other elements, while this book serves to document the O'Shea approach, plus its elaboration for complex cases, with the intention of remaining true to its origin to honor O'Shea's contribution.

Ulrich Lanius, Ph.D. — I want to acknowledge my longstanding collaboration also with Ulrich Lanius, with whom I've enjoyed many hours of brainstorming and theoretical musings which fueled our publications, but which also supported this work.

Frank Corrigan, M.D. — Our Scottish colleague, Frank Corrigan, MD, has recently joined Ulrich in guiding this cartooning psychologist with their massive understanding of neurobiology. I am very grateful for Frank's brilliant sensibilities.

Jaak Panksepp, Ph.D. — I'm especially grateful for the time I spent with the world's premier affective neuroscientist, Jaak Panksepp, in 2009, which he has described in part in the preface he wrote to the Lanius, Paulsen, Corrigan (2014) book and in his own book (Panksepp & Biven, 2012). I have had the opportunity in repeated conversations to "pick the brain" of this lovely and brilliant man who has elucidated concepts that otherwise escaped me. His definitive experimental study of affective neuroscience is bedrock foundational to my understanding of how best to approach processing very early trauma.

D. Michael Coy, M.A. — I also wish to acknowledge D. Michael Coy, M.A., who is familiar with both my teaching and Katie's teaching, for his review of the draft of the book. He began as a consultee, became a protégé in the all the methods I use and teach, and now emerges as a trusted colleague.

Katy Murray, MSW — Katy Murray contributed a valuable late review of portions of the book related to how this approach compares with the standard protocol of EMDR, for which I am most grateful.

Jim Hermanson — I wish to thank my husband, Jim Hermanson, for his patient attention and care during the countless weekends spent at home while I wrote, when we could have been out playing and exploring the wilds. His kind and patient ministrations and wonderful cooking have sustained me through many challenging hours. Additionally, and extraordinarily, he performed several last minute saves on file problems, careful proofreading, and other labors of love without which this book would not have launched.

Other Contributors Yogita Aggarwal has been indispensable in assisting with checking references and their formatting. Finally, I wish to acknowledge Cindi Paulsen, for her careful proofreading and copy editing of the entirety of the book, and Nicola Bain for her earlier reading and comments.

1 Introduction: Why is the Early Trauma Approach Necessary?

1-1 Why another EMDR protocol?

(O'Shea, 2009, 2001, 2003a, 2003b, 2006) and O'Shea & Paulsen (2007) have described the use of the early trauma (ET) approach to solve the problems associated with using the standard approach to address early trauma for non-dissociative clients with early trauma or neglect. In fact, both the author and O'Shea construe this approach as consistent with the standard protocol of EMDR, but with procedures added to make it systemic and efficient for the early time frame.

Purpose This book has several purposes:

- To describe the ET approach in greater depth than elsewhere.

- To provide a theoretical introduction to the ET approach, framing it in both psychological and neurobiological context.

- To describe the modifications to the preparatory steps and the trauma processing step of the ET approach and the extra steps that are needed when using it with dissociative clients.

- To make comprehensible a theoretical and practical approach to integration here referred to as temporal integration (Paulsen & Lanius, 2009) for highly dissociative and complex trauma clients.

When There Are No Words - Sandra Paulsen

Overview   We'll begin by describing:

- The standard EMDR therapy protocol to trauma processing, and the challenges of using it when applied to very early trauma, neglect and attachment injuries

- What's different about very early trauma that occurs in the attachment period, including neurobiological considerations related to traumatic experience and brain development, as well as the implications of those considerations for the treatment of early trauma

- The elements of the ET approach for non-dissociative clients

- The application of ET to more complex and dissociative cases, including modifications that use ego state or somatic maneuvers

- Particular specifics of mechanics, session structure, and how to conduct intensive treatment sessions ethically

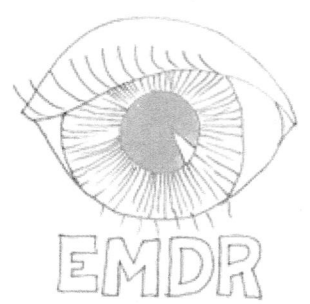

1-2 Standard EMDR therapy

About EMDR therapy's standard procedure   Eye movement desensitization and reprocessing (EMDR) therapy has been used as a treatment for trauma since 1987, utilizing an approach that targets experiences accessible in explicit memory (Shapiro, 2001).

In the standard EMDR therapy protocol, whenever possible, the client identifies seven different aspects of a consciously recalled, unresolved traumatic memory:

- a mental image or picture that represents the most disturbing aspect (worst part) of the memory;

- a negative, self-referencing cognition (NC) that accompanies this 'worst part' of the memory;

- a desired positive cognition (PC) that contrasts with the negative cognition;

- a scaled measure of the feeling of 'trueness' of this desired cognition);

- the disturbing affect associated with the memory (emotion);

- a measure of the emotional and somatic intensity accompanying the worst part of the memory;

- and the location of corollary body sensations.

In the standard EMDR therapy approach, a careful manualized process is used to process the traumatic memory to an adaptive resolution. On reassessment, once the processing is complete, the original (often vivid) traumatic memory seems less immediate, and either more distant, or positive, or just 'part of a story' rather than fragmented, intrusive, and painful. Additionally, the positive cognition feels entirely true, absent the disturbances that previously prevented it from feeling so.

The challenge of using EMDR therapy with implicit memory

As is evident from that procedure, having an avenue of access to the memory in the form of a picture and cognition associated with it is necessary. Although EMDR therapy may sometimes be used in the absence of those requisite elements, e.g., utilizing dreamlike images or a symbolic picture representing an issue rather than a memory of an event, the use of an explicit memory is the prototypic application of EMDR therapy. The standard EMDR approach does permit processing in the absence of cognitive, narrative, or image elements, if it is not possible to identify them.

Cleaving as closely as possible to standard protocol

Both Katie O'Shea and Sandra Paulsen were EMDR Institute facilitators since the early 1990s, and EMDR International Association certified consultants since that category was established. We both have great appreciation for the importance of adherence to the EMDR therapy approach wherever possible. Therefore, in our collaboration, both have earnestly and meticulously ensured that the ET approach cleaves to the standard approach where it can. Primary example: though initially there is no narrative or picture memory and therefore no negative or positive cognitions can be worked up prior to processing, we capture them as they emerge, for installation, for checking the work, and later, when appropriate, for generalizing by use of future template when that becomes possible.

Efficacy of EMDR therapy:

Numerous controlled studies have found EMDR therapy to be efficacious in the treatment of post-traumatic stress, and case studies report its broader use with a range of applications. See www.emdr.com or www.emdria.org for a review of research.

Big T Trauma

The prototypic application is with traumatic experience associated with shock trauma, that is, an experience that is life threatening or otherwise outside the realm of normal human experience, which is referred to as "big T" trauma in EMDR parlance.

Shock trauma is a severe event that causes, typically, an adrenaline response with flight, flight or, if neither fight nor flight is possible, a freeze response. It is also, however, used with "small t" trauma, namely those experiences that are not life threatening or even overwhelming, but rather may have resulted in maladaptive life lessons being learned. In such cases, there might not be the same level of disturbance or fight/flight/freeze reaction.

Adaptive information processing theory

- Adaptive information processing (AIP) theory explains EMDR therapy's effect by positing that at the time of trauma, information that can't be processed at the time is set aside in neural networks where it remains trapped in the nervous system in its raw uncatalyzed form (Shapiro, 2001).

- EMDR therapy accesses such a neural network containing that raw traumatic information, catalyzes the brain's innate information processing system, and enables the experience to be processed to an adaptive resolution.

- In big T traumas, there is certainly an expectation of finding a visual image and cognition to represent the most disturbing aspect of the memory, to serve as the treatment target.

- In small t traumas, the most salient disturbing picture representing the issue or memory is still required, though it might be more symbolic, to access the neural network.

- In either case, the client processes through the material cognitively, with imagery, emotions, body sensations.

- The therapist occasionally checks progress by returning to target, if status is unclear or when the end of a channel of information has been reached.

- In sum, the standard EMDR therapy approach in its prototypic form focuses on the explicit memory for targeting, and assessing progress of the work. It can however be modified as in the Early Trauma approach to work in implicit memory.

Challenges of using EMDR therapy with very early trauma

Explicit memory (episodic subtype) refers to an autobiographical memory of events of one's life and imagining of events in the future. That capacity is not found in babies and young children and is only found in the human species. There lies the challenge of trying to apply EMDR therapy to attachment injuries or complex trauma cases, in which early attachment injury is part of the substrate (Barach, 1991).

Early experience is held in the right hemisphere in implicit memory, and is not subject to direct recall in the way that one can recall explicit memory (A. Schore, 2009).

Implicit memory can be accessed upon turning attention to the felt sense (Levine, 2010, 1997) which is held by the right hemisphere of the brain (A. Schore, 2001).

However, the territory is murkier working in the absence of cognitive milestones, and it is challenging to obtain Subjective Units of Distress (SUD) levels for experience implicitly held, and nearly impossible to assess cognitions and VOC levels. In short, standard EMDR therapy is silent on how to systematically access and process information in implicit memory for very early trauma.

Although some writers have identified strategies for processing early experience (e.g.,(Kitchur, 2009), the mysteriousness and vagueness of very early experience leaves it outside the realm of what can be easily or systematically addressed. This vagueness means that attachment-injured individuals have a hard time remediating and clearing their disturbances with EMDR therapy.

Challenges of using EMDR therapy for complex trauma and dissociation

The challenges of using EMDR therapy for complex trauma and dissociative clients have been well known for two decades (C. G. Fine & Berkowitz, 2001; Sandra Paulsen, 1995, 2014; SL Paulsen, 2009a), because the potential for affective overwhelm and flooding must be closely managed. Abreaction (extremely strong emotional release) can occur.

Although practitioners of EMDR therapy should not avoid the unavoidable abreactions that may occur, and are advised to simply hold the course for non-dissociative clients, with highly dissociative clients, communication must be reliable enough to ensure that the client is not being retraumatized by the intensity. If the material is resolving and symptoms improving, the intensity is not too great.

If the client is abreacting but the material isn't resolving and the client is getting worse, the work is retraumatizing and must be done differently.

Although EMDR therapy can often process through such intensity, sometimes the intensity is too great for the client to stay in the process, or to maintain the requisite dual-attention awareness required for successful EMDR therapy (awareness of being in the office at the same time as being in the memory).

Moreover, in complex trauma and dissociative disorders, the client's defenses will commonly prevent standard EMDR therapy from completing normally. This can result in at best incomplete EMDR therapy, and at worst, can precipitate a suicidal crisis, an increase in suffering, or destruction of needed dissociative defenses rendering the client defenseless.

For these reasons, Paulsen has, since 1992, cautioned that EMDR therapy should never be conducted unless the therapist has proactively determined that the client is not highly dissociative, or if they are, that EMDR therapy not be conducted unless an appropriately modified approach is used in which the therapist is trained and experiences (Paulsen, 2009a, 2009b, 2014).

Conveyed in gray boxes throughout this book

Any such approach will need to use a fractionated (Richard P. Kluft, 1993) approach for affect titration purposes, in addition to extended preparation and suitable ego state maneuvers at various stages and as interweaves.

The early trauma approach described in this book can be used, also in a modified form, in conjunction with ego state and somatic approaches, with dissociative individuals, with all clinical cautions in place. **Those modifications have been inserted in the text in gray boxes.**

Extensive portions of the temporal integration step are organized separately to describe modifications of trauma processing needed for dissociative clients, so the "gray box" goes on for many pages. But first, the basis for the use of the early trauma approach of EMDR therapy will be described here.

Criteria for a therapy for early trauma

Fosha (2000) described four criteria that a therapy must have if it purports to be able to treat early trauma. They are:

1) the ability to secure the client's felt sense of safety in the therapy relationship,

2) the therapist's capacity and willingness to engage in "hard emotional work" with the client,

3) a means of working with defensive responses associated with fight and flight on a direct basis in order to obtain access to the emotional states that the client may fear that they cannot bear,

4) tactics for working with emotions that do not overwhelm and retraumatize the client, in order that the client can integrate the experience and achieve "coherence" (Siegel, 2015).

The ET approach and criteria for repairing early trauma

The ET approach accommodates all four of the Fosha criteria because it includes, in its basic form,

a) containment strategies that enable the work to be fractionated and paced, which keeps the client from being overwhelmed with extreme sympathetic arousal,

b) directly focuses on engaging the client's ventral vagal/social engagement system with resourcing and somatic empathy and other considerations,

c) clears the affective circuits so processing can complete while minimizing blockages and decreasing arousal, which minimizes defensive responses,

d) systematically accesses and processes trauma held in implicit memory to an adaptive resolution, with a systematic approach that negates the requirement for mileposts in explicit memory,

e) ensures clients have the felt sense of getting their needs met on their own terms, meeting developmental milestones in preparation for subsequent work,

f) clears early trauma by fraction of time, which, by it systematic approach, makes it possible to tell where in the work one is. With complex cases, there often need to be additional use of ego state procedures to reduce defensive processes and/or somatic work to work directly with the experiential aspects of fight/flight responses and to enable the client to have the felt sense of embodiment.

History of the early trauma approach

Katie O'Shea (O'Shea, 2009, 2001, 2003b) initially developed what she called the Early Trauma protocol of EMDR therapy as an offshoot of several contributors including, but not limited to:

- Sandra Paulsen's ego state work (e.g., 1992, 1993a,b,c, 1995, 2014, 2009b)
- Maureen Kitchur's strategic development model (Kitchur, 2009)
- Joan Lovett's story telling approach (Lovett, 2007)
- Landry Wildwind's early repair for anaclitic depression (Wildwind, 1992)
- Phyllis Klaus's work with neonates and mothers, (Klaus & Klaus, 2000)

1-3 Conference room (dissociative table–Fraser).
(This figure originally appears in Paulsen, 2009, "Looking Through the Eyes" book.)

Paulsen brought ego state therapy to EMDR practice in 1992

Paulsen had first presented on the combination of EMDR therapy and ego state therapy in 1992. An early part II training handout from Honolulu (Paulsen, 1992) was distributed widely by an EMDR therapy trainer in EMDR circles, causing Paulsen's seminal contribution integrating EMDR, ego state work and the dissociative table (Fraser, 1991), also called "conference room technique," to become widely dispersed within EMDR circles, but without citation. Paulsen also presented on ego state maneuvers and EMDR therapy at the International Society for the Study of Multiple Personality Dissociation conference (Paulsen, 1993a, 1993b) describing the need to resource clients by bringing the self-system collaboratively into the work. Similarly, this work was presented at the Honolulu Psychology Association (Paulsen, 1993) and at the 2nd International Conference for EMDR (Paulsen, 1993a, and 1993b).

The earliest contribution by Paulsen in integrating EMDR and ego state work was in a handout created in 1992 for an EMDR Part II training in Honolulu, which handout was subsequently taken and distributed widely without citation).

Paulsen influenced O'Shea directly in the early 2000s with her use of ego state work to conduct EMDR therapy for not only dissociative clients but non-dissociative clients with ego state conflicts as well.

In one presentation Paulsen gave, the client in the case vignette had ego states which the client called, "anger," "sadness," "shame," "fear," and "party girl." These ego states match closely with several of the Pankseppian affective circuits (Panksepp, 1998). Paulsen was experimenting with the addition of ego and object awareness, consistent with the hypnotherapeutic strategies of Jack and Helen Watkins (Watkins & Paulsen, 2003; Paulsen & Watkins, 2005).

O'Shea adopted Paulsen's ego state approach and experimented with it to arrive at the circuit resetting steps. Originally, she called it reinstalling innate emotional resources, and included a much longer list of emotions. In 2006, Paulsen introduced O'Shea to Panksepp's research on hardwired affective circuits, and they collaborated on a formulation of ET that incorporated affective neuroscience. Paulsen had extensive discussions with Panksepp during a year he was in Seattle, which informed her understanding of the early trauma approach. O'Shea proceeded to process those ego states directly in the conference room (a.k.a., dissociative table, described by (Fraser, 1991, 2001)).

Object awareness (a.k.a., "object cathexis" or "in-object energy") in ego state work (Federn, 1952; Watkins & Watkins, 1997) refers to the client or the therapist relating to a specific part of the self in the third person, ("he," "she," "they," or "it,") by looking at the part "over there."

Object awareness contrasts with ego awareness, the latter of which involves the therapist relating to a specific part of the self in second person "you," which evokes a first person response of "I" or "we," from the client.

O'Shea subsequently experimented with processing ego states directly including the use of the conference room. She also incorporated elements of early childhood experience and its treatment with EMDR therapy such as the work of Phyllis Klaus, Maureen Kitchur, and others.

Although EMDR therapy training emphasized the need for the client to be sufficiently resourced prior to conducting EMDR therapy, O'Shea found available stabilization methods unsatisfactory either in result or in time and cost efficiency.

Paulsen's additional contributions

It was Katie O'Shea who developed the four step procedures of the ET approach over years of experimenting clinically. Paulsen's contribution to the development of the ET approach was not only in the beginning with the provision of ego state methods to be integrated with EMDR therapy procedures, but after 2006, with collaboration with O'Shea directly. At that time, Paulsen proposed several theories included in this chapter as explanatory mechanisms for the effect of the procedure, including especially:

- Porges' ventral vagal nervous system (2011) as the mechanism of action for step 2,

- Panksepp's subcortical affective circuits, and the three levels of affective brain processing, which provide an understanding for the mechanism of action that underlie the early trauma approach.

- the use of what Federn called "object awareness," which Paulsen understands to be neo-cortically based, to reset the affective circuits in combination with bilateral stimulation in step 3,

- the formulation of the temporal integration theory, described elsewhere in this book, first presented in 2009 (ISST&D),

- Subsequent elaboration of the modifications needed to use the approach with more complex clients,

- Reframing the work in terms of attuning to multiple subtle sources of information by which the story is revealed in the non-verbals as well as the verbal messages,

- Articulation of the addition of ego state and somatic work in the preparation and desensitization phases of EMDR therapy in the early trauma approach.

- Other contributions.

2 A Few Points from the Neurobiology of Affect, Trauma, and Attachment

Challenges revealed by neurobiology

This chapter will touch on a few of the recent developments in the neurobiology of affect, trauma and attachment, covered more extensively elsewhere (Lanius, Paulsen, Corrigan, 2014). These findings will provide a theoretical basis for understanding the procedures needed to clear and repair early trauma and point to ways to proceed safely.

Healthy brain develops in healthy relationships

The presence of positive emotional experience or affect states in the relationship between parent and infant is the basis for secure attachment, which unfolds in the moment-to-moment attuned interaction between mother and baby (Siegel, 2015).

A loving tender relationship, then, is not just nice to have, but is the basis for a solid foundation of mental health and emotional resilience (A. Schore, 2003; Siegel, 2015).

2-1 Attuned mother-child relationship is the basis of healthy self

Neurobiology of implicit memory

Amnesia studies have revealed that the neurobiology of implicit memory is different from that of explicit memory (Schore, 2001).

Whereas implicit experience is held in the right hemisphere and is unconscious, non-verbal and relational, explicit memory is held in the left hemisphere, is conscious, verbal and logical.

Early trauma and neglect are held in the right hemisphere of the brain (Schore, 2001), but are experienced by the client as being in the body. This is consistent with the findings of Luria (1973) who stated that the right hemisphere of the brain is essentially concerned with body sensation much more than verbal or logical concerns as in the left hemisphere.

Early trauma and neglect is associated with somatic syndromes, including somatoform pain disorder, conversion seizures, chronic fatigue, and other somatic syndromes (Scaer, 2014; Schore, 2001), or, as van der Kolk famously expressed, "the body keeps the score"(van der Kolk, 2014).

Right hemisphere basis of relationship, attachment and trauma

Alan Schore has marshalled an army of evidence to support the idea that early attachment experience is an attuned right hemisphere to right hemisphere relationship between mother and child, that both unresolved trauma and emotional processing are held in the right hemisphere.

From this basis, it is evident that talk therapy cannot begin to access all that needs accessing in order to repair early injury of attachment (2001, 2003). Schore (2009) proposes a paradigm shift in which attachment trauma is understood to engender a right-brain based pathogenesis of psychiatric disorder, similar to what Bowlby suggested more generally, before him (1969).

How to access the right hemisphere

The import of these findings for therapy for early trauma is that:

- There needs to be a way to bypass the left hemisphere and access the right hemisphere with its implicit memory, because that is how early experience is stored, the same early experience that has caused the somatic symptoms that memorialize the trauma the body is keeping the score about.

- Another implication is that the therapist's stance in the relationship must be kind and engaging, relationally oriented, because that is the state the client needs to be in, to access infant states somatically and relationally.

Right/left or top/down

Whereas Schore is primarily interested in right/left brain differences, the great experimental neuroscientist, Jaak Panksepp, finds the important dimension in affective processing to be top/bottom brain differences.

The left/right vs top/down competition can be reconciled, perhaps, by the awareness that relational attachment trauma interferes especially with right brain's top-down (cortical to subcortical) limbic autonomic circuits, which Schore says inhibits its capacity to cope with future stressors, making it vulnerable to PTSD (Schore, 2001).

Panksepp's three levels of the affective brain

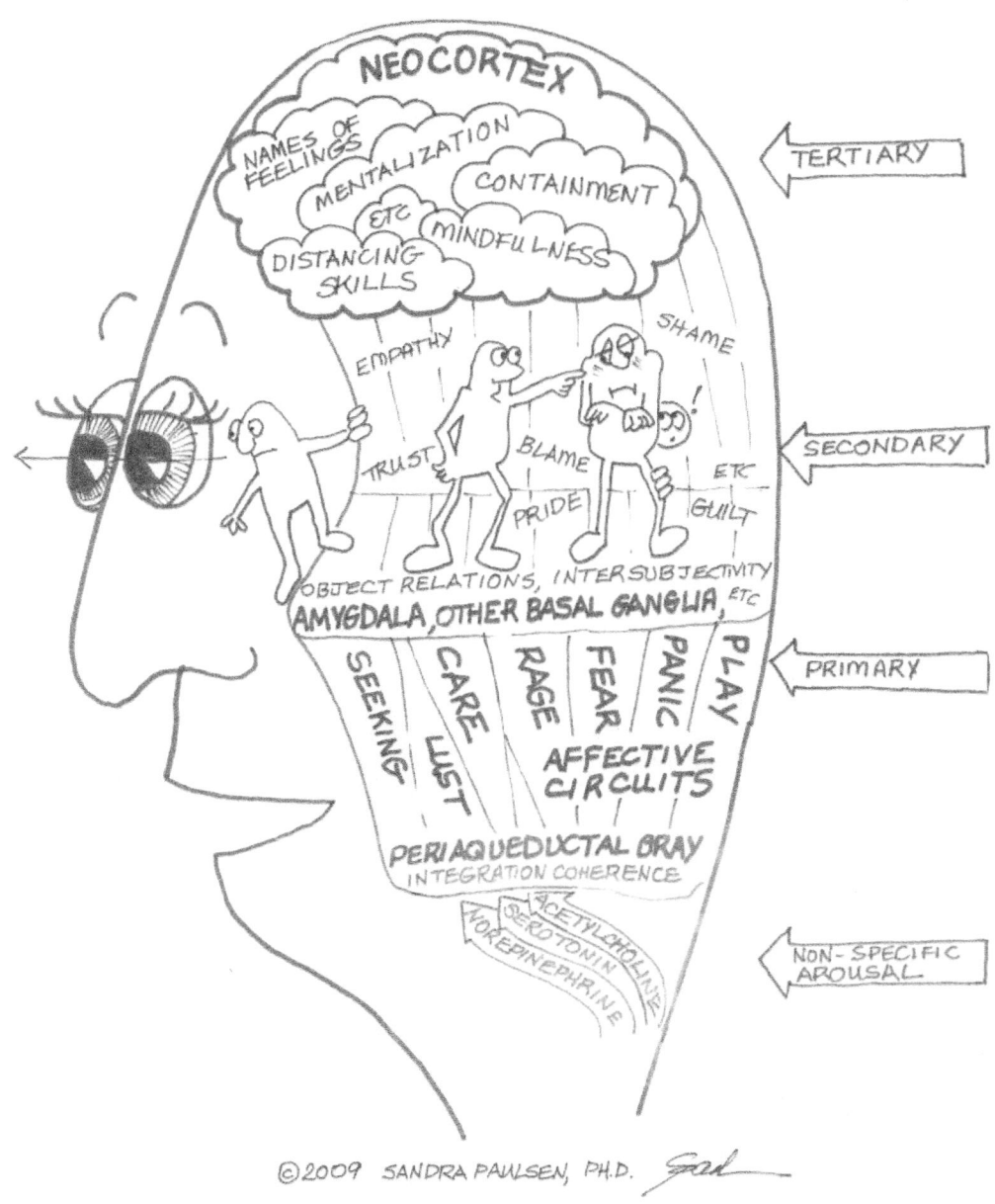

2-2 Panksepp's affective brain processing*

*This figure was jointly created with Jaak Panksepp, who reviewed and commented on earlier version. It appeared in Panksepp & Biven, 2012, in another graphic form)

Hard-wired affective circuits

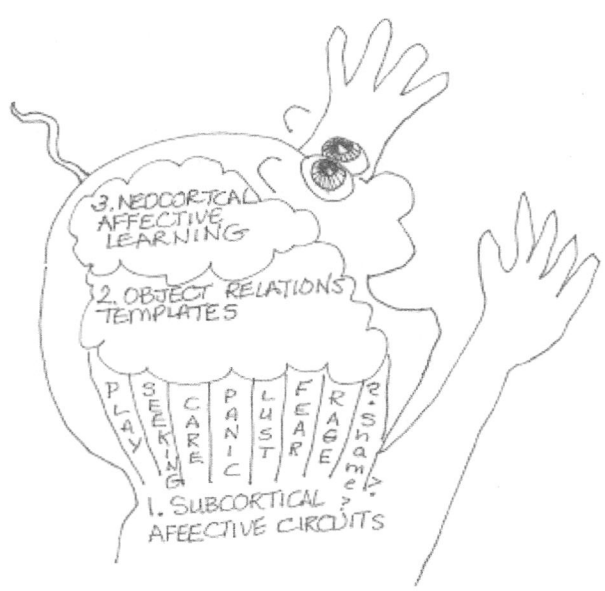

2-3 Pankseppian affective brain processing levels in baby

Affect regulation during the attachment period

The subcortical affective circuits that comprise the primary processing level serve as conduits for information that the organism needs, just as a car needs dash board gauges to provide information about the car and the environment. The circuits are unmodulated in the infant, who depends on the mother for containment. In that relationship, at the secondary processing level, the baby needs to learn essential affect regulation skill and will create a self, if all goes well.

According to Dan Siegel, "Human emotions constitute the fundamental basis the brain uses to organize its functioning, so brain organization reflects self-organization..." and "parent/child communication about emotions directly shapes the child's ability to smoothly organize his or her self," (Siegel, 1999).

If that period goes badly, the infant will not pass the next developmental milestones, or the subsequent ones. It is rather like building a structure on top of a poorly poured foundation. All the floors above will be uneven and at risk. Maladaptive lessons learned at these early ages will affect decisions for a lifetime.

Insecure attachment in this time period results in a tenuous relationship going forward, whereas secure attachment between mother and child will result in an adult capacity for sustained relationship (Bowlby, 1973; Fonagy, Gergely, Jurist, & Target, 2002; Fonagy, 2001; Fonagy, Roth, & Higgitt, 2005). Schore describes this as right-hemisphere-held internalized working models in procedural memory about what the infant has learned to expect, the lack of which predisposes the person to PTSD and other psychiatric disorders. Moncher (1996) reported positive correlations between insecure attachment in mothers and the incidence of subsequent child abuse.

Insecure or (chaotic) attachments have been associated with adult syndromes such as dissociative disorders, anxiety disorders, depressive disorders, somatic disorders, conversion disorders, and more (Scaer, 2014).

Early relationship trauma and state switching

When a baby's earliest needs for attachment in a safe and loving relationship are not filled, the effect is no less than bona fide trauma. This early relationship trauma has an injurious impact on the child's ability to smoothly switch affective states.

When affective states cannot be integrated within the stabilizing effect of the mother/child relationship, the hardwired subcortical affective circuits (Panksepp, 1998) cannot be integrated appropriately in the context of secondary brain processing related to relationship templates.

When all goes well in a secure attachment relationship for an infant, s/he will naturally learn, in time, self-containment, affect regulation, and social relationship learning. When that attachment learning goes poorly, not only are those containment- and affect-regulation skills missing, and acquired relationship templates maladaptive, but the child's capacity for state-switching does not develop smoothly. This results in a lack of integration of states and dissociative state switching (Putnam, 1988) due to disrupted affective circuits (Panksepp, 1998) and maladaptive state dependent learning.

This early failure to acquire smooth state shifting and resultant acquisition of habits of state switching instead is the genesis of subsequent development of affect dysregulation and dissociative disorders (Putnam, 1988; Barach, 1991). This is discussed elsewhere in terms of the Columnar Theory of Dissociation (Lanius et al., 2014).

The right hemisphere & affect

In doing very early trauma work, a fundamental concept to keep in mind is that early experience, affect, relational-and attachment-learning, as well as unresolved trauma, are all held in the right hemisphere of the brain in implicit memory. The particulars of these findings are beyond the scope of this book but are substantiated in the work of Alan Schore (2001, 2003).

2-4 Right hemisphere holds unprocessed trauma, emotions, somatic sensation, implicit memory, attachment relationships

When There Are No Words - Sandra Paulsen

Implicit memory is on the right

According to Schore, implicit memory is right hemisphere, unconscious, non-verbal and relational compared to explicit memory which is verbal, logical, and more likely to be accessible to conscious recall.

Early trauma is right hemisphere

The following considerations apply to both dissociative and non-dissociative clients, but the intensity of flashbacks is often more severe in dissociative clients, because it has been sequestered and is under pressure.

- Early trauma is held in the right hemisphere of the brain, but is experienced subjectively as being in the body.
- This fact is hard for many clients to fathom because remembered emotion and/or body pain, feels as if they are occurring in the present moment.
- If one believes that a pain isn't historical but rather is occurring now, the client may feel currently in jeopardy
- Therefore, the customary EMDR therapy stance of maintaining dual attention awareness (one foot in the memory, one foot in the office) is still key, but challenging, because there may be no narrative or image that clarifies for the client that the event isn't occurring now.
- For example, the memory of shame, without narrative or image, may feel to the client as if in the current moment, in the therapist's presence, one is shameful or being shamed.
- This form of reenactment of that traumatic memory held in the right hemisphere contrasts with adult memories of, say, a fiery car crash at age 22 that is held in explicit memory.
- Generally, clients recalling, for example, a fiery car crash at age 22 are unlikely to think it is happening now, because there is a picture memory of the accident at the same time as the fear or pain is present, unless they are fully pulled in to a flashback and have lost awareness of the therapist and/or the office.
- However, when re-experiencing a felt sense of abandonment or annihilation or fear from infancy, clients commonly mistake the feeling as from current time rather than being a memory, a kind of flashback that is affective and somatic.
- Infant annihilation flashbacks are the most disorganizing and frightening because they occur when the baby had insufficient caretaking, and the requirements of the situation outstripped the infant's capacity to cope. Experiencing the memory of that terror in the office can cause the client to feel again alone, or lose awareness that this time there is someone there to help.
- Paulsen alerts clients to the possibility of this memory of aloneness to inoculate the client to the idea of an emotional flashback, or relationship flashback, so that it will be experienced as a memory rather than as a present time experience of terror and jeopardy in the therapy office.

When There Are No Words - Sandra Paulsen

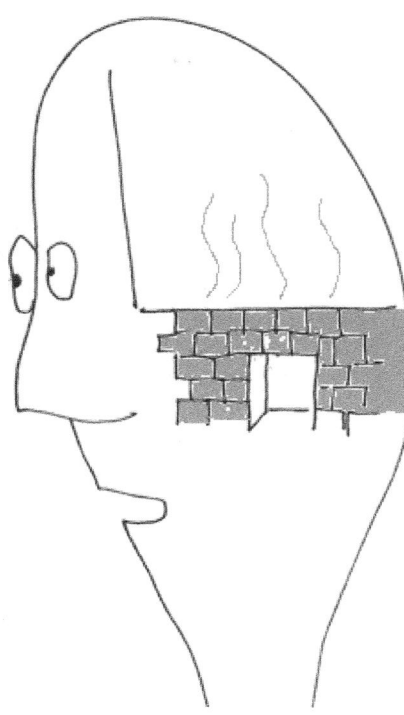

2-5 Emotional and somatic flashbacks are nuances of memory wafting from implicit memory, like vapors leaking up from King Tut's tomb

The catch and release program

It is critical that the therapist introduce to the client the following ideas, both in terms of informed consent, and education, but also as inoculation to decrease reactivity, namely, that:

- We are listening to baby's story tell itself in the re-experiencing of flashbacks of any of the information channels, including: somatic, affective, cognitive, behavioral and more, The trauma and neglect isn't happening now, but rather is a memory,
- The material mustn't be avoided but listened to with curiosity and acceptance so that it can be part of the "catch and release" program of baby's painful story, finally told and received with compassion.
- That we are offering the same compassion that we would wish for any child. The use of a hypothetical and objectively viewed other child will be indispensable in decreasing the subjective felt sense of shame as the work of clearing trauma from implicit memory proceeds.

We'd wish for a gestating mother to be attuned to and cherish her unborn baby

Many clients cannot imagine for themselves a mother who communicates with and cherishes them as a human being while they are still in the womb. Yet, healthy attachments begin in utero, as described by (Rubin, 1975, p. 145) who stated:

"By the end of the second trimester, the pregnant woman becomes so aware of the child within her and attaches so much value to him that she possesses something very dear, very important to her, something that gives her considerable pleasure and pride."

That prenatal attachment begins, in theory, before pregnancy, between a parent and wished-for child. (Doan & Zimerman, 2003) speak of this wished-for possibility of a child as an ecological system. If a prospective mother, and father, have the capacity to wish for and imagine life with a child, that resonant and cherishing context is the substrate and foundation in which the conception occurs, like a nest awaits eggs.

Brandon, *et al*, 2009, review the history and diverse application of the study of perinatal attachment experience across many fields of study.

Symptoms as a shrine to baby's story

Rubin (1975) described the following tasks as what she observed in women before childbirth in preparation to mother their babies: (1) Seeking safe passage for self and baby, (2) ensuring that the baby is accepted by significant others, (3) "binding-in"[3], and (4) giving of herself.

If for any reason mother cannot engage in this authentic ancient way with her baby, baby's experience is disappointment, hurt, aloneness, rejection, turning away, shutting down and, ultimately, death. The panoply of symptoms that result is a memorial to the story of what happened to baby, and how far the injury went.

Somatic syndromes are right hemisphere

Early trauma has been associated with the aforementioned panoply symptoms, including, though not limited to, somatic syndromes, notably, somatoform pain disorder, conversion seizures, chronic fatigue, other somatic syndromes (Scaer, 2014).

Nightmares

Nightmares also represent traumatic disturbance held in implicit memory erupting into awareness during sleep, as if the dream processing architecture is attempting to process the trauma to an adaptive resolution, but partially or unsuccessfully. The capacity of the processor is insufficient for the task.

2-6 Nightmares are evidence of the brain's failed attempt to process disturbing memories in REM sleep

Body keeps the score

Bessel van der Kolk immortalized the essence of the approach in his famous expression "the body keeps the score" van der Kolk (2014).

The symptom picture acts as a memorial to the untold story, like a silent child at a concentration camp. Though wordless, if we listen with our intuition, we can begin to hear the tragedy, despair, and sometimes even horror of baby's story in the somatic symptoms.

Right hemisphere to right hemisphere attunement: a mother's love

One of Schore's contributions is the understanding that in a healthy mother/infant relationship, the right hemispheres of both mother and child come into a synchrony of attunement.

This is the primordial mutual admiration society, the love affair in which there is no separation of the two, there is only the single heartbeat and unity.

In this ancient mammalian dance, the mother's attention, time and affections are wholly dedicated, with frequency, to the care and attunement with the tiny non-verbal communications from and with her baby.

Synchrony and coherence are the delicious results of an attuned and resonant attachment to an attentive mother (Siegel, 2015), but trauma and neglect produce asynchrony, incoherence, disorganization and a panoply of symptoms (Scaer, 2012; van der Kolk, 2014; Schore, 2001, 2003).

When There Are No Words - Sandra Paulsen

3 Approaches to Integration

ET approach for affect regulation through temporal integration

Many of the efforts to treat affect dysregulation (as is found in borderline personality disorder, bipolar disorder, and dissociative identity disorder) rely on strategies of cognitive behavioral intervention, though some are increasingly emphasizing attachment and resonant relationship in the repair.

In the early trauma approach, there will be some cognitive behavioral interventions, some hypnotic methods, some use of resonant attunement, and some processing of material to an adaptive resolution, amidst psychodynamic understandings, all lending to a systematic approach and outcome.

Three theories of integration:

Temporal, strategic and tactical

The method of integrating by time period, from the earliest pre-verbal experience, is here referred to as temporal integrationism, in contrast to strategic and tactical integrationist approaches of Kluft (1984) and (Fine, 1993) respectively.

Both O'Shea and Paulsen were influenced by the contributions of Maureen Kitchur (2009), whose strategic developmental model was also temporally based, but differed from the ET approach described here.

Paulsen first used the term "temporal integration" (Paulsen, 2009b) to describe the approach and the effect of O'Shea's clinical approach when applied to dissociative individuals. Temporal Integration is put forward as an approach to the treatment of dissociative disorders and some affective dysregulation in contrast to the strategic integration (Kluft, 1984) and tactical integration (Fine, 1991) models.

Strategic integration emphasizes integration by means of gradual diminution of dissociative barriers as co-consciousness increases and internal conflicts are resolved. Fractionation involves targeting a piece of a memory at a time, to titrate affective intensity.

Tactical integration emphasizes making use of dissociative barriers as protection while the necessary painful work is done behind the amnesia barriers. Though fractionation may be widely used within this approach, the first and essential use of it is protecting the parts of self that function in the outside world from the painful processing. Then, other aspects of the self do that necessary painful work, initially, and only later being processed by the parts of self that "do life" in the outside world. These approaches are discussed later in this book.

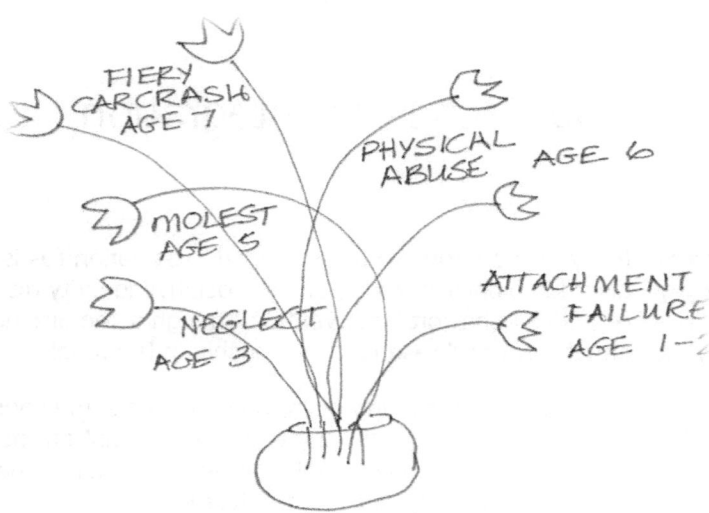

3-1 Unprocessed and unintegrated traumatic experience held in disparate sequestered neural networks or ego states/alter personalities frozen at the time of trauma

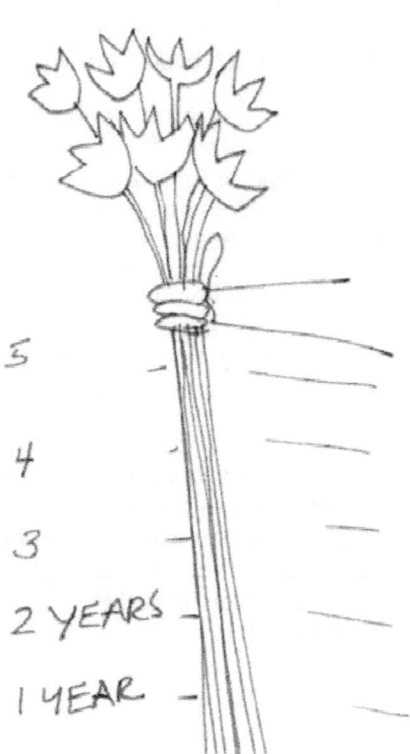

3-2 Once processed in temporal sequence, networks can be linked and integrated and missed developmental milestones achieved

Temporal integration   In contrast to these pioneering methods, temporal integrationism fractionates by containing all but the earliest material being worked upon, activating the client's ventral vagal nervous system, and ensuring that the affective circuits are free to function well. For highly dissociative individuals, other preparation methods are also likely needed.

Once preparation is complete, the fourth step of the ET approach involves integrating from the earliest experience for purposes of both fractionating and titrating affective intensity as well as clearing and repairing earliest unmet developmental milestones. This is done systematically by time period.

As the work progresses, each unmet developmental milestone is repaired and the repaired milestones become a layer of foundation for subsequent steps and subsequent repair.

Because temporal integration is a new approach, it is introduced here in the book, and expanded later in the book, when trauma processing is described in full.

4 Introduction to the Preparation for Trauma Processing

ET approach purpose

The purpose of the ET approach of EMDR therapy is several fold: to increase the client's stability and resources, to repair very early trauma and attachment injury in a way that is both systematic and efficient, and to increase the client's confidence in their own capacities and healing potential.

Premises underlying the work include:

1) the processing of early traumatic experience, including early attachment injury, can only be successful if the client's processing capacity exceeds the volume of material to be processed Watkins & Paulsen (2003), Paulsen & Watkins, (2005).

2) O'Shea's statement that everything we do must empower the client and work collaboratively with the client and with the client's nervous system and intrinsic healing potential.

Painters spend much time on prep—so must we, for complex cases

4-1 As in house painting, preparation is everything and makes the work go easier and faster

Introduction to the ET basic preparatory steps

The prior discussion introduced the theory and background of the Early Trauma approach (O'Shea, 2009; O'Shea &Paulsen, 2007). The ET approach was generally reviewed within the context of how the phases of EMDR therapy are similar and how they are necessarily tweaked when working in implicit memory.

Next, we will describe the preparatory steps of the approach and the modifications needed to utilize the approach with highly dissociative clients.

There are three preparatory steps in the ET approach in its basic form: 1–containment, 2–safe state, and 3–resetting affective circuits. This chapter will first explain the basic Early Trauma steps as defined by O'Shea (2009) and O'Shea and Paulsen (2007). After that description of each basic ET preparatory step, there will be a discussion of how each step must be modified for working with highly dissociative clients.

Increasing processing capacity

4-2 When the processing capacity is too small for the volume of material to process, the EMDR therapy can't complete normally

When There Are No Words - Sandra Paulsen

4-3 When the processing capacity is greater than the volume of material to process, the EMDR therapy can complete normally

ET benefit: increased processing capacity for volume of material

If the client's processing capacity is less than the volume of material to be processed, one or both of the following must be employed for processing to successfully proceed to an adaptive resolution:

a) the material must be fractionated (Kluft, 1993, 1990) into smaller pieces or

b) the processing capacity must be increased, whether for the duration of the process, e.g., via the addition of the therapist's resonance, or as an ongoing adaptive resourcing and strengthening of the client (e.g., Phillips & Frederick, 1995; Watkins & Watkins, 1997).

The ET approach does both of these things. The first step, containment, and the fourth step, processing by time frame, both serve to fractionate the volume of material to be processed. The second step, safe state, and the third step, resetting affective circuits, both serve to increase the client's capacity to process. As the work progresses through step four, that step also tends to increase the client's capacity to do subsequent work, as early injury is repaired systematically.

ET benefit: increasing

One of the most profound of injurious impacts of early trauma and neglect is the client's tendency to doubt the information they get from their own emotions and *client trust of their system* — body. Typically, the child had to jettison their own point of view to adopt the point of view required by their parents or caretakers.

The ET approach is specifically designed to reliably increase the client's confidence in both affect and soma and sources of necessary information.

It does this by: psycho-educational means that normalize fight/flight/freeze responses, the presence of emotions and other mammalian responses, increasing compassion for self by normalizing the developmental requirements, strivings, and yearnings of any child.

ET benefit: decreased abreactive intensity — The procedures described here as basic early trauma work have been used on many dozens of individuals over several years with uniformly good results.

The preparation seems to greatly reduce the possibility of unintended abreaction or other untoward result.

5 Preparation in Complex Cases: Ego State Maneuvers and More

5-1 ISST&D Treatment Guidelines 3rd Edition address the safe use of EMDR therapy in complex cases

ISST&D treatment guidelines   The International Society for the Study of Trauma & Dissociation (ISST&D) has promulgated treatment guidelines for highly dissociative clients (ISST&D, 2011). The third edition of those guidelines state that there is a consensus in the field that treatment should include a period of stabilization prior to metabolizing traumatic memories.

The third edition of the guidelines also includes discussion of the use of EMDR therapy for dissociative clients, to which several senior EMDR therapy practitioners contributed including Sandra Paulsen, Catherine Fine, Joanne Twombly and Denise Galinas. The guidelines are important reading for all EMDR therapy practitioners and reflect the standards of the community of professional practice for treating dissociative clients.

For highly dissociative clients, much more preparation is needed

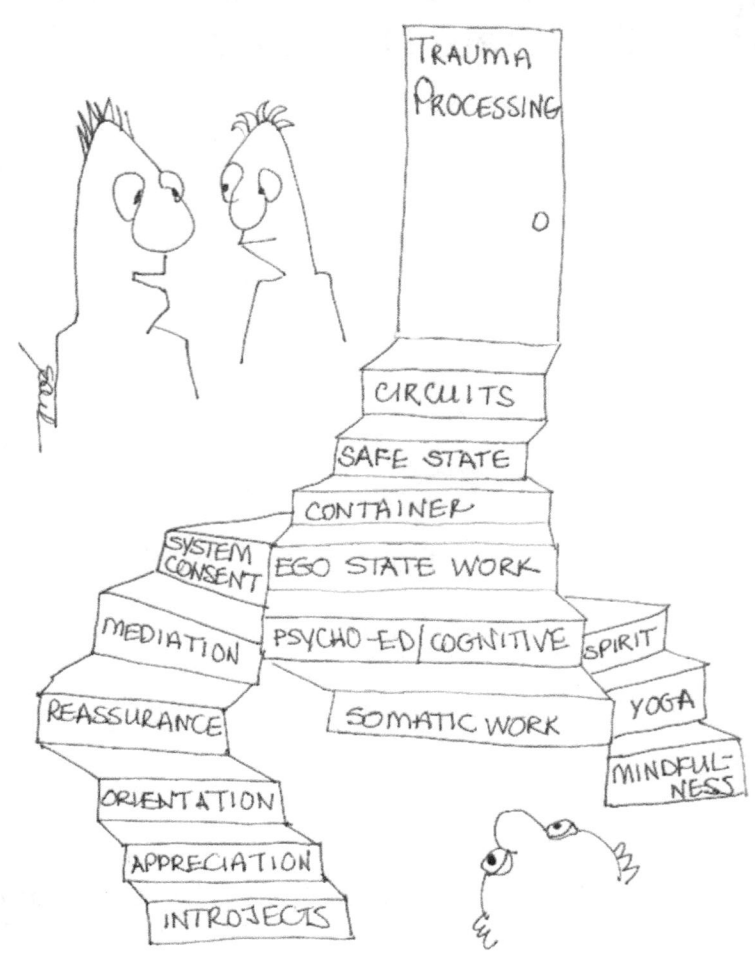

5-2 For highly dissociative clients, much more preparation is likely needed prior to temporal integration

Special considerations for severely dissociative clients

In addition to the three preparation steps already described for non-dissociative individuals, namely, containment, ventral vagal (safe state) resourcing, and resetting the affective circuits, for highly dissociative clients, additional preparation steps are commonly needed.

Although the above three steps are those that are "officially" part of the early trauma approach (O'Shea & Paulsen, 2007; O'Shea, 2009), therapists should consider and utilize the following when working with severely dissociative clients.

- Ego state therapy usually must be utilized before using even the preparatory steps in order to enlist the self-system in the work.

- It is critical to orient early, not late, in the work, any perpetrator introjects or other problematic alters to person, place and time, as described in Paulsen & Golston (2014b) and in Paulsen, (2009). Perpetrator introjects are the locus of the loyalty to the aggressor that is responsible for most thwarted therapeutic interventions and considerable therapist and client confusion and even despair. This point is so critical, that it will be mentioned several times and way.

5-3 The child introjects the point of view of the perpetrator, the locus of identification with the aggressor
(This figure originally appears in Paulsen, 2009, "Looking Through the Eyes,")

- Ego state interventions are necessary for each of the preparatory steps and are certainly essential for interweaves in temporal integration. Moreover, the therapeutic relationship is considered to be insufficiently developed to attempt the early trauma work if that relationship is not held between the therapist and all key parts of self--not necessarily every part of self, but the most powerful or important ones.

- If the most powerful ego states and the ones most central to the traumatic dynamics are not engaged with the process, they will block therapy in general, and early trauma processing in particular as is the very nature of traumatic defensive states

- Additionally, Paulsen & Golston (2014) enumerate a range of containment and stabilization efforts that will not all be necessary for each client, but some of which will be necessary to get the entire self-system to a point where the ET approach can be employed. Having said that, it is very useful to the therapy if the ET approach is employed as early in the treatment as it can be successfully tolerated.

Additional stabilization for complex cases

In Lanius, Paulsen & Corrigan (2014), Paulsen & Golston identify numerous stabilization and containment strategies that may be necessary or beneficial with dissociative clients.

It will be rare that the use of the single four steps of the basic ET approach will be sufficient to prepare a dissociative client for trauma processing with the ET approach.

The following are necessary but not sufficient, surely, for preparing a highly dissociative client for the fourth step of temporal integration.

- Establishing safety internally (See Paulsen & Golston, 2014b; Paulsen, 2009)
- Establishing safety externally
- As mentioned, conducting extensive ego state maneuvers to orient and deconflictualize the self-system (See Paulsen & Golston, 2014b)
- Grounding skills training
- Skills training such as mindfulness, relaxation, meditation, yoga or other body-related therapy to facilitate the client's capacity to evoke a ventral vagal or resourced state.
- Somatic therapy (e.g., sensorimotor therapy, somatic experiencing, somatic transformation, or other suitable somatic procedures that help the client to be able to notice, tolerate, track and gently metabolize somatic experience including traumatic somatic experience)
- Cognitive behavioral skills training, e.g., decatastrophizing, resolving internal double binds or other conflicts
- Psychoeducation about fight/flight/freeze responses and other emotional responses to trauma and to relationship dynamics
- Normal developmental milestones for infants and young children
- Understanding relationship contracts in families
- For some, reiki or other energy-based procedures that enable gentle releasing of trapped traumatic experience as an introduction to metabolization and release of held energy.
- Other preparatory methods as warranted by the therapist's skills and the client's needs.

Additional reading for stabilization and preparation

For complex dissociative clients, additional preparation steps may be needed. For further reading, please see: :

- Paulsen & Golston (2014a, 2014b)
- Boon and Steele (2011)
- Loewenstein (2006)
- Paulsen (2009b)
- Paulsen (2009a)

5-4 A keystone intervention to stabilize clients is to work with perpetrator introject parts of self, to reduce loyalty to the aggressor.

For the ET approach, ego state maneuvers are needed at each step for highly dissociative clients

For dissociative clients, ego state interventions will be needed before, during and after each of the basic ET steps.

- Notably, for dissociative clients, the ET process should not be undertaken without, at a bare minimum, ego state maneuvers at every step and as a first order interweave when processing is stuck.

- Most important, maternal introjects need to be worked with directly to shift loyalty to the caretaker that may have been the price of survival for many infants. Even for non-dissociative clients, loyalty to the mother's point of view and abdication of the baby's own viewpoint is the origin of a great many clinical symptoms. It is the fulcrum which will enable healing using ego state therapy and other maneuvers.

- If the reader remembers only one thing from this book, it might be this point about baby's learned loyalty to the mother's point of view.

- If there were other "big T" traumas in infancy, those other perpetrator introjects would also need to be worked with directly.

- At many junctures, it will be necessary to orient, appreciate, and reassure ego states, especially perpetrator introjects, and mediate conflicts between states using ego state therapeutic maneuvers.

5-5 Before attempting temporal integration, in cases of DID, appreciation, orientation, and consent of the "honchos" is extremely important.
(Figure originally appears in Paulsen, 2009, "Looking Through the Eyes")

Protective elements in complex clients

The most elemental obstructions to trauma processing in complex trauma include:

- insufficient processing capacity due to scarce internal resources and structure, and sparse affect-regulation ability resulting in shutting down or hyperarousal, and

- loyalty to the aggressor, in the form of introjection of the parent and/or perpetrator's viewpoint, to the exclusion of owning, and processing, the client's point of view from infancy.

Much of the preparation is dedicated to addressing the first point above, increasing processing capacity, internal resources and affect-regulation ability to expand the window of tolerance.

Loyalty to the aggressor requires ego-state maneuvers, which are addressed separately throughout each step, because that loyalty interferes with the work at every step until and unless it is addressed. Failure to address this step results in aborted trauma processing or greatly and unnecessarily lengthened treatment for many clients.

See Appendix C for specific language and methods for working with perpetrator or parental introjects.

When There Are No Words - Sandra Paulsen

Looking at something over there is object awareness.

Looking through my own eyes is ego awareness

5-6 Looking at something "over there" adds objectivity, which brings neocortical resources to bear

Ego and object awareness

Although the topic is abstruse, an understanding of ego and object awareness is imperative in doing ego state work. The therapist's most powerful tool is the deliberate addition or subtraction of ego energy (ego cathexis).

We use both for different reasons to untie sticky knots in shame-shoelace

- **Ego cathexis is powerful.** Just as calling a student's name in a classroom causes that student to sit up and pay attention, calling an ego state by name causes it to be awakened, pulls it forward into awareness and may also make it executive.

- **Indirect is weaker.** It weakens the power of this effect to insist, in a highly dissociative client, that a front part speak for each back part, as some clinical approaches do.

- **Indirect shows favoritism.** Arbitrarily choosing one front part as a kind of "spokespart" to be executive shows a kind of favoritism that can be harmful to rapport with other parts of the self-system.

- **Object cathexis is also useful.** There are occasions to deliberately subtract ego energy (and add object energy) by having a front part <u>look at</u> one or more other parts, to gain insight or compassion or objectivity. Jack Watkins asserted that this was a keenly important tool to use, so he was not only advocating ego cathexis, though he named his therapy ego-state therapy (Watkins & Watkins, 1997). It might well have been named ego-and-object state therapy.

- **Direct access is powerful and faster.** Anecdotally, this author has heard repeatedly from clients who received or practiced ego-state therapy from other traditions, that they were quite frustrated at how much time they had previously spent working the other way, namely, with all internal communications through one front part. In Paulsen's practice, they reported,

33

the movement was much quicker and the work far deeper when dissociated parts were ego cathected to engage them more potently in the work.

- **Direct access is integrative.** Although some practitioners are concerned that speaking directly to parts is reifying or disintegrative, the author finds that quite the opposite is true. After a skillfully conducted direct access, appreciation, and orientation of parts, and mediation of conflicts between parts, the self-system is far more integrated than it was prior to direct access. If direct access results in disintegration or decompensation, then an error has been made clinically, most especially:

    - Failure to work first with perpetrator introjects (or other parts of the self, such as angry teen or shamed child parts, powerful enough to derail the work). This has been described in various locations including: Paulsen, 2009a, Paulsen, 2009b, and Paulsen & Golston (2014a).

    - Failure to use closure and containment procedures at the end of session. It is simply imperative for safety and maintaining stability that any session where ego state therapy is conducted must be closed with an appropriate containment procedure, as described in the "monster sequence" in Paulsen's illustrated book (2009) and elsewhere in this book.

- **The front is not "the client."** If the clinician fails to recognize that a front part is only a porch of the self-system, and acts as if that front part is, in fact, "the client," the clinician has allowed him or herself to be in trance, the same trance that the client is in, in this regard.

The front part is only a <u>part</u> of the client, though it may be the part that does life, drives to therapy or writes the check. It is the sum total of all of the parts in the self-system that is actually "the client." This is the single most prominent error in ego state work with dissociative clients, and so it will be referenced repeatedly in this book.

5-7 De-conflictualizing the relationship between self-states increases inner peace and stability, making energy and resources available

Somatic therapeutic interventions for dissociative individuals

- Somatic interventions are often needed to increase soma tolerance and affect-regulation, and are discussed by Ogden & Fisher, (2014) and Paulsen & Lanius (2009).

- It is important that the client has some capacity to tolerate somatic sensation without dissociating or the early trauma method can hardly be employed without abreaction.

- For many individuals, the entirety of somatic methods need not be undertaken prior to using the ET approach, but for dissociative individuals a more intensive course of somatic work is more often needed. Indeed, beginning at the beginning, and reviewing, releasing and repairing unprocessed traumatic experience for the first years of life will go a long way to resolving proscriptions against having body sensations, needs and affect for all but the most injured people.

- Once those time periods have been repaired in temporal integration, the client's compassion for self will typically be much greater. So too will be there understanding that their bodily and emotional responses are not shameful at all, which will increase their capacity to do all subsequent therapeutic work

- Achieving this compassion and understanding will itself be somewhat integrative even before later traumas have been processed. The ability to tolerate the subjective felt sense of an emotion and its opposite, the ability to envision the objective image of an emotion, are the two bookends of inter-subjectivity in the I-and-thou of relationships

- The development of those two bookends with somatic therapy and with the affective resetting experience go a great distance in repairing the intersubjective milestones of infancy, the capacity for relationship, attachment, and empathic attunement

5-8 The client's sympathetic nervous system can be activated by slow motion fight or flight responses, with careful resistance where appropriate--here the resistance requires no touch

Somatic techniques The preparation for highly dissociative individuals requires not only extensive use of ego state therapy, but, if the client has limited tolerance of body sensation, specifically somatic work including, but not limited to:

- Somatic empathy (Stanley, 2016)
- Somatic resourcing (Levine, 2010)
- Somatic tracking
- Somatic micro-movements
- Evoked oscillations
- Spontaneous oscillations

Other steps, in addition to the described four steps, are needed, including extensive use of ego state therapy and somatic resourcing. This point cannot be made too much, and will be emphasized frequently in this document.

Just as harm can come from EMDR therapy practitioners doing EMDR therapy unbeknownst on undiagnosed dissociative clients, harm can be done by even well-trained ET practitioners doing ET with dissociative clients without the necessary preparation and ego state modifications.

Getting permission from defensive protective alters to help the baby It is both extraordinary and important that even resistant, uncooperative parts of the self that would ordinarily not consent to participating in trauma-focused treatment at an early point in therapy, can often be asked for permission to help the baby, with surprising results.

The fierce defensive state often agrees to stand down in the name of helping the baby state(s), if a certain level of trust is in place.

For some clients, then, where safety is less of an issue, an early introduction of the goal of doing ET work to "help the baby," and psycho-education and other preparation needed to do the ET approach, can greatly economize on time necessary to prepare a dissociative client to be helped with the ET approach.

The willingness of fierce alters to stand down if the baby can be helped, says volumes about their origin in infancy as a survival strategy for a tiny child.

Therapeutic rapport still key In the ET approach, the establishing of therapeutic rapport and a trusting relationship are still important, but undertaken at the right time, these procedures can reduce preparation time for EMDR therapy considerably.

5-9 Cooperative alters will quickly stand aside, but ego state maneuvers will be needed to enlist the cooperation of the fierce protective parts who came into existence early in life to protect the same small child by identifying with the aggressor

Dissociation Informed Consent

D. Michael Coy and the author have undertaken to explicate an assessment process that describes initial interview questions that guide whether the client has indicators of a dissociative disorder, in addition to such screening devices as the DES-II (Bernstein & Putnam, 1986) and the SDQ-20 or SDQ-5, (Nijenhuis, Spinhoven, Van Dyck, Van der Hart, & Vanderlinden, 1996), or diagnostic devices such as the MID (Dell, 2006) or the SCID-D (Steinberg, 1994)

Structural dissociation. It is necessary to assess the presence or absence of structural dissociation, which will determine whether aspects of the self-system of the client are likely to structurally impede trauma processing, especially perpetrator introjects disoriented to present circumstances and loyal to the aggressor.

- Soma tolerance. It is important to understand whether the client has the capacity to mindfully be aware of body sensations, both positive or negative (or comfortable/uncomfortable).

- Affect tolerance. Some clients are alexythymic, or have an absence of capacity to notice, tolerate or describe emotions. Positive and negative affect tolerance should be assessed separately.

- See Lanius, Paulsen & Coy (2016) and Coy (2016) for more on the decision process and assessment of these and other elements in initial inquiry. Coy (2016) is putting forward an assessment device to support the integrated psychotherapy described as neuroaffective psychotherapy (Lanius & Paulsen, 2015; Lanius, Paulsen & Coy, 2016).

6 Technical EMDR Therapy Modifications within the Early Trauma Approach

EMDR therapy phase I – history

History & Treatment Planning. The full review of domains to assess is outside the scope of this book, and varies with the therapist's training and discipline's understanding of relevant history. However, it is absolutely necessary to assess for the presence of a dissociative disorder prior to conducting EMDR therapy on any client. If the presenting issue is an attachment problem, or if the therapist discerns that early experience is contributing to the presenting issues, history-taking can be challenging.

Some individuals know facts of their infancy, namely, that they had surgeries, were adopted, that a twin died, etc. Others know little or nothing about the facts of their first years or of their parents' lives. However, many individuals can find a bodily answer if the question is framed as, "I realize none of us remembers much of anything before age 3, 4 or 5, but if you had to guess whether your earliest needs were met, whether you were loved and cherished, or whether those first years were difficult or lacking, what would you guess?"

Typically, after a moment's reflection, many clients will say, "I think it was lacking." Some individuals will obtain detailed historical information from family members prior to conducting the ET approach, while for others that will not be possible or advisable. In either case, the unfolding of processing of early years tends to involve surprises of various types to be covered under temporal integration.

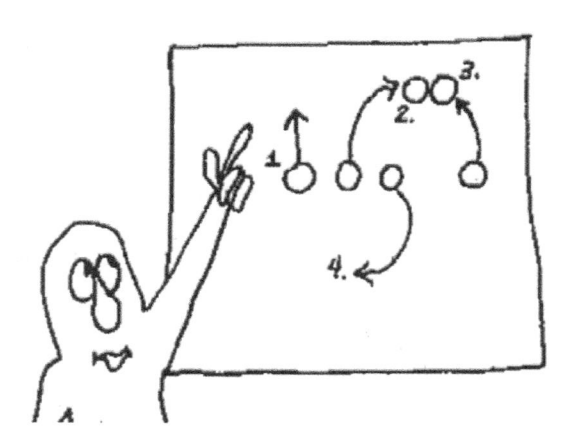

6-1 Tactical maneuvers needed in preparation for temporal integration

EMDR therapy phase II – preparation

Phase II of EMDR therapy is about preparation, and in the standard EMDR therapy approach, preparation typically includes the installation of safe place, and possibly resource development and installation (RDI), along with informed consent processes.

All three of the ET preparation steps--containment, safe state, and resetting the affective circuits--may be construed as occurring under the rubric of EMDR therapy phase II. Any additional preparation steps needed for complex clients are also part of phase II, preparation. At the same time, those methods may need revisiting in subsequent phases, including especially phase IV, desensitization. These preparation steps will be described, along with the modifications required to use them with dissociative clients, in the next chapter.

6-2 Targeting in standard EMDR therapy aims at the elements of trauma held in explicit memory: picture, cognition, emotion and body sensation

EMDR therapy phase III assessment

In EMDR therapy phase III, the target that is selected is generally a memory that typifies the issue that the therapist and client have agreed upon collaboratively.

The target is "worked-up" by:

- Articulating the picture that represents the most disturbing aspect of the memory
- In addition to that image, a negative cognition (NC) is articulated that expresses the client's negative belief about him or herself, as well as the positive cognition (PC) that the client would like to have replace the NC
- The validity of cognition (VoC) is assessed, from 1 to 7, where 1 is completely false and 7 is completely true, to determine how true the positive cognition feels in the gut, not intellectually, at the outset
- As well, the emotion associated with the memory in the present moment
- Along with the subjective units of disturbance (SUDS), from 0 to 10, where 0 equals no disturbance and 10 equals maximal imaginable disturbance
- The location in the body of sensations associated with the memory are also identified

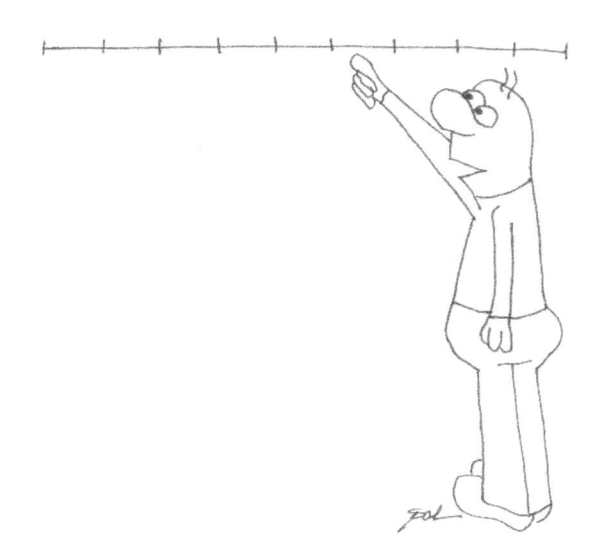

6-3 Targeting in the early trauma approach, by time frame, from the beginning

How to work up the target without explicit memory

With the above standard target workup, EMDR therapy processing is ready to begin when the standard approach is used. However, none of this target work-up is typically possible for experience held in implicit memory from the first years of life.

- There may be no image or images may be dream like or symbolic.

- There is little by way of cognition accessible.

- There may or may not be an awareness of affect or body sensation at the outset.

- Numeric ratings of VoC and SUD are meaningless when the material is nebulous at the outset, and after the material is activated, too cognitive and adult for the somatic "baby state" the client will be in.

- Without these mileposts, the standard approach is impossible to use for early experience.

- Pre-verbal material that does emerge may not be readily recognized as such by the client or the therapist, making it more difficult or impossible to enable an age-appropriate release and/or repair.

Some have suggested targeting key relationships such as the relationship with the mother or the father, but there, processing tends to access associations for later childhood or later life, where explicit memory is available.

Targeting by time period

In the ET approach, target workup is transformed from the above exercise to the selection of a period of time. Images or dreamscapes may emerge, and the therapist will not take a strong position on their veracity, though the client will typically place some trust in what emerges as time proceeds. The therapist will encourage the client to suspend judgment and rather emphasize repair of what is manifesting.

Revisiting phase III with each time period Because of the unique nature of the targeting in the ET approach, EMDR therapy phase III –target assessment will be revisited with each time frame worked on in this method. Because in the ET approach targeting is done by time frame without access to explicit memory, it is not possible to articulate negative and positive cognitions as it done in the preferred format for standard EMDR therapy. Rather, they, and emotions and body sensations, will be captured as they emerge in the course of processing, in the Early Trauma approach.

6-4 Because there are no cognitions in implicit memory, we capture them as they emerge during processing of implicit memory

EMDR therapy phase IV- desensitization through phase VI–body scan Similar to phase III assessment, in EMDR therapy phase IV desensitization, the processing that is core to EMDR therapy recurs for each time frame. Indeed, the same is true for phase V installation, and phase VI body scan. That is, one conducts installation of captured PC's, with bilateral stimulation, and body scan to ensure completeness, after repeatedly checking that the time period is clear and repaired. Only then does one move on to the next time frame.

EMDR therapy phases VII and VIII Phase VII closure is conducted at the end of an ET session no matter how many time frames were covered within that session, whether structured to be a short or extended session.

Similarly, phase VIII reevaluation is conducted subsequent to the ET session, whether at the next regular session, the next extended session, or by remote communication if the ET session was conducted using an intensive structure of one or more long days.

Structure of treatment Psychotherapists will likely need to conduct ET sessions within 45-50 or 90 minute sessions. Preferably, however, extended sessions of half- to full-day sessions, structured with breaks, are the ideal way to employ the ET approach. This is because in brief sessions clients and therapist are more typically operating in a left-hemisphere frame of reference.

As both get into the nuances of ET work, however, especially in temporal integration, time slows down and the work becomes more of implicit memory in the right hemisphere, wordless, somatic and held in the field in the room. As such, in a short session one only begins to get into the material when one runs out of time.

In an expanded session, there is time for the nuances to reveal themselves, be verbalized, appropriate processing and interweaves to occur, and have the client re-contain in preparation for the world outside the session.

See the appendix A for a discussion of considerations in conducting intensive psychotherapy ethically. There are certainly risks and should not be undertaken without full awareness of the risks and benefits.

Modality of bilateral stimulation

Other considerations include the modality of bilateral stimulation:

Tapping is often used, as O'Shea finds that the sensory domain is especially salient for infant ego states. Paulsen typically uses tapping in this work, but may use eye movements when the client can readily access the material, or to assist the client in moving through abreactive material.

Although there is no research on this point, clinically it seems that eye movements are more likely to produce cognitive responses, and somatic stimulation more likely to produce somatic responses, or responses from implicit memory.

Although all laws and ethical considerations regarding touch should be taken into account, where appropriate, therapist proximity and tapping on the ankles may be a source of reassurance.

O'Shea &Paulsen (2007) recommend the use of reclining chairs, or a comfortable chair and ottoman, so the client may be recumbent, with feet up and resting comfortably. The therapist can ergonomically tap on the client's ankles with client reclining or otherwise well supported. Comfort is especially important for longer sessions. If the therapist is in a chair on wheels, adjustments can easily be made to the therapist's proximity to the client, even if the therapist is not tapping, but rather utilizing tactile bilateral stimulation equipment or auditory equipment.

Because the work causes clients to associate to very young states, for many people, the therapist's proximity is important. Across the room may work for talk therapy, but for this work, clients will often want the therapist closer, because babies want people close. We strongly recommend against any kind of acting out such as holding, rocking, etc., in an attempt to supply in physicality the holding and touch that the client would have needed as a child. Rather, the repair will be supplied in the mind's eye. The therapeutic relationship is boundaried and structured appropriately and without acting out, even as the therapist's tone of voice may be soft and maternal, and the therapist's physical presence proximal.

Therapeutic stance and grounding

Other considerations include the therapist's use of a gentle and comforting tone, (to avoid triggering), soft lights, and ready access to items that will evoke a resourced state. These may include canines, equines, the outdoors, fragrant oils, or other items that activate the client's ventral vagal nervous system, to be discussed more fully elsewhere in this book. Any well-intentioned soothing effort that ends up being triggering should be replaced with something less triggering; perpetrators often use soothing tones in their seductions. If the therapist inadvertently says or does something triggering, it can be helpful to ask the client, or parts of the client, what the similarities are between the perpetrator and the therapist, and <u>then</u> what the differences are. As needed, the therapist should reassure that the specific feared boundary violations will never happen in this office.

Possible time & session use   Non-dissociative clients may require as few as two preparation sessions to conduct steps 1, 2, and 3, although several sessions of preparation is more typical.

Dissociative clients take longer by far   Highly dissociative clients may take months or even years before the ET approach can be attempted because of fragility, resistance, risk and the challenges of establishing rapport under conditions of profound mistrust. A common error is for a front part of a client, in collaboration with the enthusiastic but perhaps naïve therapist, to agree to move forward based on the front part's attestations of trust in the clinician. Both the front of the client and the therapist may be unaware of the reluctance and mistrust of other parts of the client beneath the surface. Embarking in trauma work in this circumstance will result in no progress at best, or more likely, destabilization and retraumatization.

7 Preparation--Containment

7-1 Containment imagery helps fractionate the target to titrate intensity

Purposes of containment methods

The use of containment imagery and procedures have several purposes in the containment step of the early trauma work, namely:

- to increase overall client stability,

- to increase the likelihood that the client can stay in the "window of tolerance" (Siegel, 1999) during the ET processing,

- to provide convenient imagery to enable focus on one piece of the work, called "fractionation," (Kluft, 2013) and pacing of the work as it unfolds during the ET process, and

- to create a clear "desktop" for detail work, much as when doing beadwork or repairing jewelry. If one works amidst clutter, there isn't the clarity needed to attend to and work with the details. With a clear desktop, the details of the beads or chain links are revealed. Similarly, when one contains all except what one is working on, the beads are easy to focus on and there isn't as much distraction and background noise from other memories or contemporary problems.

- to create a distance from the client's executive part(s) and the material, which might be overwhelming if it were accessed simultaneously in conscious mind.

- to enable partially processed material to be set aside between sessions until it be addressed,

- to lower the background noise and chatter during trauma processing by keeping later material at bay, for a better "signal/noise" ratio,

- to have the skilled capacity, in the client's life in general, to set material aside and stay focused as needed, compartmentalizing life segments.

The hypnosis tradition Containment originates in the hypnosis tradition, and is a distancing maneuver. See for example Kluft (2013), Watkins &Watkins (1997). The use of containment imagery is familiar to many EMDR therapy practitioners and hypnosis practitioners over many years (Kluft, 1990). Though its historical review is beyond the scope of this book, it must be mentioned that this is not new with EMDR as has been erroneously supposed (Kluft, 2013).

7-2 Having one alter "looking through the eyes" at a time also fractionates the work in complex trauma/dissociation

When the client acquires the ability to set aside disturbing experiences in order to cope with the demands of daily life, confidence tends to increase along with life functioning. The containment ability then, when practiced consistently for a time, is a self-management skill that can be life changing for many clients.

In child development theory, containment occurs with maternal "scaffolding" (Winnicott, 1960) that allows babies to begin to develop a self. Baby develops an internal representation of the mother's view of baby as a person with needs, feelings and a self. In her reassurance baby learns that reassurance is possible, down regulation is possible, and mother can be counted on to acknowledge baby's feelings and needs.

In the therapeutic use of containment, then, the benefits are not only the immediate down-regulation of affect, but also, over the long term, development of a skill in self-regulation as well as a repair in development of this internal mental construct of self. The use of containment imagery can be an important key to pacing psychotherapeutic work (Kluft, 1989). The skill helps the client to compartmentalize in a deliberate way not only in therapy but in life.

Deliberate containment may or may not use hypnotic imagery, and is different than involuntary (pathological) dissociation. With containment imagery as used in the early trauma approach, we are evoking the brain's capacity for dissociation in a deliberate and healthy manner, to pace the work. Having containment skills increases client sense of mastery and internal locus of control, with resulting positive impact on stability.

The setting aside of disturbing material in dissociative clients generally requires ego state work which will be described later in the chapter.

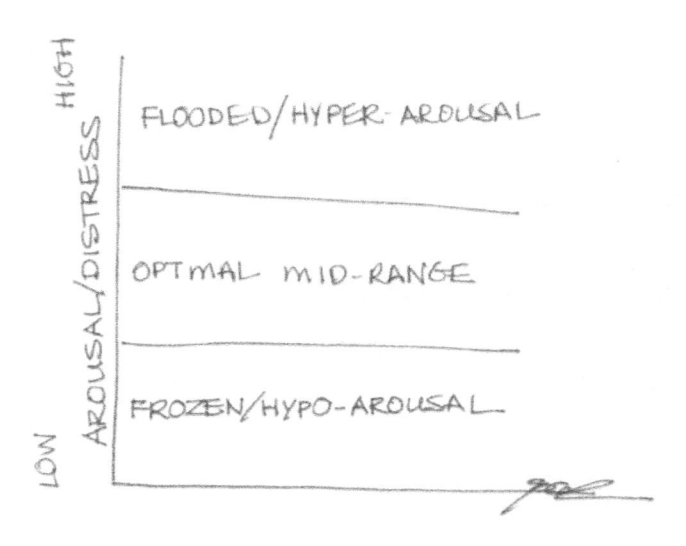

7-3 It's important to keep the level of activation within the optimal arousal window, neither hyper nor hypo-aroused (Siegel, 1999).

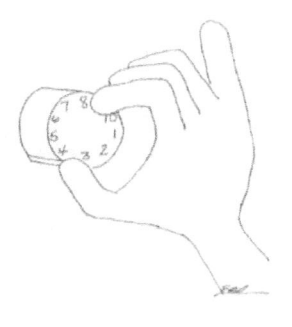

7-4 With practice, the client can use an imaginal rheostat to down regulate emotion

Staying in the window of tolerance

Daniel Siegel (1999) described the "window of tolerance" which refers to a level of optimal arousal.

- If the client is too affectively aroused during trauma processing or even during therapy in general, healing change cannot occur. This is because the client is either flooded and overwhelmed or numb and shut down.

Porges' polyvagal theory (2011) states that:

- High levels of arousal are associated with sympathetic nervous system activation that occurs when the organism mobilizes for action, whether fight or flight, in an adrenaline response.

- Conversely, if the client is hypo-aroused, they are frozen, shut down, surrendered, collapsed or dissociated, change cannot occur. This hypo-aroused state is associated with what Porges calls the dorsal vagal nervous system, the first parasympathetic nervous system.

The optimal mid-range In the optimal mid-range of arousal, the client is able to grow, change and heal.

Porges's introduction of a second parasympathetic nervous system, the ventral vagal nervous system, or the social engagement system. The goal for therapy and for well-being is to be readily in this engaged and connected state, when it is safe in present time to do so.

The therapeutic relationship is a key means to activate the ventral vagal nervous system so that change can occur within the safety and support of social engagement.

ET benefit: increased affect tolerance Where prior to ET work, clients may too readily feel that their trauma processing porridge is too hot or too cold. Once their window of tolerance is increased, they will more likely feel that they can tolerate trauma processing, and that the intensity is just right. Paulsen refers to this as "Porges Porridge Theory," with Porges's approval (personal communication, October 2010).

7-5 When containment strategies are well-practiced, the client can do the work and remain in the optimal arousal zone, not too hot (sympathetic arousal), not too cold (dorsal vagal shutdown), but just right (which Paulsen calls Porges porridge theory).

Containment of affect regulation When a containment ability is in place, the client can more readily remain connected to the present time, engaged in the therapeutic relationship and stay in the optimal arousal window. This enables trauma processing to occur even though the material being processed is very early and the client as a baby had few if any internal ego resources to draw upon. The material would likely be overwhelming if approached all at once.

The window of tolerance for dissociative clients

For dissociative clients, staying in the window of tolerance is more challenging.

- There is often a brittleness that accompanies any stability the client has been able to achieve, which can be disrupted by internal or external events.
- Ego strengthening methods can enhance the person's window of tolerance. In particular, somatic resourcing (Ogden &Fisher, 2014) can be a potent means to expand a dissociative client's window of tolerance.
- Having said that, the procedure below will be narrowly described in terms of the modifications needed to apply it to dissociative clients.

Containment imagery

The notion of a container is a universal idea, but its use in treating complex trauma was formalized by Richard Kluft (1984). Initially, containment imagery was used in the form of formal hypnotic trance, but it is also useful without formal trance induction, in the form of simple imagery created imaginally at a moment's notice.

This method utilizes the almost universal innate capacity to compartmentalize and distance. It is a skill related to mindfulness, because it requires an observing stance to begin to allow material to be set aside. The stance of curious observing distance is critical to containment, and with practice becomes readily available for many.

It may well be related to the capacity to dissociate, but it differs from pathological dissociation because it is voluntary, conscious and deliberate.

See Appendix D for samples of language for evoking container imagery.

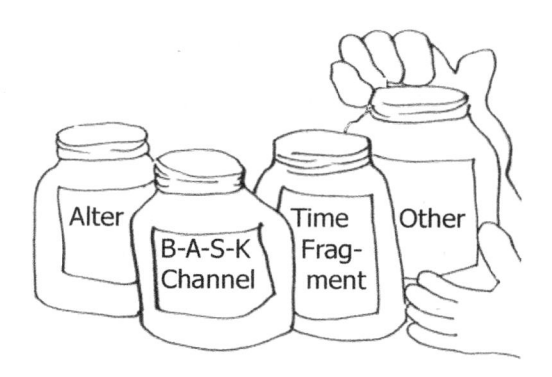

7-6 Memories can be fractionated by many dimensions including by alter/ego state, BASK channel, time fragment or other ways.

Containment to fractionate: the work

In the early trauma approach, containment is used to fractionate (Kluft, 1990) the work and to increase the client's ability to stabilize him or herself.

Whether the client chooses a box, a vase, an oil refinery, a post-office box, a police locker, a gym bag, or anything else, the image can be personalized.

The client can practice using the container imagery over days or weeks and achieve considerable mastery, learning to set aside that which might otherwise distract until it can receive full attention.

Used in an ET session, it is a readily available and convenient image.

Once the full panoply of disturbance is contained, a single piece can be "pulled out" and worked, rather like a single tissue can be pulled out of a box of tissues without pulling out more than what can be useful in the moment.

Errant memories that slip out ahead of their time can be redirected gently back into the container.

7-7 As in beadwork, temporal integration is detailed and nuanced, requiring a "clear desktop" free of distractions in the client's mind

A clear desktop Once most disturbing material is set aside or "contained," it becomes possible for the client to discern subtle shifts in the felt sense as it emerges.

If daily distractions, big intrusive memories, relationship problems, life challenges, etc., were not set aside, the subtle felt sense would likely be lost in the din.

With those matters temporarily set aside and contained, the client's focal attention can go to the moment-to-moment emergence of subtle body sensation, affect, cognition, symbolic imagery, or other memory fragments.

This emerging ability in the client brings with it a new problem for many individuals, namely, enactment of emergent memory.

For dissociative clients

7-8 Containment strategies will be helpful in closing down incomplete sessions or sessions where ego state work has touched on traumatic memories

Enactment as leakage of contained or dissociated material

One of the most common problems of any trauma work is traumatic transference, in which the relationship dynamics of the original traumatic experience are mistakenly attributed to present time.

This problem is less of a hazard with standard EMDR therapy when the narrative is known to the client and therapist. This subject will be covered more extensively later, but is introduced here to alert the therapist to inform the client about leakage of material contained unconsciously. Dissociative clients already have a capacity for containment, but because it is unconscious and reflexive, it is a dissociative characteristic.

As that capacity is deliberately and consciously utilized in step 1 containment, the dissociative client especially, but also the non-dissociative client, needs to be aware of the phenomenon of leakage of traumatic material from contained or dissociated places into present time in the form of reenactment material.

Enactment to distinguish then from now

As is evident in this book, Paulsen often uses cartoons and metaphors (see also Paulsen, 2009) for psycho-educational purposes. To communicate with clients about the phenomenon of enactment, she often uses the notion of King Tut's tomb with the client.

She says, "when that first archaeologist opened King Tut's tomb, the air that hit him was thousands of years old. If he wasn't aware of that, he might think he needed a bath, as if the staleness was caused in present time. In fact, it was ancient history that was only accessed in present time. In the early trauma work, all that isn't being worked on is contained, and then systematically and deliberately accessed by time frame." When ancient "vapors" leak up from their containers in early trauma work, the client may think and feel that it is coming from present time or the current relationship with the therapist.

Between sessions, those ancient vapors may be attributed to a spouse or a boss or a current relationship. So the therapist will be asking, "is this the first time you have felt that feeling (dynamic) or could this be part of baby's story?"

With a few repetitions by the therapist of this query, the client will typically come to realize that the cognitive, affective, somatic, or behavioral material attributed to present time may be leakage from baby's contained experience. This will be taken up again in the next chapter.

Case example Mary Lou is a 37-year-old Asian-American female with a history of immigration to the United States at age 2, when her family left Vietnam and moved to California. Shortly after the move, Mary Lou's mother died, and she and her sister were raised by her father and her father's mother, who came to the United States with the family. Mary Lou's first language is English, for all purposes, and she is a medical technician by trade. Mary Lou's relationships have been impaired due to her mistrust and inability to believe that anyone will be there for her. She presents to therapy with the chief complaints of difficulty with relationships and trust, and also with difficulty managing emotions and outbursts at home and on the job.

In the preparation to repair her early attachment experiences, the first step of containment was initiated. Her therapist suggested that she practice the use of a container, using the following language:

"Mary Lou, how would it be if we had you practice using a container image to hold things that we have yet to address? It might help you in several ways: one, it would hold disturbing things aside until you had time to fully address them, two, it will help us have a "clear desk top," so we can do our early trauma repair, which might be rather subtle. It's like doing bead work or some other detail work, where it's important to have a clear desk top so you don't lose track of beads. Here, if you practice this skill, we'll use it to work on a bit of disturbance at a time, and hold the rest aside until we can address it.

Thirdly, if we have incomplete sessions, at the end of such a session we can use the container to save the work until we can get back to it, but you'll be able to comfortably and safely drive home after the appointment. Are you willing to practice?"

Mary Lou said she was, and she selected the image of a Vietnamese ceramic urn. She agreed to practice the use of the urn as a container between appointments.

She practiced every day for two weeks and at the interim appointment the therapist checked with her to see how that practice was going. Mary Lou said she was using it to focus better at work and be less distracted. She also noticed that she was slightly calmer at work because she was not worrying in the background.

Complex case Example Greta Lynn is a 42-year-old Caucasian female who has a complex trauma history, and has worked with her therapist for a year on stabilization using ego state therapy, breathing exercises, grounding exercises and establishing rapport and trust. She has also attended yoga in a nearby yoga center. Greta Lynn and her therapist have also worked on somatic resourcing, and certain other somatic methods, to begin to connect Greta Lynn with her body sensations.

Greta Lynn and her therapist engaged in a number of preparation steps, prior to doing trauma work and one of them was the container image. The therapist introduced the idea similarly to the example of Maureen, above, but differently. With Greta Lynn, the therapist invited any parts of the self who had something to say about the idea of containing disturbance until it can be fully addressed to come into the conference room to discuss it. One part, Greta Lynn II, said that it didn't sound much different than what they normally do, namely, protect Greta Lynn, the front part of the self, from disturbing memories, so she was not opposed. The therapist agreed there was a similarity, but said this is deliberately done instead of unconsciously or habitually.

Another part of the self, mother part, is an introject of the client's external mother, who is deceased. Over the months, the therapist has several times oriented mother part to the current circumstances, including the date, the client's home state (far from where her abuse occurred in childhood), the fact that her mother was deceased, and other facts of her current circumstances. mother part was, then, willing in general to support and allow the therapy. Mother part said that she thought the idea of a container was silly, but that she wouldn't stop the practice of it.

Another part of the self, father part, is an introject of the client's external father, who is alive. The therapist has worked studiously to orient the father part of self to present circumstances as well, but with mixed results.

In addition to frequently forgetting the present circumstances requiring repeat orientation, father part was suspicious of the therapist's suggestions. He angrily objected to the idea of containing anything between appointments, and the therapist determined by asking the father part that he thought all disturbance should be left in front of mind at all times.

On further inquiry, and reminders that the bad old days were over, that the client was now 37 and had a life of her own, and that the external father was far away and no contact for twelve years, father part said reluctantly that it would be ok to do an experiment to see if the client could stay safe if she weren't continuously aware of risks and disturbances.

After several weeks of repeating the orientation and mediation between parts, Greta Lynn was able to conduct the experiment of using a container and successfully practice it. Although Greta Lynn was only intermittently successful or willing to use it (because father part kept forgetting it was ok to use it now), she came to understand its benefit and developed the skill.

When the therapist checked in, Greta Lynn said she was feeling better but didn't know why. The therapist thanked the parts who allowed the container image to be used, with special thanks to father part.

When There Are No Words - Sandra Paulsen

8 Preparation–Ventral Vagal Resourcing

8-1 Learning to evoke a felt sense of safety or "safe state"

Language O'Shea refers to this step as "safe state" resourcing, and the reason for that language is described below. The author is calling this section ventral vagal resourcing because there are myriad ways to evoke the neurobiological state of the ventral vagal nervous system, which achieves the needed goal of enhancing the client's capacity for processing and expanding the window of tolerance.

Purpose of ventral vagal resourcing The purposes of step two are:

1) to ensure that clients are adequately resourced prior to approaching the processing of difficulty material, and that their ventral vagal nervous systems are activated,

2) to further ensure that clients can stay in the optimal arousal window to the degree possible, and

3) to increase the likelihood the client can tap into adaptive resource neural networks. The following expands on those purposes:

Ventral vagal nervous system and adequate resources Before Porges, it was accepted that there were two nervous systems:

- the sympathetic system, and
- the parasympathetic systems.

Steven Porges (2011) hypothesized that there are two para-sympathetic systems, with very different functions, one dorsal vagal, and one ventral vagal. Porges formulates the three systems as follows:

- the sympathetic nervous system is in charge of fight and flight responses.

- the dorsal vagal system is responsible for the freeze response, the shutting down that occurs when neither fight nor flight is possible.

- the ventral vagal nervous system described by Porges is also called the social engagement system, and it is the one implicated in attachment and connection itself.

Although Porges describes it in the context of connection between individuals, in the opinion of the author, the ventral vagal nervous system may also be activated in any other kind of connection, including connection to community, as well as spiritual and intuitive connection with others; ventral vagal engagement is only possible in conditions of safety.

Optimal arousal window in safe state

This subject was covered previously. The only expansion specific to the safe state step is that when a client has access to their ventral vagal nervous system, it increases their ability to remain in the optimal arousal window.

Therefore, considerable time in session and between sessions may need to be invested to arrive at this capacity.

Paulsen practices in the forest, and almost everyone feels safe there because of the inherent tranquility of nature. Therefore, in cases in which the client has flown in to do intensive treatment over several days, the work proceeds if the client reports and exhibits sufficient safety to do the work. In that case, the client is encouraged to practice safe state upon return to their home.

Accessing adaptive neural networks

The more time one has spent in the ventral vagal state, the more associative linkages and connections there are, resulting in readier access to the ventral vagal state, and the greater likelihood of accessing adaptive neural networks.

Establishing a ventral vagal or safe state

Much trauma work is painful, frightening, deep, and potentially disorganizing for many clients.

Therefore, in order for the client to sustain processing without being overwhelmed or collapsing, s/he must have sufficient levels of safety and resource to tolerate and thrive in the work.

This has been called the optimal arousal window or the "window of tolerance" (Siegel, 1999). The therapist must ensure that:

- the client has sufficient activation of their ventral vagal nervous system before and after the activation of memory, which will evoke the sympathetic nervous system, and likely also memory of dorsal vagal surrender and shutdown, and

- during processing, there must be sufficient social engagement by means of the therapeutic relationship or other resources to ensure that dual attention awareness can be retained or processing will arrest.

Language for the client: "whole self" or "safe state"

- O'Shea has described a process of identifying what she calls a "whole self-state" which is a deeply resourced state intended to include many dimensions of self. Therefore, she also uses the term "safe state" and "whole self-state" interchangeably.

- O'Shea's emphasis is on the term "safe state" rather than the commonly used "safe place" device taught in EMDR therapy trainings because she wishes to impart to the client an understanding that the state is a natural part of the client's system.

- The term "place" sounds like it is external to the client, whereas "state" is understood in lay thinking to be within the client. Therefore, for example, a client who uses the "beach" for his "safe place," might think that there is magic in the beach. With the language, "safe state," we intend to communicate that it is not the beach that is magic, but, rather, the client's capacity to turn attention to the beach at will to evoke a sense of safety that is resourcing.

On the challenges of achieve a "whole self-state" in dissociative clients

- Dissociative clients will not be able to evoke a felt sense of safety by evoking their whole self-system simultaneously, because some parts of the self are holding sequestered and unprocessed traumatic experience. Therefore, a more reasonable tactic for resourcing is for therapist and client to become acquainted with the specific functions and attributes of various alter personalities or ego states, and enlist their agreement to step forward and become executive as needed.

- Conversely, obtaining the agreement of parts holding unprocessed sequestered material to step back and contain the material at a distance will facilitate functioning and increase the likelihood of the client feeling as resourced and safe as possible, given the challenges of being highly dissociative.

Increasing the window of tolerance

All of these lessons need to be in place, along with:

- the felt sense of being grounded in present circumstances, namely, that all parts of the self are in one body

- orientation to the present year and orientation to the present location

- awareness that the abuse isn't happening any more (if it isn't)

Once these have occurred, the client may be more capable of tolerating positive affect and positive soma, resulting in an increased window of tolerance and greater capacity for processing without dissociating.

Means to strengthen ventral vagal state for processing

Various means can ensure this, including for example:

- the presence of a therapy animal,

- the kind voice and presence of the therapist,

- therapist patter such as, "it's not happening now," "it's a memory," "that's it,"

- ventral vagal reminders, "this time you're not alone, I'm right here with you,"

- the therapeutic environment itself is also important in creating a sense of safety. For example, at the time of this writing, Paulsen has created a healing center in the woods on an island, with an ambience of gentle sweetness of the cedar trees, tranquil colors and natural surrounds inside and outside the building.

- Resourcing the client with appropriately chosen stories, songs, or other methods is well within the understanding of connection, if it serves to reliably activate the client's ventral vagal nervous system in a cost-effective manner.

This is very important when the work is very early and attachment-related, because the work is based far more on the felt sense of that explicitly remembered material. The present felt sense needs to be a strengthening holding environment. Physical holding or other boundary violations are strongly discouraged as misguided attempts to repair early attachment injury.

8-2 The therapeutic relationship may activate the client's ventral vagal nervous system, especially if gently, over time, they share life-enhancing experiences, so the client learns ways to stay in the window of tolerance.

On spiritual resourcing

Regarding spiritual practice, there are several things to keep in mind:

- Many therapists were trained to eschew spiritual practice in their therapy practice, for reasons ranging from academic to agnostic to scope of practice, all of which are reasonable.
- There is at least one compelling reason to consider using spiritual resources in strengthening clients for trauma processing where appropriate. For many individuals, spiritual resources are their highest and strongest resources, making other resources pale in comparison.
- Spiritual resources should not be foisted on clients where unwelcome, of course. Many clients have great reluctance about organized religion and may have experienced clergy betrayal with resulting spiritual trauma and alienation.
- Paulsen has found that nature tends to be spiritually profound and grounding for many, and is absent the human betrayal and bureaucratic elements of organized religion, so is more acceptable for many.
- Any client for whom organized religion is resourcing might well be encouraged to bring that element into the therapy for the client's sake, regardless of the therapist's own frame of reference.

8-3 Usually, even those without a formal religious frame of reference or spiritual understanding can activate their ventral vagal system in nature

Natural spiritual resources

- Paulsen has found that Native American spirituality is natural, non-bureaucratic and profoundly resourcing for many.
- In Paulsen's life and practice, the Red Road has been a spiritual path. Her telling of Native stories and songs is with permission, ongoing consultation, humility and a practice of daily gratitude.

- This spiritual practice imbues the healing center with ephemeral qualities that serve the client, the work and the therapist well.
- The therapist is cautioned not to pick only the parts of any cultural traditions that they like while leaving behind the more challenging parts of a cultural tradition. Such a practice is called "cherry-picking" and is profoundly unwelcome and resented by Native cultures.

Felt sense of safety is paramount

Whether spiritual, nature, animal assisted, human or other resources are employed, ensuring the client has a felt sense of safety and resource is critical.

This practice utilizes the brain's innate capacity to be in a resourced state, activates the ventral vagal nervous system, and tends to enhance a felt sense of self efficacy.

It brings the adaptive neural networks online, evokes neocortical functioning, and increases the likelihood that the client can spontaneously shift into adaptive understandings and resolutions in the course of the processing.

Spontaneous shifts are scarce

In early trauma work, spontaneous shifts often do not occur.

- The therapist, then, will likely need to employ an interweave to access adaptive neural networks.
- There are numerous possible interweaves to consider, namely imaginal, experiential, ego state, somatic, cognitive, objectivity, or other interweaves as needed.
- Having primed the pump with adequate resourcing means that there won't be as much groping in the dark for a resource, for a way to shift perspective, for a way to bring in adult, spiritual or compassionate resources during processing.

Prognostic and diagnostic red flags

- If a client cannot access a felt sense of safety with any of the above described means, the therapist should consider that s/he has overlooked a dissociative disorder.
- Considerable additional preparation may be necessary, including: properly and formally assessing for a dissociative disorder, extensive psycho-education regarding the role of the polyvagal systems in appropriate language for the client.

Additional trust building will be necessary, likely by means of extensive somatic and ego state work, prior to conducting EMDR therapy.

Safe state for dissociative clients

Safe state is much harder to achieve for many dissociative clients.

- Dissociative clients may never have felt safe in their lives. If they were to begin to relax they would feel especially endangered, as if relaxation were an invitation to predators.
- They often blame themselves for the predatory behavior of others, saying they should have prevented the predation with additional vigilance. They believe that they were stupid to not expect the predator to do what s/he did and prevent, even though they may have been a small child at the time of the traumatic experience

- It is often necessary to do ego state maneuvers to address directly the ego states who either:

  are disoriented and believe the old harm is happening now, if it is not, or

  are oriented to present person, place and time, and yet believe that they should not permit a felt sense of safety, because then if something bad happens it will be their fault

- The language for working with ego states to orient them to present body, place and time, as well as the language for working with introjects to get them on board with the treatment, are covered in Paulsen (2009) and summarized in an appendix to this document.

- The use of canine assisted therapy to evoke a felt awareness of present safety can be very useful in conjunction with working with alters for present orientation to safe circumstances (in the office, or at home, if they are indeed safe at home).

Many sessions may be needed

- At the same time the client is working on being able to reliably evoke a sense of safety, the client should also be developing an ability to use containment imagery to set aside material not actively requiring attention in the present moment,

- For some individuals, there will be a need to practice both skills outside of the sessions. Therefore, the therapist will be checking on both of those skills as needed as the work progresses.

- For some individuals Steps 1 and 2 can be demonstrated in a single session and the client's capacity to do both will be completely adequate.

- For many others, more sessions and for those with highly complex trauma histories, many more sessions and methods will be needed.

- For clients who do not have Dissociative identity Disorder (DID), EMDR therapy trauma processing should not begin until both steps 1 and 2 skills are well in place and the client can reliably evoke them.

- For DID clients, considerable additional resourcing steps may be necessary before there is readiness for EMDR therapy trauma processing. See (Paulsen & Golston, 2014a; 2014b).

Emotional first aid methods and healthy habits

- O'Shea emphasizes the need to teach and/or review what she calls "emotional first aid methods," for which she has developed a "healthy habits" handout for clients. These teach basic emotional skills and coping techniques including the use of: imagination, dream sleep, the "butterfly hug" (Jarero, Artigas, & Hartung, 2006) etc.

Somatic resourcing non-dissociative

- Somatic resourcing can also be used to evoke the ventral vagal nervous system in the client. With a non-dissociative client this can be done by asking about something they find resourcing or life enhancing.

- If the client, for example, says, "the ocean," the therapist might say, "what is it about the ocean?" joining the smiling client with a smile of their own. This tends to activate both therapist and client's ventral vagal nervous system. The client might answer, "the majesty, the rhythm of the waves, the sound and the salt air."

- After lingering over these words and matching the client's enjoyment in a shared experience of the ocean, the therapist might say, "and where do you notice that in your body," or "what do you notice in your body as you think of that majesty and salt air?"
- The client may answer, "an expansion in my chest," or "lightness all over my body." Such a discussion can expand and enrich over some minutes, with a slow, relaxed tempo, in a non-dissociative client.
- As a caution, any client with unworked trauma may trip into the memory of the trauma if the resource is held too long.

8-4 Highly dissociative people may feel they have no body
(This figure originally appeared in Gomez & Paulsen, 2016 children's book All the Colors of Me)

Dissociative clients and somatic resourcing

Somatic resourcing is often challenging for DID clients:

- A dissociative client may be able to get as far as describing what she likes about the ocean or some other resource.
- However, if the therapist asks about the client's bodily experience, the client may feel tense, report confusion, or even say "We don't have one of those."

Such a direct question about body sensation can evoke muteness or paralysis if it is specifically a triggering question that is reminiscent of a perpetrator's question. Therefore, the therapist is wise to initially stop well short of direct inquiry about bodily sensation with a dissociative client.

After some time or weeks of somatic resourcing, the therapist can begin to inquire of a dissociative client, where in the body they notice the "expansive feeling of the ocean's waves," etc. Often ego state work will be necessary to orient and resolve concerns of alters advising against bodily awareness for various reasons.

Some alters may insist there is no body. Such an alter personality shouldn't be forced to have body awareness before they are ready, but other alters can be grounded and oriented to the present circumstances of safety in the body.

It can be helpful to orient to the present facts such as, is the perpetrator alive or dead, and, if alive, whether they are they near or far, elderly and infirm, or pose a present danger. Orienting to the present body of the client can help child parts to feel safe in present time, e.g., to their height reaching up in a bookshelf, etc. (Twombly, 2009a, 2009b).

eg

8-5 "Whose hand is that?" can orient parts to the body they live in (This figure originally appears in Paulsen, 2009, "Looking Through the Eyes")

Slowly resourcing without referring to body

With a dissociative client, it is initially more helpful to develop a list of resources and join the client in a pleasant discussion of what they find resourcing about those resources, to the degree they can tolerate positive affect.

The shared enjoyment, again, tends to activate a shared ventral vagal experience between the two, and that helps to remediate any impoverishment of somatic mirroring from the client's childhood.

That list of resources can be used to slowly expand the client's window of tolerance.

With psycho-education, gradually over time, about the importance of being able to notice and tolerate positive body sensation, the therapist may gently begin to invite discussion of body sensation, without lingering on the topic very long.

Tolerating positive sensation

The therapist may find that the client cannot tolerate positive body sensation because it evokes double binds in the client about pleasure and culpability for pleasure, or shame over having had a perpetrator stimulate youthful tender tissues to arousal. To remedy such blockages, direct ego state work with parts of self that punish for felt sense of resource of positive soma or pleasure is necessary.

This is often two parts, at least, a shame child part and the introject of an external perpetrator, who shames the child. The therapist should work with the introject first, according to the "monster sequence," (Paulsen, 2009). See also Appendix C about working with perpetrator introjects.

Psycho-education about body sensation

Additional psycho-education is often needed, such as:

- Reading to the various aspects of the client the laws of the state regarding the definitions of child abuse can be helpful for providing objective information about what is permissible and impermissible and how seriously the current courts take child abuse, contrary to what the child learned in the family about the value of their own humanity, or their culpability for what happened to them as a child,

- A child is never responsible or guilty for having felt a sense of sexual pleasure or arousal, even if that arousal was wrong, because it was caused by an adult either directly or indirectly, even if the adult blamed the child,

- Tender tissues in erogenous zones are designed to be responsive to stimulation, so if arousal occurred as one of several responses to a non-violent molestation, the tissues were only doing what they are designed to do.

- The nerve endings of genital tissue are very sensitive and close together, but they are supposed to be activated by normal sexual maturity, not by predatory behavior in adults that prematurely sexualizes a child.

- If sexual arousal is prematurely activated in a child in molestation, it is not ever the child's fault, or the body's fault for doing its job, and the child could not have stopped it if the adult is intent upon molestation.

- If the child subsequently learned to truncate the experience of arousal of any kind or resource of almost any kind, the remedy needs to be to restore those normal sensations and experiences.

Case example

Mary Lou, who was introduced in the containment step (step 1), came to therapy with a history of practicing Buddhism, which she was raised with in her family. She had set it aside for a time while assimilating with her American friends. On inquiry, her therapist helped her realize that she found comfort in the practice of meditation and Buddhist mindfulness. Her therapist helped her to understand that when meditating she is using her own capacity to deliberately shift her own neurobiological state. When she meditated, she reported feeling connected to the universe and to her ancestors. This brought her comfort and tranquility.

Mary Lou agreed to practice meditation again as an experiment to see if it made her life better or worse. She set about to meditate at least once a day, sometimes twice a day. After several weeks, Mary Lou reported increased confidence in her ability to regulate her internal state. She was able to be more dispassionate about the highs and lows of life and daily stressors. This meant that her tolerance was increased and she felt stronger. Together, Mary Lou and her therapist concluded that she was almost ready to do trauma work.

Added prep for complex clients

In addition to the above considerations, dissociative clients will require additional preparation beyond the containment and safe state steps described here.

Complex case example

Greta Lynn, introduced in the containment step (step 1), and her therapist had engaged in numerous preparation strategies as earlier described. The therapist wanted to help Greta to learn to activate her own internal ventral vagal nervous system or "safe state," but she knew she needed to consult with protective parts of self, first.

The therapist first approached the father part, who was the "highest ranking honcho" in Greta Lynn's self-system. The therapist asked, "father part, I'd like to help her [stated ambiguously about who "she" is, namely, the front part or the total self] to feel stronger and safer and calmer, but I don't want to do that without your permission."

A slightly smug smile appeared on the client's face, and the therapist knew that the father part was nearby, and was pleased to be consulted. "I know I can't accomplish anything without your permission. By the way, father part, are you remembering that you aren't the external father, who is dead, but an internal likeness of him? That you came for protection, in your way? And that its 2016 and she's here in Seattle?" The client answered, in a deeper voice, "oh yeah. Hard to remember that. you pretty sure about that?"

The therapist was relieved to see that the orienting of the Father Part took far less time now, after several repetitions over time, and she knew the work was progressing. "Well, don't take my word for it, here's a mirror, so you can see whose face it is. Here's the newspaper to see what year and place it is. Given that, and given that the external father is dead, is it okay if I help her to feel safer?"

Suddenly and unexpectedly, in popped another part of the self, uncle part of self, who said, "no way is it ok for her to feel safe. I'll show her! That's when the bad stuff happens, and it's her own fault for putting her guard down."

The therapist said, "thank you, uncle part, for coming! Nice to meet you. Thanks also for protecting her in that way, and for reminding us that when she was little, if she put her guard down, something bad would happen. Thank you for making sure she never put her guard down. Now, uncle part, are you remembering that the bad stuff isn't happening now? the uncle is in prison? The father is dead?

So if she puts her guard down now, it's not exactly the same as before. I mean something bad <u>could</u> happen, to her or to me or anyone, but not like when she was 6 and 9.

Never again will she be a little girl without a grown up to protect her, because grown up Greta Lynn is 42 years old, so the little ones will always have grown up Greta to make grown up decisions to help keep her safe. I think she's listening, but I'll help her remember how important this is. And as long as I'm around, I'll be another grown up to help her make good decisions. What do you think, uncle part?"

He answered, "I don't know."

The therapist answered, "Well, you don't have to decide anything today. But maybe we could do an experiment for a couple of weeks? How would it be if I worked with her on ways to feel safe, and you and I can reconvene and decide if it makes things better or worse, and you can decide."

"Well, ok," the client answered, in the voice of uncle part. "But what will I do?"

"She'll always need protection, uncle part, we all do need to stay safe. I don't get rid of parts though uncle. If you like we can look at another job for you that might be more fun. Or maybe you're ready for a nice deep healing sleep?"

The client shifted in her chair and a voice said quietly, "he's gone."

The therapist said, "I think we can proceed. If he disagrees he can speak up at any time, and he knows I'll take him into account. His job has been hard and thankless." A part of Greta Lynn answered, "we're just beginning to understand that."

9 About the Affective Circuits

Two stabilization procedures covered so far in this book are:

- Step 1–containment

- Step 2–safe state

The third stabilization step used as a matter of course is step 3 – resetting the affective circuits. This step is especially valuable for individuals who are:

- destabilized because they are flooded affectively,

- alexithymic and cut off from their affective circuits, or

- variously flooded and cut off, in a cyclic fashion

Imagination effects change   Imagination is an important component in effecting changes, including the neurobiology of change (Moseley, 2004).

Neurobiology of affect
- Sylvan Tomkins (1963) theorized that emotions are innate, and it was Tomkins' work O'Shea relied upon on in initially developing the ET approach.

- One of Paulsen's contributions to the development of ET was bringing in the affective neuroscience contributions of Panksepp, to provide a scientific and experimental substrate to the assumptions previously suggested by Tomkins based on clinical findings. Panksepp provided the empirical and experimental evidence that demonstrate that the basic human emotions were innate and basic (Panksepp & Biven, 2012; Panksepp, 1998).

- Lanius, et al, describe a columnar theory of dissociation (2014) based upon Panksepp's three levels of affective processing (1998) and evidence of columnar circuits in the brain.

Hats off to the seminal contribution of Jaak Panksepp   Panksepp's work on affective neuroscience was hard won because he did his seminal research on emotion at a time when funding was scarce, when the prevailing zeitgeist was that emotions were epiphenomena, and when prevailing wisdom was that only behavior and cognition were of import to science. Panksepp nevertheless proceeded to work experimentally, and identified seven hardwired, subcortical affective circuits that are present from birth and require no learning (Panksepp, 1998).

The function of affect   The affective circuits function to:

- Maximize survival prospects for the individual and more broadly, for evolutionary reasons,

- Provide information about safety, relationship and other basic purposes, (Panksepp, 1998).

Alexithymia: no feeling   Paulsen, O'Shea, & Lanius (2014) described the neurobiological and affective origins of alexithymia.

Alexithymia is here understood to refer to the inability to:

- readily identify and name emotions

- experience emotions or body sensations that underlie the emotions.

- have a felt sense of appetitive desires.

- have a normal orienting response and/or movement response to novel stimuli in one's environment,

Alexithymia and early trauma   Traumatic stress and early childhood trauma have been associated with alexithymia, affective dysregulation and deficits with regard to affective mentalization. Drawing on Panksepp's notion of basic subcortical affective circuits, the present chapter looks at strategies that use neocortical resources of imagery to increase affective mentalization, as well as reset them to allow increased adaptive, relational and inter-subjectivity capacity.

Brain organization is a function of emotions   Brain organization reflects self-organization because:

- Emotions are the basis for how the brain organizes its functioning (Siegel, 1999).

- What parent child interaction teaches a child about emotions directly affects the child's capacity for self-organization and self-management.

- When a parent helps a child to navigate emotional upset by reinitiating positive affect states, the resulting repair of rupture affects the child's attachment to that parent and what to expect of relationships for life.

9-1 Affect regulation, health and resilience is learned in the reliable presence of mother in the moment to moment attunement
(Figure originally appears in Paulsen, 2009, "Looking Through the Eyes".)

Inter-subjectivity, mother & child

According to Siegel (2015), when the "I-and-thou" of an intersubjective empathic exchange successfully and reliably occurs in the mother and child relationship:

- attachment learning emerges from this ongoing navigation,

- affect regulation skills unfold in the moment-to-moment dyad experiences,

- this navigation and learning becomes the foundation of mental health and resilience (Siegel, 2015).

Attachment disorder

Attachment disorder is often at the core of dissociative disorder (Barach, 1991).

- Insecure attachment attributable to early trauma and neglect leaves a child without an adequate repertoire of behavioral and emotional responses, so they don't have a means to respond adaptively to environmental demands.

- Without that repertoire, they cannot navigate the demands of developmental stages, and so, they accumulate a trail of unmet developmental needs.

- Without the assistance of the parent in helping the child regulate their emotions interactively and ventral vagally, the child is left to auto-regulate by means of a dorsal vagal response.

The use of dorsal vagal shutdown for down-regulation of affect is the difference between the oxytocin-based habit rooted in social engagement-acquired affect regulation, and an opioid-based habit acquired by coping alone when one cannot do it alone (Lanius, 2014 August, personal communication).

9-2 Chronic opioid activation may manifest as "rag doll eyes," or that far away "spaced out" look

Increased opioid activation

Opioid activation has several effects in the short and long term:

- In the short term, it lessens physical and emotional pain, by decreasing cortical activation, producing relief.

- In the long term, the opioid "habit" results in such symptoms as: dissociative amnesia, somatization responses, automatic emotional responses disconnected from a felt sense in the body, and a panoply of other symptoms, acting as memorials to what was not processed contemporaneously.

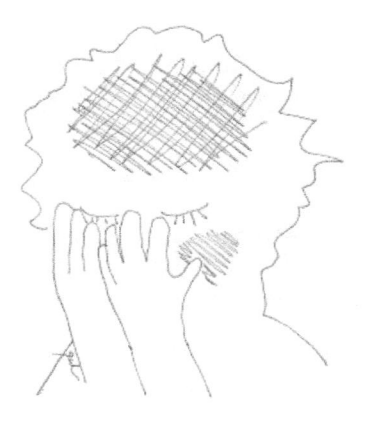

9-3 Shame is a deep brain function, switching off of the neocortex at the circuit breaker, when necessary to forsake one's own point of view to adopt the other's

Resulting shame Shame is a factor in shutdown habits as well, because;

- When parents do not help a child when the child needs help, the child typically will feel shame (Nathanson, 1992).

- The child, who is naturally the center of his or her own small universe, interprets the neglect as evidence that the child is doing something wrong.

  Therefore, core schema emerge from this unavailability of parental care, such as: "I have done something wrong," "I am bad," "I am unworthy," "I am shameful."

- The shame problem snowballs when the child struggles to achieve subsequent developmental tasks without sufficient help, and the child infers that this struggle and failure also reflects deep and abiding inadequacy.

  The experience of shame and unworthiness contributes foundationally to a range of disorders including: affect disorders, anxiety disorders, state regulation disorders, personality disorders, dissociative disorders, among others (Putnam, 1997).

Panoply of injury to self The child's efforts to establish a self, one of the prime early developmental imperatives, is compromised by the following, as a result of trauma or neglect in the first years:

- neurobiology of affect is disrupted especially in the secondary affective processing function,

- the child does not learn to expect support in relationships, but rather, conflict, neglect, or abandonment from others.

- relationships are disappointing and connection is either not possible or compromising.

- adaptive emotional responses do not develop,

- a core maladaptive schema is acquired,

- avoidance or hostility is adopted as a preemptive strike relationally,

- shame pervasively organizes the coping repertoire.

When There Are No Words - Sandra Paulsen

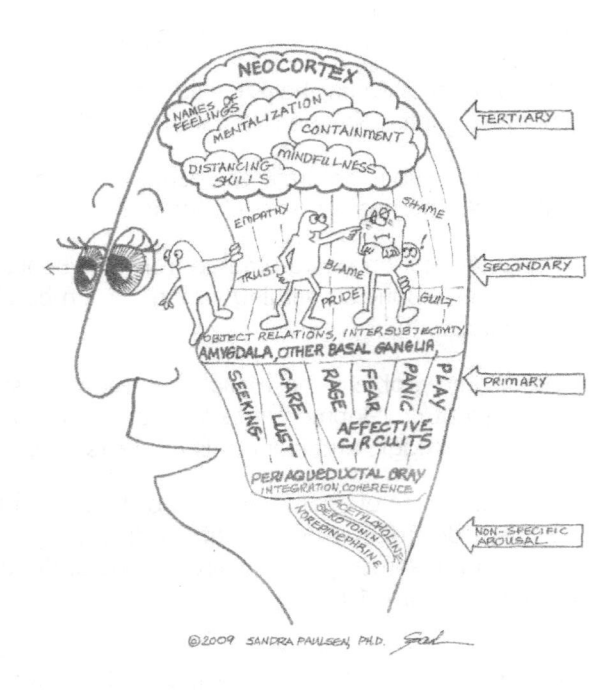

9-4–The Pankseppian three levels of affective processing in the brain

Panksepp's three levels of brain functioning: the first – subcortical circuits

As mentioned previously, Panksepp describes three levels of affective brain processing.

- Primary brain processing of affect is the level of the subcortical affective circuits. The seven circuits he found in rats, capitalized to show they are actual hardwired subcortical circuits, are:

  - SEEKING (which Panksepp calls the mother of all circuits)
  - RAGE (a defensive circuit for fight)
  - FEAR (another defensive circuit for flight)
  - PLAY (activates more of the brain than any other circuit)
  - LUST (in its myriad yearnings and urges)
  - CARE (the substrate for love and nurturing) and
  - PANIC. (the substrate for sadness, grief, loss, and depression)

The panic referred to in the PANIC circuit is not that of panic attacks, but, rather, infant separation distress. PANIC serves to cause the infant to engage in the distress cry, which evokes nurturing and the mother's return because it activates her CARE circuit.

- If all goes well, the mother returns to her distressed infant, comforts and cares for its needs, and the attachment is secure.

- If all does not go well, and mother does not return or provide for the infant's needs for any reason, then the melanchony that results by the thwarted PANIC response serves as the substrate for sadness and depression, according to Panksepp.

- This is consistent with the idea that lifelong or anaclitic depression begins in infancy with emotional deprivation.

- These hardwired circuits are common to all mammals and integration of them occurs at the level of the Periaqueductal Grey (PAG) in the midbrain.

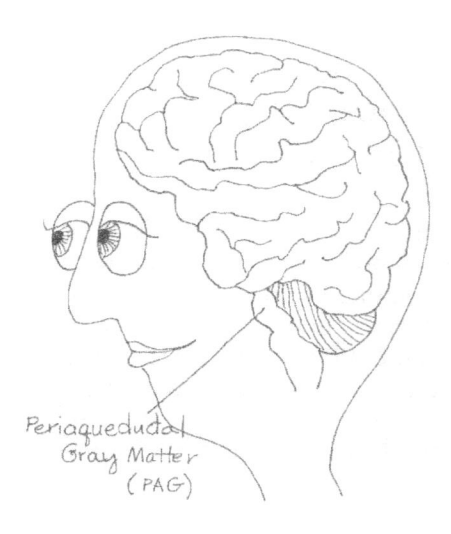

9-5 The affective circuits are integrated at the periaqueductal gray

Paulsen, O'Shea, & Lanius (2014) suggest that the affective circuits are the basis of the development of separate self-states. The circuits will be revisited in more depth after reviewing Panksepp's secondary and tertiary affective processing.

Secondary affective processing: relationship templates/ object relations

Panksepp's secondary affective processing is the initial learning of an infant during the attachment experience with the primary caretaker(s), and subsumes object relations, intersubjectivity, and classically conditioned relationship templates.

This learning occurs at the level of the amygdala and other basal ganglia. With normal attachment, a baby has full use of affective circuits, because a loving caretaker helps to provide containment and regulation of affect, both by providing loving arms that contain, being in synchrony or coherency in the energetic biofield (Siegel, 2015), and by demonstrating acceptance and the capacity to self-regulate.

With a loving caretaker, then, a baby acquires healthy use of emotional circuits for affective information about connection, curiosity, danger, injustice and the need to fight.

- Out of this experience, a lucky baby acquires self-efficacy, an integrated self, continuity of time, perception, self-and smooth-state switching.

- An unlucky baby acquires relationship templates based on classically conditioned fear responses to danger, rejection, or insufficient care.

The expectations baby acquires during the first two years of life define for a lifetime the successes and failures the individual is likely to experience.

- If baby is chronically hurt, disappointed, and helpless to get relationship needs met, the result is an avoidant or reactive approach to relating to others, unless repair is made by life experience or therapeutic means.

- Many syndromes likely have their basis in the first years of life including many cases of personality disorders, neurotic styles, dissociative habits, eating disorders, somatoform disorders, mood disorders and more.

Third level neocortical affective processing

Panksepp's tertiary brain processing of affect is subsequent learning that is neocortical in nature, such as mindfulness skills, labels for emotions, assertion skills, etc.

Neocortical learning includes coping strategies, functional capacities and social skills, and all other knowledge and understanding about emotions. Traditional talk therapy most often works on this level. Cognitive behavior therapy attempts to change affect top down, by examining beliefs and experimenting with alternative beliefs and conclusions, practicing new behaviors, and not being led by one's emotions. EMDR therapy and somatic therapies tend to work bottom up, processing affect, which potentiates subsequent cognitive shifts, either spontaneously or with assistance from strategically timed brief cognitive interventions.

Non-specific arousal factors

Panksepp additionally describes what he calls non-specific arousal factors that affect affective processing, especially, the neurotransmitters acetylcholine, serotonin, norepinephrine (Panksepp, personal communication, 2009). The critical role of the opioid system in traumatic disturbance is discussed in Lanius, Paulsen &Corrigan (2014), in Section 1, Chapter 8, Dissociation and Endogenous Opioids.–with suggestions for involvement of the cannabinoid system as well.

9-6 The SEEKing circuit is the mother of all circuits according to Panksepp (1998)

More about basic affective circuits   With the conceptual framework in place for the three Pankseppian levels of affective processing, it times to return to a discussion of additional considerations about the basic affective circuits.

The SEEKing system   Basic affective circuits–the foundational role of the SEEKing system

The most basic of these emotional circuits is the SEEKing circuit. It refers to the brain's basic impulse to search, investigate and make sense of the environment (Panksepp, 1998). SEEKing:

- Is concerned with, affects, and is affected by general arousal. It is the interplay of interaction with our external environment.

- Is a motivational system for appetitive learning.

- Results in acquiring expectancies based upon having learned to associate previous cues with arousal and disarousal (Panksepp, 1986), We then seek based on that appetitive conditioning.

- Causes us to initiate play, lust, and general activity and to investigate and be curious.

- Inspires invention and pursuit of goals. In many individuals with complex trauma histories, seeking was discouraged or punished.

Inhibited SEEKing   When SEEKing is inhibited, there are far reaching consequences for all manner of behavior, with clinical implications.

- Passivity, phobic avoidance, attachment avoidance, and other inhibitions are often related to blockage of SEEKing. In the treatment of traumatic stress syndromes and dissociation, SEEKing is important, as its function will affect the overall level of arousal of the client and thereby the client's relative position in the 'window of tolerance' (Siegel, 2015, 1999).

- SEEKing has a profound impact on the elicitation of an orienting response. A person who is dissociated and in a withdrawn emotional state no longer responds or orients to the external environment.

- When someone is chronically immobilized and dissociated, he or she is no longer able to orient to present time and becomes stuck in the past, disoriented to present circumstances. Like a mosquito frozen in amber, life goes on around them but dissociated ego states or alters remain disoriented to present circumstances, frozen and immobilized.

- Finally, appetitive learning no longer takes place under these conditions. The person does not exhibit any new learning with regard to having specific preferences. Rather they will only exhibit automated responses to previous conditioned stimuli, regardless of what other underlying emotional system they are concerned with.

How SEEKing dysfunction might affect other circuits

Specific examples of how dysfunction of the SEEKing system affects appetitive learning and other emotional systems in trauma survivors include:

- Habitual avoidance of a feared stimulus (FEAR system),

- Dissociation and immobilization in response to external stressors (PANIC system),

9-7 When the SEEKing circuit is suppressed, life is suppressed

- Fetishistic sexual behavior (LUST system),

- Inability to protect oneself when under attack or alternatively an inappropriate responding with anger and rage to minor frustrations in life (RAGE system),

- Inability to play and interact socially with others (PLAY system), or inability to have caring and nurturing relationships (CARE system).

- Incapacity to initiate novel responses, or assert oneself

- Chronic high anxiety from the demands of inhibited seeking

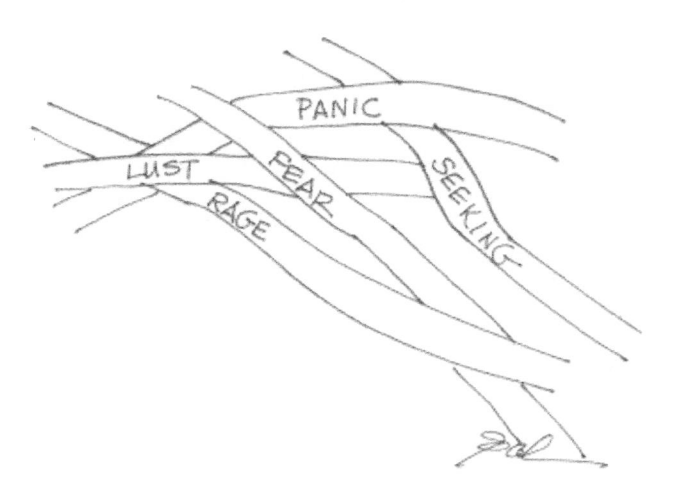

9-8 Conditioned responses at the time of trauma can wire together circuits that are otherwise unrelated, in over-coupled responses

Functions of Pl

PLAY is important in emotional survival in the following ways:

- The PLAY circuit is recognizable in many animals and certainly human children.

- It can be intra- or inter-generational or intra- or inter-species.

- It can be social or practice for more serious survival skills.

- In children, sometimes parents punish children for play, or discourage it. This essentially interferes with SEEKING and exploratory behavior in general.

- PLAY is at the core of practicing emotional and adaptive functioning and engaging in all of the basic affective circuits from a safe base.

- PLAY is important for socialization of animals and humans.

- 9-9 The PLAY circuit activates more of the brain than any other circuit.

- PLAY may promote certain types of neuronal growth, as well as "serve to exercise and extend the behavioral options under the executive control of inborn emotional systems" (Panksepp 1986, quoted in Panksepp 1998 p 295 (72).

- Panksepp suggests that PLAY may indeed be the waking equivalent of dreaming, promoting information processing and emotional integration in a similar way to REM sleep. When we imagine, then, we may be utilizing the PLAY circuit to process and integrate experience and lay down new pathways.

The PLAY Circuit

9-9 *The PLAY circuit activates more of the brain than any other circuit.*

Attachment Book Ends

PANIC and CARE

9-10 *The PANIC and CARE circuits are evolutionary bookends, mother and child, the chicken and egg.*

The social affective circuits: PANIC and CARE

The PANIC and CARE circuits are adjoined evolutionarily in order to ensure maternal care in animals which require caretaking of the young, as follows:

- The PANIC circuit is that emotion evoked in separation distress when a child is separated from its mother. It is there so that the infant's distress cry evokes a nurturing response in the mother/caretaker. (Panksepp, 1998).

- Although Panksepp's seminal research was on PANIC and CARE in rats, its extension to human attachment injuries have been addressed by others, e.g., Lanius, et al (2014).

- If mother/caretaker comes, infant's needs are addressed and Baby is again secure.

- Many individuals have other outcomes. For reasons benign or malignant, mother may not come. Baby's distress heightens and becomes panic.

- If there is still no one forthcoming, Baby may give up, a result the first author calls "tender hearted hurt," which in the presence of disappointment after disappointment, eventually becomes chronic and unbearable.

- A baby cuts off emotions, perhaps habitually, because the pain is that much greater than the baby's capacity to tolerate distress. This is where good circuits go bad; it is not safe to feel, because no one is coming with help and comfort for the baby.

- Chronic desolation and despair becomes associated with giving up. Guarding becomes chronic, as does feeling invisible.

- Not all of the developmental milestones associated with the beginning of life can be completed successfully in this despaired and unattached state. In such circumstances, the baby is quite alone with the challenges of growing and learning, and moreover, with the task of becoming a person which the child is also hardwired to do

- Excessive activation of the PANIC circuit is not only related to depression and possibly to autism, as suggested by Panksepp (1998), but it also is at the core of the dorsal vagal response and the dissociative collapse.

- The child's emotions, rather than being interactively regulated by the parent through ventral vagal engagement, a process mediated by oxytocin, are now autoregulated by means of a dorsal vagal response, e.g. shutting down by means of excessive opioid activation

- With this chronic state, the child has become capable of self-regulating excessive arousal, but at a significant cost. The child learns to rely upon dissociative switching and shutting down.

9-11 The CARE circuit is typically stronger in the female, but not always.

The CARE circuit

The CARE circuit enables caretaking of infants, offspring and other people.

- The CARE circuit is stronger in the female, typically, but also present in the male in the human species (Panksepp, 1998).

- Nurturance, when provided at optimal levels, protects a child against lifelong insecurities and worry.

- In some cases infants not properly cared for may find their own CARE circuits prematurely activated, in an attempt to provide care to unavailable mothers.

- This may result in those social disorders that involve preoccupation with controlling another, such as stalking, or domineering behavior, as found in some paranoid individuals.

When There Are No Words - Sandra Paulsen

9-12 Some children are parentified to meet the unmet dependency needs of their parents, which causes life-long symptoms in the child

The LUST circuit
- The LUST circuit is a basic one that make reproduction possible, of course, and that draws people together in relationship, even though the genders are different enough to make shared experience challenging or unlikely if LUST weren't operating.

- The LUST circuit is the basis for a variety of sociosexual relations (Panksepp, 1998) and both temporary and enduring bonds.

- The disruption of this circuit early in life may be the basis for some of the sexual disorders.

Defensive responses: FEAR and RAGE
As an overarching statement, an incomplete active defensive response or a blocking or inhibition of such active defensive responses like FEAR or RAGE will bias the person to respond to an external threat with helplessness and PANIC. This tends to increase the likelihood of a passive defensive response, e.g. dorsal-vagal shutdown.

Fight or flight………………….. And if that fails…………….surrender.

9-13 The FEAR circuit–involved in flight, and in surrender, is a defensive circuit. Adrenalin is stimulated in sympathetic arousal, and if flight, or fight, is not possible, then surrender and dorsal vagal shutdown is the remaining path.

The FEAR circuit The FEAR circuit is part of the survival system and the flight response when threatened or endangered. The following statements describe the role of FEAR:

- According to Panksepp, mild fear may produce inhibition or avoidance, but intense fear results in actual physical flight responses.

- We are wired to run and attempt to escape when there is an external threat. An inability to escape is maladaptive and a threat to survival. It has been suggested that the FEAR circuit is the basis for dread and it may be at the basis of phobic and other anxiety disorders.

9-14 The RAGE circuit is a defensive circuit, powered by adrenalin, which activates the sympathetic nervous system response to prepare us for fight.

The RAGE circuit The RAGE circuit is present, evolutionarily and practically today, as part of a fight response. Like other animals, we are wired to fight when attacked and also when there is injustice. The following describes additional considerations about RAGE:

- The RAGE response is so integral, that a newborn infant will have its RAGE circuit activated as easily as by having its arms held to its sides (Panksepp, 1998).

- On one hand, this circuit reflects a profoundly protective emotion, e.g., warding off helplessness under threat.

- However, the RAGE circuit may also be at the very basis of violent behavior.

10 The Neurobiology of Resetting Affective Circuits

10-1 The brain's capacity for visualization allows us to create repair, in imagination, that provides the biochemical "marinade" that the brain has waited for all these years.

Thanks to Ulrich Lanius The following neurobiological review of key elements that appear to be related to the affect regulating effects associated with resetting the affective circuits are included here courtesy of Ulrich Lanius's extensive neurobiological understandings and are from Paulsen, O'Shea, & Lanius (2014).

Fractionating the overwhelming affective load The client's learning history of trauma and neglect results in an unprocessed affective load, with several implications for early trauma repair:

- The intensity of unprocessed affect is an excessive load similar to the excessive electrical current that trips a circuit breaker or blows a fuse.

- The thalamus acts as a circuit breaker to avoid over-excitation of the neocortex.

- The respective fixed action patterns for the expression of a specific emotion may still occur, but, as a result of the disruption at the level of the thalamus, the neocortex is no longer informed about the events that occur at the level of the lower brain structures.

- Nor can the neocortex influence the expression of these fixed action pattern's, as top-down processing is impeded by the disruption of the thalamic relay, as well as by deactivation of the neocortex.

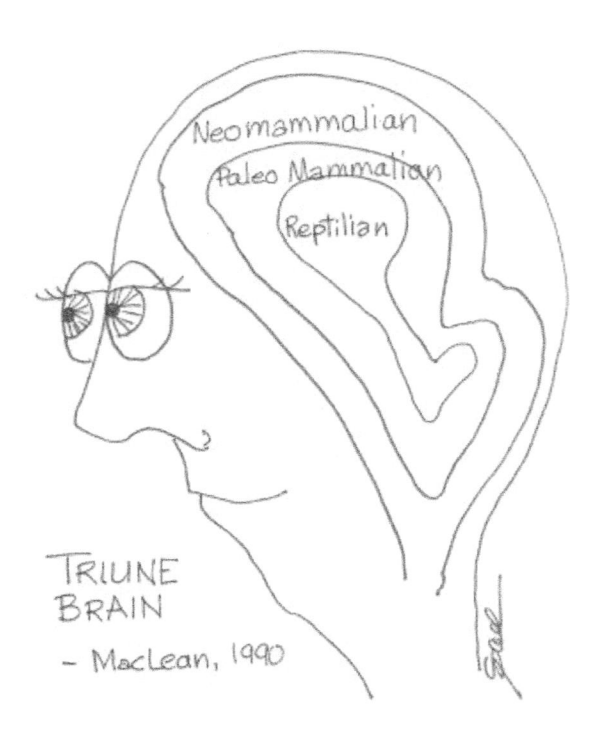

10-2 Imagination is a uniquely human function of the neo-mammalian brain, the neocortex. Visualizing what is needed in order to have a different outcome enables the client to obtain a biochemical wash of the "marinade" of what they wanted on their own terms.

The role of imagination in repair

The following discussion is here to inform the reader about why, neurobiologically, and how, clinically, imagination can be used reparatively in early trauma work, and why it is not the same as pretending something didn't happen. The effects found in this step are not typically found elsewhere in psychotherapy, and therefore, a more extensive discussion of proposed neurobiological bases seems warranted.

- Imagination, imagining and the imaginal: about visualization and PLAY:

- Imagination or imagining involves forming mental images, sensations and concepts, when they are not perceived through the external senses.

- Imagination is the work of the mind that helps the individual--and their brain --to develop.

- Imagination helps provide meaning to experience and understanding to knowledge. Not only is it fundamental to making sense of the world (e.g., Sutton-Smith, 1997), it also likely plays a key role in learning (e.g., Egan, 1991), as well as neural development (e.g., Panksepp, 1998).

- Visualization, imagination and imagining are essential underpinnings of the capacity to pretend and play.

- They facilitate the envisioning of multiple social contexts and different affective responses to them. This allows for the strengthening and development of those very affective responses and practicing them in a non-threatening environment, readying the organism for the challenges encountered in different life situations.

Imagination and pain Pain informs us of several key lessons about imagination (Paulsen, O'Shea & Lanius, 2014).

- Long standing complex regional pain syndromes can be affected by graded motor imagery (Moseley, 2004).

- Moseley worked with clients suffering from phantom limb pain who had been unsuccessful with regard to using a mirror box (e.g., Ramachandran, Blakeslee, & Sacks, 1998) -- a method that recreates an illusion of the existence of the missing limb – that, apart from EMDR therapy, is one of the few successful treatments for phantom limb pain.

- Moseley began by using graded motor imagery rather than creating a visual illusion. That is, he asked clients to simply imagine pictures of their limbs and associated movement.

- Specifically, treatment utilized sustained attention to the phantom limb, followed by imagined motor movements, and ultimately mirror movements (e.g., McCabe, et al., 2002; Ramachandran, Blakeslee, & Sacks, 1998).

- This occurring-in-sequence, consistent with sequential activation of cortical motor networks, was most likely to reduce pain activity (Moseley; 2004). This manner of proceeding is consistent with the premise that observation, motor imagery and execution are associated with partially overlapping increases in activation of parieto-frontal areas.

- The combination of sustained attention and imagined motor movements was the preparatory activity necessary for clients to benefit from the mirror box treatment that had previously failed to yield results for them without preceding imagery.

- The imaginal step seems crucial for individuals who do not initially respond to treatment with mirror movements. The work by Moseley and colleagues suggests that "a completely novel body image can be constructed solely by internally generated mechanisms (Moseley, 2004)."

Imagination & emotion   Imagination is also relevant to understanding the transformation of emotion, as we observe in the resetting-affective-circuits step, as follows:

- Similar to the motoric imagery utilized by Moseley and colleagues, we can use emotional imagery, experimented with objectivity (object cathected not subjectively experienced in the procedure) to alleviate emotional dysfunction in traumatic stress syndromes.

- For instance, Bausch & Stingl (2011) suggest that even highly alexithymic subjects are capable of differentiated emotional imagination. Moreover, when they imagine emotions, they experience normal electrodermal activity and are capable of rating valence, arousal and vividness of the imagined emotion.

- Various writers have suggested a number of therapeutic mechanisms for the efficacy of emotional imagery.

- Sabatinelli, Lang, Bradley, & Flaisch (2006) propose that emotional imagery activates an associative network of stimulus, semantic, and response (procedural) information including response mobilization.

- Kim et. al. (2007) suggest that the imagery of emotion activates amygdalar function, as well as multiple other structures including the midbrain, the area that contains the PAG and that is relevant to affective circuits (Panksepp, 1998).

- Peelen, Atkinson, & Vuilleumier (2010) suggest that the perception of basic emotional states activate the medial prefrontal cortex (mPFC), an area implicated in affective processing, mental state attribution, and theory-of-mind that is commonly deactivated in PTSD.

- Finally, the experience of emotional arousal has been associated with gamma band activity (Keil et. al., 2001), the binding frequency in the brain, a phenomenon that may potentially be involved in the underlying mechanism of EMDR therapy treatment.

10-3 In the resetting-the-circuits process, the client's neocortical capacity is utilized to look at each emotion with objectivity, and without the subjective felt sense. This enables the circuit to process without an affective load on it, the same way an electrician turns off the circuit breaker before tinkering with electrical circuits.

Mentalized affectivity

- Mentalized affectivity refers to the capacity to feel an affective state, and to retain reflective thinking about that state (Fonagy, et al., 2002, 2005). Mentalization requires a meta-cognitive stance, i.e., to be able to think about one's feelings. This premise leads us to several insights:

- The use of affective mentalization with regard to basic affective circuits, in a way is a form of motor imagery, where the experience of emotion is experienced as a form of movement or energy within one's body.

- Based on our clinical experience, by using visualization or imagery of the quasi-motoric aspects of an emotion, e.g., engaging in affective mentalization as described in more detail below, we can induce the experience of feeling again.

- This kind of affective resetting may counteract changes in emotional processing in PTSD as reported by Phan et al. (2006).

- Not only does such imagery appear to alleviate alexithymia, it also much increases affective regulation. It allows reinstatement of clients' normal adaptive function of emotion. We believe that we are able to bring about human neocortical functioning to bear on emotional expression and experience, rather than reptilian emotional functioning. We consider this type of intervention to be an essential part of stabilization prior to embarking on trauma-centered treatment, e.g. trauma processing.

Jurist (2005) differentiates three elements of affectivity that are delineated and divided into basic and complex forms:

- Identifying affects, e.g., naming, distinguishing
- Processing affects, e.g., modulating, refining
- Expressing affects, e.g., outwardly and inwardly, communicating

These elements bear much resemblance to the stages suggested by Moseley (2004) in treating pain syndromes:

- Laterality recognition and focused attention,
- Imagined movement and finally

Execution of such movement. Indeed, this sequence of identification, imagination and execution may reflect the intrinsic stages of problem solving in general.

11 Resetting the Affective Circuits– the Procedure

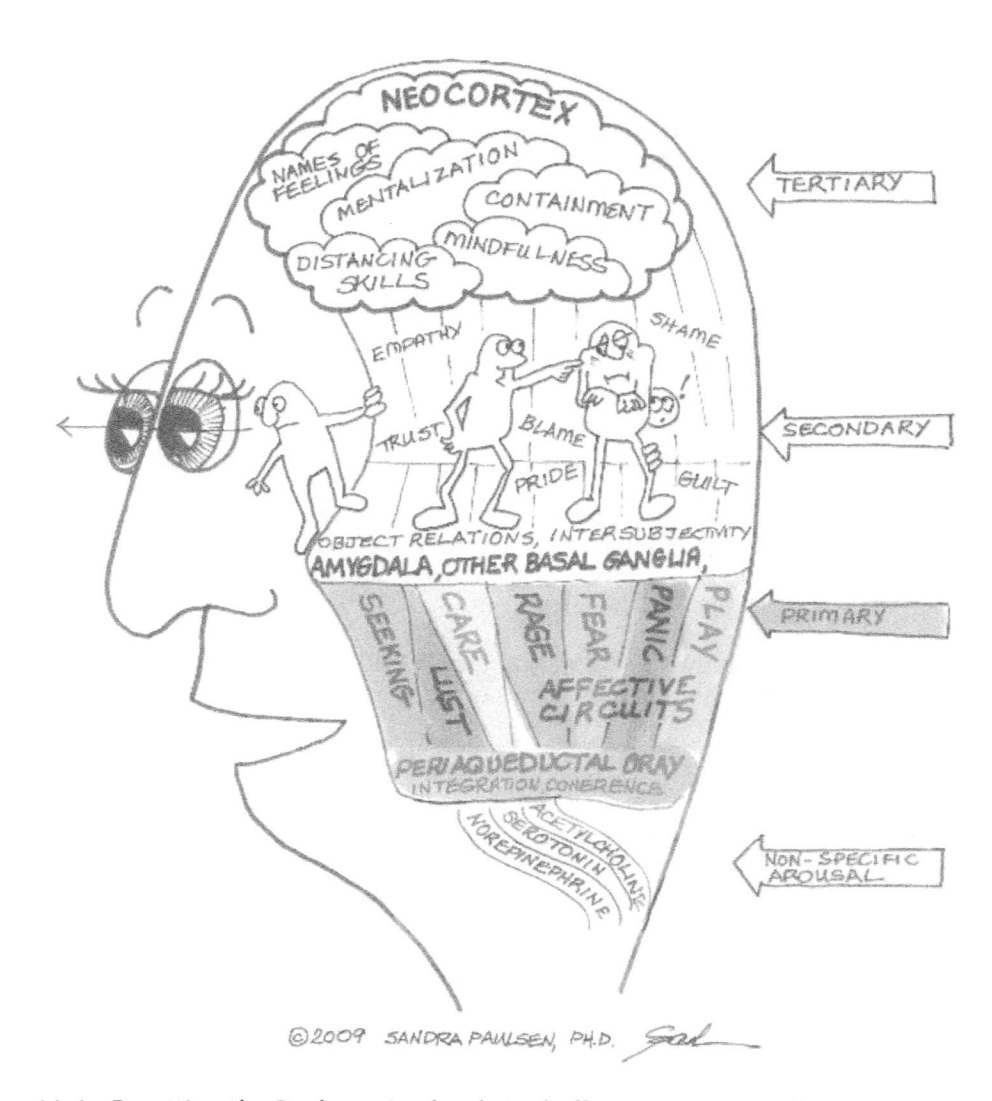

11-1 –Resetting the Pankseppian hardwired affective circuits so the emotional information can freely flow through them during processing

Introduction

O'Shea's terms

Katie O'Shea uses the terms "reinstalling innate emotional resources," instead of "resetting the affective circuits." O'Shea prefers her phrase because it emphasizes that emotions are resources that we are born with, and this step makes them again available. Paulsen prefers the language of "resetting the affective circuits," because the phrase refers to Panksepp's important experimental findings that we are born with hardwired sub-cortical circuits that require no learning (1998). In both cases, the understanding is that this step makes those emotional circuit resources available, or back online.

Stabilization Stabilization is necessary before attempting any form of trauma work, including the Early Trauma approach of EMDR therapy, for clients who are:

- complex,
- attachment-injured, and/or
- dissociative

Affective mentalization and affective resetting Katie O'Shea initially developed, and subsequently Sandra Paulsen co-developed and extended, with O'Shea, a procedure that involves affective mentalization for working with clients with very early trauma and neglect. That procedure includes bilateral sensory stimulation as is used in Eye Movement Desensitization and Reprocessing (EMDR therapy).

Step 3 of the early trauma approach O'Shea initially developed the approach because of challenges of applying the standard EMDR therapy approach in clients with a history of very early trauma and neglect –similar to Moseley pain clients. O'Shea's clients were frequently unable to benefit fully from EMDR therapy approach because:

- EMDR therapy ideally targets an image in explicit memory, and does not address how to work with early experience held in implicit memory, so is easier to address systematically with shock trauma than with developmental trauma and neglect in infancy. Knowing where one is in the work is difficult.

- even when very early experience can be accessed with EMDR therapy using symbolic imagery as a target memory, it can overwhelm the client and cause flooding especially when used with a dissociative client (Paulsen, 1995, 2007, 2009).

The early trauma approach of EMDR therapy has four steps, the first two of which are familiar from the hypnosis tradition, namely,

- step one uses containment imagery for distancing from affective disturbance,

- step two establishes a felt sense of safety and a capacity to evoke that felt sense when needed.

However, steps three and four are innovative in that:

- step three uses affective mentalization and imagination, which are believed to clear affective circuits and reestablish adaptive emotional functioning; it is examined in this chapter

- step four targets traumatic disturbance and neglect by time frame, and will be examined later. That step is here called "temporal integration."

Containment-- using imagery of a container The container maneuver reduces the affective load on the circuits, as follows.

- The therapist suggests to the client to create a container within which the client places all of their respective trauma history including not only any current stressors," but also:
- "everything that has yet to be learned from or sorted through," in O'Shea's words.
- "everything from current time, adulthood, childhood, really everything, so we have a clear desktop," in O'Shea's words.

- The use of containment imagery for emotional containment has a long history in the hypnosis tradition.

- When the therapist has the client "set aside" in a container image everything that isn't currently being systematically reviewed, released and repaired, it fractionates the work into manageable pieces.

Fixed action patterns
- The work of repairing the learning history will address the habitual fixed action patterns (fixed action patterns) that were acquired in lieu of working through traumatic experience at the time of the trauma.

- The fixed action patterns reflect:

    basic emotions which were not able to be normally utilized and worked through at the time of trauma

    appetitive responses to stimuli, including a lack of response to the external environment

    conditioned responses, including a lack of response to the external environment.

Targeting a fraction of traumatic experience
- Targeting as conducted in EMDR therapy processing is always targeting of a fraction of mental contents, but here, containment imagery enables the client to envision setting aside other distracting material, which serves to titrate the experience of affective load.

- The setting aside of affective disturbance is akin to turning off the appliances which might trip the circuit breaker anew.

- This allows the client to experience the affect, sensations, and movements needed during processing of traumatic experience with dissociating and shutting down due to excessive intensity.

- Once disturbances are set aside using containment procedures, there is a readiness to proceed to the imagining of basic emotions with objectivity.

- O'Shea originally used the procedure with a far longer list of emotions, conceptualized as on continua from negative to positive. Paulsen brought the Pankseppian emotions to bear and added the conceptualization that these emotions were innate circuits, whereas the longer list included learned circuits.

- Paulsen further posited that the continua with negative and positive emotional valences originally used by O'Shea was more speculative and theoretical than the hardwired circuits known to exist due to Panksepp's experimental work, and therefore were

Results of resetting the circuits
Resetting the innate affect circuits serves to:

- remove the affective load from the circuit, and prepare the nervous system for more adaptive response in the future

- allow neocortical learning and neuroplasticity to emerge, rather than the ongoing habitual expression of a conditioned trauma response,

- engage the emotions in an imaginative and therefore playful manner, which may stimulate appetitive circuits, e.g. SEEKING.

- Activating the SEEKing circuit may assist in bringing the brain's reward system back online. This phenomenon has been associated with both increased amygdala and medial prefrontal cortex activity in conjunctions with activation in the nucleus accumbens (Costa et al., 2010).

- Whether the above surmised biomechanisms are correct or some others are, the resetting circuits procedure rather reliably produces such a calming result, when successfully conducted with objectivity, that some sort of biomechanical action must be occurring.

11-2 Typically after circuit resetting, the client feels more calm, though an exception might be when feeling calm is startling. It's important for the therapist to keep the client in objectivity, lest premature trauma processing be evoked by subjectivity.

Benefits of resetting the circuits

- When the procedure is conducted properly, that is, without allowing the client to slide into the felt sense, clients nearly uniformly report an increased sense of calm. The rare exception is that some clients report feeling strange or weird, and then realize it is because the sense of feeling calm is new so it feels unusual. That new calm is not just a state shift but also a downshifting of the static internal sense of anxiety or arousal with which the client lives.

- The calm is a new normal or new baseline for the client which will habituate in about two days. When step 3 is conducted with time in between steps 3 and 4, it becomes obvious that the new calm is a new normal, not a state shift, around which variability will occur but with more of a sense of regulation and with less reactivity. When resetting the affective circuits and temporal integration are conducted with little or no time in between, as in the intensive treatment format, the resulting calm the client reports is harder to attribute.

- Resetting the affective circuits without an affective load has several notable benefits, including: increased capacity to tolerate affect and remain in the window of tolerance;

    - improved ability to bring adult resources to bear on affective function rather than just slide in to affect with no capacity for distancing,

    - improved ability for the front part of self to stay oriented to present time and maintain dual attention awareness (Shapiro, 2001),

    - improved ability to approach disturbing material without overwhelm,

    - an overall increased sense of calm that endures between sessions,

    - improved ability to engage in relationship with empathy for others

Impact of the circuits resetting procedure on early trauma processing

- The significance of these hardwired affective circuits is that when the adaptive expression of these circuits has become blocked, the individual will be unable to express these emotions or will be conflicted about having emotions at all, and then won't use them as information about the environment.

- If emotional expression has become associated with traumatic experience or the child has learned that expression of such emotions is associated with a threat to survival, accessing these emotions will increase the likelihood that activation of such emotions will result in stress or dissociative response. Moreover, such learned inhibition of basic affective responses is likely to contribute to affect dysregulation, behavioral disorders, and the capacity to achieve developmental milestones.

- When EMDR therapy is attempted in such cases of inhibited or "clogged" emotional circuits, difficult abreaction frequently occurs. In such cases, information processing may fail because the processing capacity isn't great enough, possibly because of decreased thalamic connectivity. Alternatively, habitual defensive responses may result in resistance and interfere with processing.If, however, adaptive emotional processing has been re-instated through affective resetting prior to trauma processing, subsequent trauma focused work tends to proceed much easier.

- Once affective resetting has been achieved, the affective information flow. including feelings, seems to flow freely without inhibition or blocking or excessive overwhelm.

- The resetting results in an overall reduction in phobic avoidance of mental contents, meaning the client can finally face the music of their own story without having to run away from, at least, the emotional part of it. There may still be avoidance of body sensation and painful insights, but those need to be addressed with somatic work and cognitive work, respectively.

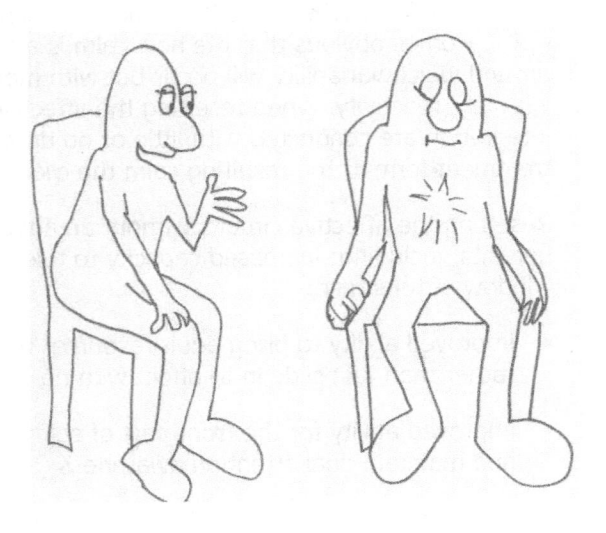

11-3 Once the circuits are available for information without reactivity, the client can better sit in the felt sense of body and emotion during trauma processing

More benefits of circuit resetting

- Additionally, because the procedure is calming—it allows emotional distancing and perspective taking--it tends to decrease arousal and thus increase affective regulation.

- This appears to increase processing capacity which is not surprising given what we know about the fact that arousal decreases thalamic activation.

- Because the client can stay with the affect longer, becomes more aware and more capable to tolerate soma, the self becomes more strong, resilient and embodied.

- That is, the client is better able to tolerate sensation of any kind because, like free flowing rain, it flows through unobstructed, and without flooding.

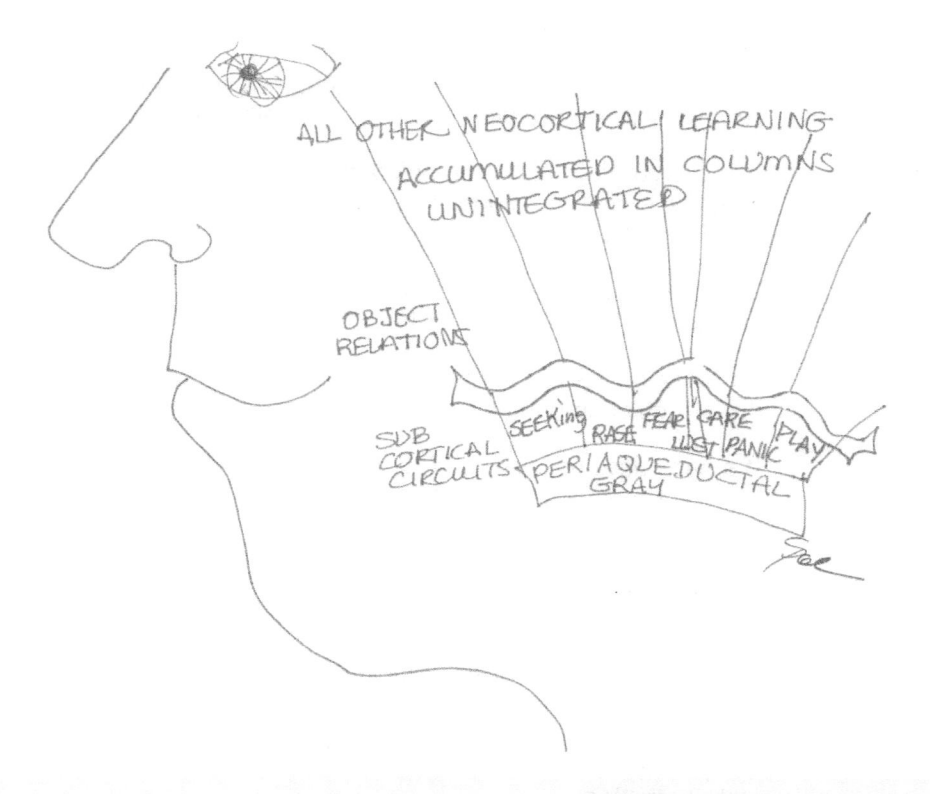

11-4 When the circuits are not horizontally integrated in the attachment period, state dependent learning accumulates vertically in columns, which manifest as alter personalities

Benefits for the treatment of dissociative disorders

- In dissociative clients with traumatic attachment histories, the affective states are not integrated horizontally across the circuits, and so they stand alone in a columnar fashion.

- The horizontal integration represents the acquisition of learned smooth state switching in the attachment period. See Lanius et al. (2014) for an exposition of the columnar theory of dissociation.

- As state dependent learning is accumulated over time without integration, ego states and even alter personalities result.

- Putnam (1988) has described smooth state switching as being an artifact of normal child development, and dysregulated switching of abnormal child development, early trauma and attachment failure.

- Without horizontal integration across affective circuits, smooth state switching cannot occur. In its place we see sudden state switching or even the amnesic switching of true dissociative identity disorder. That switching can be subtle or florid.

- Observation of florid switching reveals the utter absence of associative linkages between affective circuits and the sudden state switching of chronic dissociation.

The waveform nature of emotions One of the benefits of resetting the affective circuits that accrues to many clients and certainly to those dissociative clients who can allow the resetting to be successful is to become aware of the waveform nature of emotional experience.

It is evident that it is in the first year of life that infants in healthy families typically learn that emotions have a crescendo and decrescendo, like a wave on a beach that builds and then recedes.

Babies are born with the affective circuits, and accelerate rapidly to full emotionally intensity without having to learn how.

However, babies are not born with a braking system up and running, and learn down regulation in their mother's loving arms, if they are lucky.

If a baby does not have sufficient care, and help with down regulation in the form of a mother's care and comforting, then the child has no way to down regulate.

That leaves only switching the emotion off at the "circuit breaker," in an all or nothing way. This is the basis of dissociative state switching.

The successful experience of maintaining an objective viewpoint of the sequence of an emotion will enable clients to learn the waveform nature of emotion, and begin to override the wagon-rutted road of dissociative state switching that many complex trauma clients have relied upon in lieu of a more attenuated form of state switching.

How to The Procedures for Resetting the Affective Circuits

Procedural overview The method of resetting circuits is described also in O'Shea (2009) and Lanius, Paulsen, & Corrigan (2014).

Shame as circuit breaker: If baby isn't permitted to have emotions in the attachment period, shame is evoked, which serves to cut off those emotions like a circuit breaker, at the secondary level of affective processing.

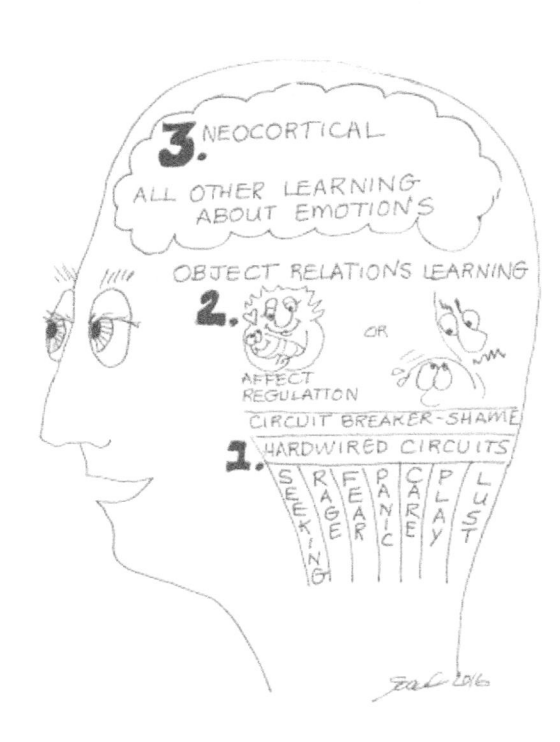

11-5 In the Pankseppian formulation, the first affective processing level is the hardwired subcortical circuits, the second affective processing level is object relations learning and relationship templates, including introjection, and the third affective processing level is the neo-cortical, which includes all other affective learning.

Sequence of affective circuits There is no research on point, but we are clinically guided. In general:

- We reset shame first, although it is not a Pankseppian circuit, because we understand it to function like a circuit breaker that can interfere with resetting the others.

- This author recommends next targeting RAGE and FEAR, the self-protective circuits, then CARE and PANIC, the circuits related to attachment, then LUST, ending with SEEKing and PLAY. Others prefer to use other sequences.

- Lanius, (2014) recommends working first with SEEKing and PLAY, then with the affective defensive responses like FEAR and RAGE, as reestablishing active defensive responses, then emotions that have a passive defensive or dorsal vagal aspect like PANIC.

- Moreover, LUST in particular is frequently difficult to work with in cases of sexual abuse. If a path can be found to reset it, however, there can be considerable reward in stabilization.

- As discussed earlier, SEEKing is foundational and PLAY allows other emotions to be accessed while at the same time increasing emotional valence and distance.

- Rather than focusing on the subjective feeling of each of the emotions, the client is asked to describe what the emotion looks like, which evokes a further distancing from the felt sense of the emotion.

- This distancing and objectivity likely evokes neocortical resources, and removes the affective load that would be likely to trigger overwhelm and result in dissociation and the shutting down of the thalamic relay.

- Moreover, having the client look at the emotion, rather than feeling it, likely maximizes interest and the SEEKing response, thereby engaging the medial prefrontal cortex, according to Ulrich Lanius (personal communication, May, 2014).

Bilateral stimulation and affective circuit resetting

- Bilateral stimulation likely increases neural connectivity within the affective neural network.

- We liken this activity to "flushing out" of the circuits, "like clogged gutters."

- Bilateral stimulation continues throughout the resetting process, between intermittent queries about what the emotion looks like, until the image or picture stops changing, becomes positive, or becomes neutral.

The special role of shame

- While both Tomkins and Nathanson include shame as a basic emotion (Nathanson, 1992), there is no experimental evidence for a SHAME circuit in rodents and lower animals (Panksepp, 2009 June) personal communication).

- However, higher animals appear to, and humans certainly do, exhibit shame, which plays a significant role in blocked expression of emotional responses. Tomkins (1963) suggested that shame is the primary inhibitor of positive affects and diminishes exploration.

- Shame may act as a biological tether that interferes with exploratory behavior through inducing immobilization and a dorsal vagal response.

- That is, parents can use the induction of shame to curtail a child's exploratory impulses, potentially decreasing exposure to threats, but also easing the burden of childcare.

- Shame may be the vehicle by which the circuit breaker is switched off, when baby's needs and feelings are unacceptable to the caretaker or overwhelming to the baby and must be stopped (Lanius, Paulsen, & Corrigan, 2014)

The challenge of shame

- Generally, shame affect can be profoundly difficult to work with, likely due to its dorsal vagal and dissociative aspects (e.g., Mason et al., 2001). These aspects are likely attributable to secondary processes within the client's learning and attachment history, rather than hardwired. Nevertheless, shame appears to directly impact on the PANIC circuit. Thus, before resetting Panksepp's seven emotional circuits, it is typically wise to begin by resetting shame.

- Shame is not provably a hardwired circuit, so we don't use Panksepp's capitalization convention. However it is either a circuit that can't be found in experimental rats, or it is learned during the attachment period (secondary brain processing in Panksepp's terms). As stated earlier, the author believes it to be a hardwired circuit breaker in humans, though not rats perhaps, at the level of the thalamus (Paulsen, O'Shea, & Lanius, 2014).

- Shame during session about having needs and emotions or injuries can sometimes deter people from being able to clear the other affective circuits. Therefore, it seems to be beneficial to work with shame in addition to the other circuits, and that is where we begin.

Resetting circuits as the objective picture develops

- Affective circuits are hypothesized to be reset, much as one might reboot a computer that isn't working right. Indeed, the resetting or rebooting metaphor emphasizes the nature of the circuits as an information processing system, which clients and therapist alike might readily understand.

- In order to reset the affective circuits so that emotional information can flow without blockage, one has to take them offline. This is another reason to work with them in the abstract without an affective load on them.

- The way this is accomplished is to ensure that during step three the client works with each of the Pankseppian emotions, plus SHAME, with an objective stance, rather than a subjective one, as mentioned earlier.

- That is to say, the client is instructed to prevent himself from feeling the emotion, and instead asked to simply look at each emotion.

- The image that the client begins with evolves as it develops or changes, or perhaps doesn't change, and when it stops changing it is understood to be reset, whether it is positive, neutral or simply has stopped changing.

Processing the objective image until it is positive or neutral and/or stops changing

- For each of the seven Panksepp emotions plus shame, the instruction is simply, "What does (emotion name) look like?"

- The client is instructed to just notice the image, which may be realistic or abstract, symbolic or a color, a photo or a cartoon, it doesn't matter. It is merely a production of the brain's information processing system.

- The client is further instructed to let the therapist know if client begins to have a subjective or felt sense of the emotion.

- If the client feels the emotion instead of just looking at it objectively, the therapist and client will stop and put the felt sense into the container, so that the work can continue in objectivity.

- This can also be described as looking at each emotion "at arm's length," each emotion is processed until one of the following statuses occurs:

    it stops changing,
    it becomes positive, and/or
    becomes neutral.

- At any of those points, the resetting is complete. Note: O'Shea prefers to say "positive, <u>or</u> neutral, <u>and</u> stops changing," and Paulsen prefers to say, "positive, <u>or</u> neutral, <u>or</u> stops changing." O'Shea's preference is because she doesn't want the resetting to stop too soon. Paulsen's preference is because in the case of very creative minds or ADHD, the person may continue percolating and associating long past the point of completion.

11-6 When the client is locked into toxic shame, the solution might be the objectivity interweave, "let's imagine someone you don't know, in Pocatello, in a similar situation"

Avoiding subjective vignettes

- The client is urged to use images that are not from their own life, for example, not their father's angry face, when resetting RAGE.

- Instead of the client's father's face, the therapist might instead suggest someone else's father's angry face, someone we don't know and a father we don't know, so the client is looking with objectivity.

When There Are No Words - Sandra Paulsen

- If the client says, "I'm still feeling afraid, though the father is someone I don't know," the therapist might say, "is the father looking at you? If so, let's turn the picture so the father we don't know is showing his angry face to a child we don't know."

- This removes the client's subjective viewpoint entirely from the scene, enabling the scene to be viewed with objectivity, evoking adult neocortical resources that seem to reset or reboot the affective circuit, when combined with bilateral stimulation until the picture stops changing.

Viewed with neocortical objectivity, at arm's length

11-7 When presented with a similar situation viewed with objectivity, instead of the shame held in subjectivity, the client can often see that the child is always innocent

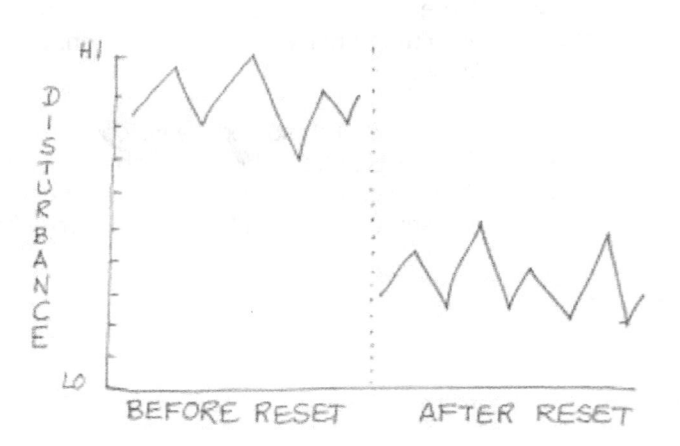

11-8 After resetting the circuits, the client will still experience emotional variations, but the baseline or "idle" will be lower, in most cases

Status inquiry upon completion

- When all the seven circuits plus shame are reset, the therapist asks, "and how do you feel in this moment?"

- Remember that during the resetting the therapist has not asked about how the client feels because the two are working studiously to keep the stance an objective one, not a subjective one, for each emotion.

- Typically, the client will report feeling calm, often much calmer, than before the circuits were reset. This calmer state is permanent one, although the client may soon forget that s/he ever felt different.

- It isn't that the client won't have emotions again, but rather, it is as if the idle has been set lower from that point onward. The client has a new baseline around which normal affective variability will occur.

- The process resembles flushing out rain gutters; once accomplished, the rain dispersal goes much more smoothly, with less overflowing and dysregulation.

- Whereas gutters must be cleaned seasonally, affective circuits only need to be reset once if properly done because the blockage likely occurred in the attachment "season" of life, and once achieved, flows more openly ever after.

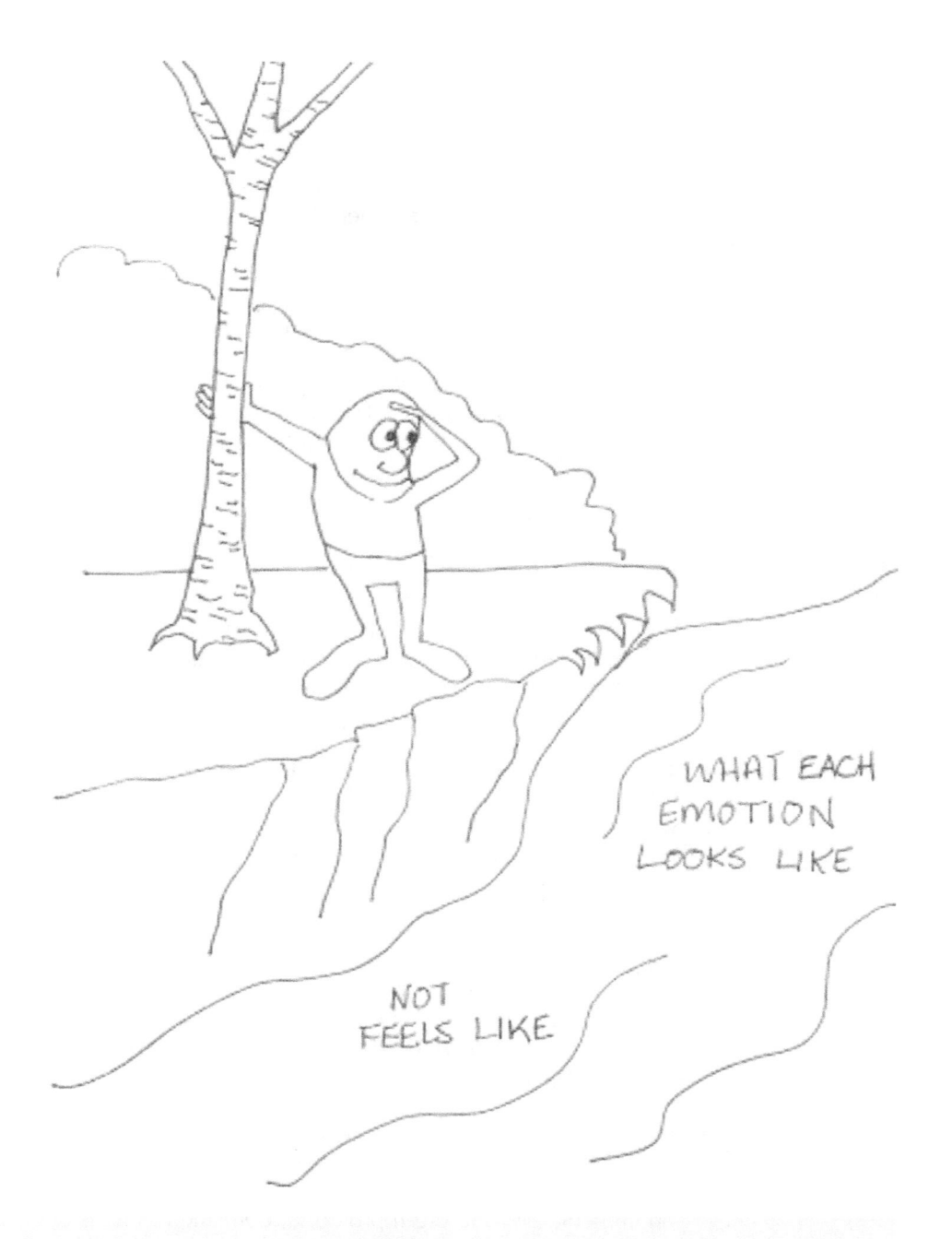

11-9 The hardest part of resetting the circuits, for many, is to look at each emotion with objectivity, and not slide in to subjectivity. The therapist advises the client to hang on to the birch tree on the river bank, and watch the river flow by, without sliding in

Trouble Shooting

What to Do When Good Circuits Go Bad

When the client can't look at an emotion and slides into the felt sense

- It is important that some clients, especially highly dissociative individuals with their early disastrous attachment histories, and certain others, may not initially have a capacity to "look at" an emotion without sliding into the felt sense of it.

- This inability to maintain objectivity about an emotion seems related to the failure of the intersubjective milestones with dissociative and non-dissociative clients. The more dissociative the client is, the harder this work is, but that is an indicant of how different life will be when the client is able to attain emotional containment and normal distancing capacities instead of sliding into affect without bound.

- With a dissociative client, it is advisable to have a discussion with the system or relevant parts, especially the "honchos," about whether they will permit a lower level of disturbance by resetting the circuits.

- With some dissociative clients, some alters appear to be columnar, that is, acquired learning histories atop basic Pankseppian circuits (Paulsen, 2014). Therefore, resetting the circuits necessitates that those alters are not executive during the resetting process.

- The author tends to leave ambiguous, initially, the question of what alter is forward during the resetting. This is because the informed consent process will typically pull forward a relatively adult part of self (or apparently normal personality, in the parlance of structural dissociation (Steele, van der Hart, & Nijenhuis, 2005).

- However, if the client cannot maintain objectivity without sliding into the felt sense of the emotion, instead of maintaining an objective arm's length stance, Paulsen will then negotiate with the emotion based alter in question to step back and allow an older alter or "apparently normal personality," (ANP) (Steele, et al, 2005) to be "looking through the eyes," or executive, during the resetting the procedure.

- Paulsen initially leaves undefined the matter of what alter is executive. This is because, if the client is able to do the task with objectivity, even though a particular alter may not be specified, the effect on the client's self-system is an immediately, and often profound, defusing of intensity of affect. This can often then be accomplished, without negotiating with alters' and their specific memories of the trauma that fuels the intensity of affect. Once the circuits are reset to the degree possible, subsequent processing of traumatic memories will be much easier.

- In the attachment period, baby and mom ideally share their affective experience and mom helps baby acquire a sense of "I-and-thou" in mirroring and acceptance and shared loving communication.

- When the method of resetting the affect circuits cannot be accomplished without the client sliding into the felt sense of the emotion, various devices can be used to help the client achieve that objective distance, which seems to help to repair the intersubjective milestone and increase affect regulation ability.

- It's helpful to ask the client to observe the emotion in question as if the client were on the bank of a river, holding on to a birch tree, and watching the river flowing by, but not sliding into the river.

- We ask the client to imagine the emotion in a scene on a TV on, for example, the shame channel or the RAGE channel. The TV can be black and white or even across the street in the neighbor's house, or viewed through the wrong end of a telescope.

- As said above, it is important that the scene not be people the client knows, but rather, people the client doesn't know, or even animals.

- If the client still slides into the felt sense, we might try asking the client to envision the scene with cartoon characters.

- If the client still slides in, the therapist can invite the client to imagine the cartoon characters are paperclips, "paperclips we don't know, not paperclips you know."

- If the client still slides in, Paulsen will use humor to say, 'you're feeling sorry for a paperclip we don't know in an imaginary story we made up this very minute? No paperclips were hurt in the telling of this story." Laughter will facilitate the client's ability to maintain an observing distance from the emotion.

- In rare cases, or when the client doesn't seem to have any idea what the emotions would look like, it is possible to use photographs or video material of animals exhibiting these basic affective responses. Similarly, if clients slide in to the felt sense while observing photographs or videos, cartoons or even stick figures engaged in the emotions may assist in obtaining the requisite objective stance.

- It is important that clients who cannot maintain the desired objectivity not feel shamed in the procedure, but rather, the therapist instructs as follows; "make sure you tell me when you slide in, don't just keep it to yourself, because I'm here to help. This time, you aren't alone with it."

- if the client expresses self-condemnation for an inability to not slide in, the therapist says, "it's okay, this is right where we need to be, and I very much think that this is going to produce a change in your life, so we'll just slow this down and take the time it needs."

- Paulsen sometimes says, "not to worry, you can't flunk this. I'm the only one here who can flunk, and I'm not going to. If you have trouble, it just shows us how much you need the step, and how important it will be when, finally, you <u>can</u> envision the emotions without sliding in."

11-10 The client views each emotion with objectivity, and without the felt subjective sense of the emotion, processing with bilateral stimulation until the image becomes positive or neutral and/or stops changing

Dissociative or just injured early?

- Although most dissociative clients have a tendency to "slide in" to the river of emotion in the subjective felt sense, rather than being able to "look at arm's length" of objectivity, not all clients with this difficulty are structurally dissociative. Some are just injured early in the attachment period. The authors have not seen examples, yet, of individuals who "slide in," to subjectivity who had lovely attachment learning.

- For individuals with this much trouble, it is sometimes helpful to begin not with the Pankseppian circuits and shame, but rather, with the basic defensive systems, including fight, flight, freeze and connection responses for those clients who cannot achieve the arm's length viewing of these functions on their own.

11-11 For highly dissociative clients, it may be necessary to reset the safety systems for fight, flight, freeze and connect, before resetting the individual emotional circuits, to increase client comfort with the amygdala alarm system and with their nervous system overall

Trouble shooting circuit resetting for complex clients

- For highly dissociative individuals, sometimes it is first necessary to use the same procedure to "reset" the safety systems.

- Resetting the safety systems may begin with psycho-education about the normal function of the amygdale or other brain functions, or about the normal mammalian fight/flight/freeze and connection nervous systems described by Porges (2011).

- Many dissociative individuals believe that emotions are to be avoided, are nothing but trouble, or blame themselves for any of the normal fight, flight, freeze fixed action patterns that they uncontrollably engage in, sometimes with episodes of amnesia.

- Many dissociative individuals do not feel safe engaging their social engagement or connection subsystem (ventral vagal subsystem in the Porges parlance), but may be able to experience it with animals, with the earth, or with spirituality, or with other parts of self.

- The actual resetting of the defensive subsystems proceeds as above, with the therapist asking what each of the fight, flight, freeze, and connection, separately, look like (with objectivity, at arm's length), not feel like (subjectively).

- Again, individuals who can't do this without feeling the defensive response will need help in the form of various degrees of "prostheses" that enable the evocation of objectivity. For example, "what does an animal's flight response look like."

- For many clients, we teach about the Porges polyvagal theory, discussing the sympathetic nervous system (for fight and flight) and the two parasympathetic nervous systems (dorsal vagal for helpless shutdown, immobilization and surrender, and ventral vagal for social engagement and connection when we are safe).

- We ask the question, "Is it ok to feel safe when we are safe," with reference to the present moment in the office. Having a sleeping therapy dog can be instructive as to the tranquility of the moment.

Resetting the affective circuits: case examples

Case examples

Simpler case example resetting the affective circuits

Mary Lou, whom the reader met in case example in the containment and safe state chapters, was ready to reset affective circuits, after the therapist explained the process to her, saying that we are born with basic circuits, but some people have to cut off their feelings so the circuits aren't available to provide information the way they are supposed to.

The therapist gave instructions saying, "for each of the emotions, just notice what picture comes to mind, mindful that we want it to be viewed with objectivity, and not with any felt sense or subjective sense of that emotion. The best way to do that is for the image to not be of someone or something you know. So if you say you see your father's face, for example, I'll say, "let's have it be someone's father you don't know, so that it can be completely objective and dispassionate. It doesn't have to be a person, it could be an animal or a color or a shape or anything. Then I'll add the bilateral stimulation, and we will just allow time for the image to process and change if it's going to change. If you find yourself feeling the emotion, let me know, because I can help you get to objectivity."

At that point, the therapist turned to her therapy poodle, Driscilla, and said, "what do you think? will she remember to <u>tell</u> me if she's having trouble? Or will she think she's failing, and hide it and not tell me?" Turning back to the client, the therapist said, "if you have trouble, it won't mean you failed, I'm the only one here who can fail and I don't intend to, but you need to let me know if you're sliding in. Ok? OKAY?"

Both Mary Lou and the therapist laughed as Mary Lou stroked the straight-man, Driscilla, and the therapist explained, "Truly, so many people don't tell me, and it defeats the purpose, because the whole point is to help <u>gain</u> objectivity if you have trouble, so why not let me help?"

The therapist began resetting the circuits, starting with one that isn't on the Pankseppian list of hardwired circuits, but is important nevertheless. "What does shame look like? Not feel like, but look like?"

Mary Lou answered, "a puppy hanging its head by a puddle it made."

"Just watch that image with curiosity and we'll see if it's going to change...." After a time of bilateral stimulation, the therapist said, "and now, what does shame look like?"

"About the same," Mary Lou answered. "About the same or exactly the same, because in this business, any change at all is change." "Well, I think it's a little lighter, and I can see the background a bit, it's a garage."

"Just notice....." the therapist said. After a time of tapping with dual attention stimulus/bilateral stimulation (DAS/BLS) the therapist said, "and now?"

"the puppy is lifting its head, and its tail is starting to wag."

"just notice..." the therapist resumed tapping, then, after a time, said, *"and now?"*

Mary Lou answered, *"it ran off playing with a boy and left."*

The therapist discerned that the processing was complete for shame, and proceeded to the next, the defensive emotions. *"What does RAGE look like?"*

Mary Lou answered, *"I see my mother's face, just furious."*

The therapist said, *"Let's let it be the face of a mother you don't know."*

"Oh okay," Mary Lou said, then added, *"it's turning purple, like she'll explode."*

"Are you feeling it?" the therapist asked.

"No," Mary Lou answered, *"it's just interesting to see it."*

"And now?" the therapist asked after a time of DAS/BLS (dual attention stimulus/bilateral stimulation). Mary Lou answered, *"she's calmer now."*

"Notice that."

"Oh she's now pouring herself some tea," Mary Lou volunteered, after a time of DAS/BLS.

The therapist ventured, *"does it seem done? If you know? Some people can tell and some can't, either way."*

Mary Lou answered, *"oh yes, it's resolved, I can tell it's done."*

"What does FEAR look like?"

Mary Lou answered, *"it's a rabbit, frozen, still."*

"Okay, just watch," said the therapist in a lilting voice, to indicate curious and mindful acceptance, while silently engaging in DAS/BLS. After a time, the therapist asked, *"and in THIS moment, what does FEAR look like?"*

Mary Lou replied, *"the rabbit ran away, and is gone."*

"Let's give it a little more time, so we can see if its still changing or done changing," the therapist said, holding the space for more development, unsure if the reprocessing was complete, while engaging silently in DAS/BLS. After a time, the therapist said, *"and now?"*

The client replied, *"well, the rabbit got back to her babies and is sniffing them to make sure they are safe."* The therapist said, *"just notice,"* and did another set of DAS/BLS. Then the client volunteered that the babies were safe and they all went to sleep, and that it felt complete.

Complex case example of resetting the affective circuits	Greta Lynn and her therapist had worked together for over a year, initially establishing rapport, handling some crises, problem solving significant life matters. They worked on containment strategies and safe state.
	They also worked on grounding and resourcing, and stabilizing Greta Lynn by deconflictualizing her self-system. This occurred by means of the therapist

appreciating and orienting the "honchos" of her self-system, which were introjects of her perpetrators.

Once the honchos realized that they were not the external perpetrators, but internal likenesses of them, that they were appreciated for their survival function, that the dangers had passed, and that the therapist wouldn't try to get rid of them but rather considered them seminal to the work, many things changed.

The honchos were able to decrease self-harm and internal revictimization, and participate in experiments to protect differently than the masochistic way they had been doing, which was the only thing they had known (internalization of a perpetrator's sadism can result in reenactments of either sadism by or of masochism in the client).

Her problem behaviors decreased as a result of these maneuvers, with temporary flare ups and setbacks which were increasingly easy to solve.

Once the honchos had "stood down" and Greta Lynn's self-system was deconflictualized, the therapist approached Greta Lynn (meaning, her self-system) about resetting the affective circuits, saying, "You know, you guys, all the emotions are there for a reason, a survival reason, to convey important information.

RAGE tells us about injustice and prepares us for fight, FEAR tells us about danger and prepares us for flight.

(The therapist proceeded to discuss the adaptive survival purpose of each of the basic Pankseppian circuits of RAGE, FEAR, LUST, PANIC, CARE, SEEKing and PLAY, as well as the important human function of shame, noting how they are all like dashboard gauges)

"We wouldn't want to clip dashboard wires in our car, just because a red light comes on, but many people learn very early to do just that regarding their emotions."

Parts of Greta Lynn protested that emotions were dangerous or otherwise troublesome and shameful.

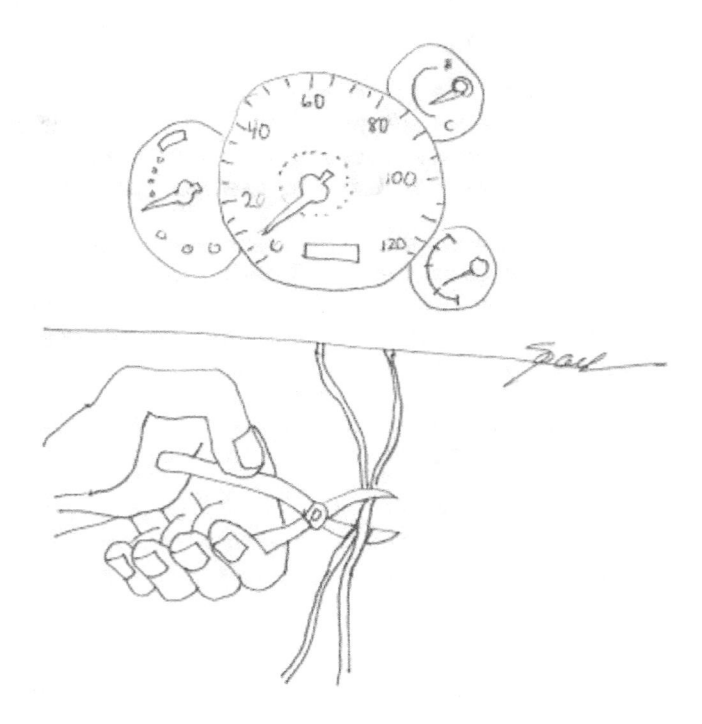

11-12 When babies don't have help down regulating their emotions, they have no choice but to "clip their dashboard wires" and dissociate their experience. This is like switching off the circuit at the circuit breaker.

Resetting the survival/ defensive/ safety circuits

Case continuation: considerable discussion with several vantage points of parts was required to normalize the idea of emotions. It was challenging enough, that the therapist backed up and talked about the survival systems of fight, flight, freeze and connection, based on the Porges sympathetic and parasympathetic functions.

Greta Lynn listened with wide eyes as the therapist described that each of those survival functions is completely normal. They used online videos and photos of animals to discuss, objectively, how fight, flight, freeze and connection are entirely normal animal and human functions. But in conditions of trauma for a child, the child is often forced to submit, and shame results, even though the fight and flight responses were entirely normal, albeit thwarted.

At last, they started to reset the defensive/survival functions before resetting the affective circuits. She double checked with the honchos to make sure they would permit the work, "Father part? Can we proceed to reset the fight/flight/freeze circuits?"

"We'll see. I have my doubts," said. 'Uncle? How about you?" "Whatever," he answered. "Thanks, guys. Speak up anytime you have concerns."

Ok everybody–and who's going to speak? Greta Lynn 2? (Greta Lynn 2 was a part that could face forward or backward, that is able to do life functions or face the internal world of parts and was supportive and helpful with the therapy). It is not required for this step, typically, to be very specific about who or what is present for resetting circuits, because that takes care of itself, *if* the honchos permit the work in the first place.

"What does fight look like, not feel like, but look like." The client was obviously switching, so after several frustrating and confusing attempt to have the client come up with her own image, the therapist said, "remember, you guys, this isn't about you or your life. It's about what fight looks like in general, and if you want we can draw from the animal kingdom. Remember those pictures we saw?" "A part of Greta Lynn answered, "yeah, we remember, the horses fighting each other in the plains."

"OK, so just allow that picture to be in your mind, and we'll have you just look at it, and NOT feel it, and let me know if you start feeling it, and I'll tap and we'll see if it will change or not change. No pressure, we'll just see what your system wants to do with it. I trust your system."

"It's scary," Greta Lynn said, in a child voice,

"OK," the therapist said, "then let's have it be cartoon horses fighting!"

Some part of the Greta Lynn snickered, but we continued. Then again she "slid into" affect, and the therapist said, "don't slide into the river, kids, stay on the river bank and just watch the picture float by…..that's it" The therapist kept up her patter to help the client stay in the present moment, saying silly things like, "don't forget you're here with me and my poodle…." (the poodle weighing 8 pounds, again making some part of the client laugh, since the client had a good relationship with the poodle).

The therapist thought enough had been done for the session, and they spent time with the affectionate poodle and in grounding and containment to make sure the client was "road-worthy," with the therapist reassuring the client that she did just fine, we knew this would be slow work, and when we get this repaired it will make a big difference.

The therapist continued to reset the fight system with objectivity in the next session, and then it was decided that not only would the horses be cartoons but they would be on a distant small TV screen.

At one point the therapist checked with the father and uncle parts of self to make sure they were remembering that it's the present year, age, location and circumstances, because else they might well interfere with the resetting.

Overall, there was an ambiguity about which part or parts were involved in the resetting, and the therapist's sense was it was a system-wide processing; although some of the parts are more closely associated with fight, it was not manifest in the resetting function, as if the various perspectives all may have benefitted from the objectivity about fight as a normal, not shameful, defensive function.

The client's vignette about the fighting of the cartoon horses was that eventually one rode away and the other grazed and joined a herd. It could have gone differently, with a more positive, more neutral, or even more seemingly negative outcome (such as a horse dying) and still be a normative processing of the fight defensive system.

Over the next weeks and months, interrupted by the demands of problem solving for current life issues, the therapist and Greta Lynn reset all of the defensive circuits (fight/flight/freeze and connect) and then proceeded to reset the emotional circuits. Sliding in was continuously an issue, so the work was punctuated with a full range of efforts to help the client to not slide in but to maintain objectivity.

With the FEAR circuit, no amount of effort would successfully prevent the client from sliding into the subjective felt sense of the emotion, because the terror was very young and wordless. After a negotiation with the self-system, it was mutually agreed to process the pain for the little one, with the blessing of the father and uncle parts, who had to be reminded more than once that they were internal likenesses of the external perpetrators, not the actual external perpetrators, so blurred were those boundaries.

When sliding into the FEAR circuit in the felt sense, there was some processing of FEAR by the terrorized infant state who was physically hit and molested, but also dialogue with father part, who originated during this very early trauma, and processing of father part's origins, including the moment when the terror of being hit again caused the infant to create a father part to keep the rest of the self silent from screaming even when external father was not present. Note that an infant would not normally have the capacity to inhibit a screaming response, but in the presence of physical abuse, pain, terror, then shutting down completely enables a kind of inhibition well over what is developmentally possible.

Summary
- Affective circuit resetting is an essential step for individuals with significant dissociative symptoms and/or alexithymia.

  It is equally essential for individuals with emotional flooding, and an inability to avoid sliding into affective arousal even when it isn't wise or appropriate to do so. This approach allows aid with the connection, as well as allowing the reconnection to previously dissociated affects; in addition, it aids in down regulating affective overwhelm, thereby increasing overall affective regulation.

- Affective resetting assists smooth state switching by conjoining the different affective circuits again, after they have become fragmented through higher order and cortical learning.

- Once these preparatory steps are in place, processing learned experience will go more smoothly because we are taking neurodevelopment into account by addressing subcortical affective circuits without an affective load, and bringing neocortical resources to bear in order to bring objectivity to the task.

- Once the affective circuits have been reset, temporal integration can begin.

- This will facilitate sensory experience being integrated with imagery, ultimately allowing for the embodied experience of emotion.

12 Temporal Integration: Introductory Concepts

Organization of the topic in three chapters

Because of the complexity of this step, temporal integration for clearing and repairing trauma by time frame, its discussion is divided into several chapters:

- Introductory concepts (this chapter)
- Basic procedures
- Procedures for dissociative clients

Discussion will begin by laying forth some history and basic concepts needed to understand this approach.

Organization of this introductory chapter

This chapter introduces the temporal integration approach by going over:

- Recap of preparation for temporal integration
- Attachment experience, affect regulation and state switching
- A brief history of integration approaches

Recap of Preparation for Temporal Integration

Three preparation steps leading to the trauma processing step

A brief recap of the sequence of the process to this point may be helpful to the reader in understanding readiness for trauma clearing in implicit memory.

The first two of the basic preparatory steps, above, are familiar from the hypnosis tradition, with some variation, and can be accomplished in many ways, although O'Shea recommended a specific way and offered specific scripting.

One specific preparatory aspect of the early trauma approach, clearing the affective circuits, is uniquely important, and was discussed at length in the prior chapter.

The fourth step of the basic early trauma approach, temporal integration, is conducted only after the first preparatory steps are complete as well as any additional preparation needed for a given client. The trauma processing step involves clearing early trauma by time frame.

Modifications needed for dissociative clients

As described previously, for dissociative clients, preparation is typically much more extensive and variable depending on the client's affect tolerance and capacity to manage stress, in the context of the developing therapeutic relationship. Elsewhere in this book, a number of representative additional preparation methods needed for dissociative clients are listed. They should be administered not as a cookie cutter checklist, but based on the needs and preferences of the client.

Original steps of the early trauma approach

In O'Shea's original approach (O'Shea, 2009; O'Shea &Paulsen, 2007), there are three preparatory steps. The language here for the basic steps is Paulsen's.

1) Containment skills

2) Ventral vagal state

3) Resetting the affective circuits

4) Temporal integration

O'Shea original language

O'Shea original language is different, as follows:

1) "Container,"

2) "Safe state,"

3) "Reinstalling innate emotional resources"

4) "Clearing trauma" or "reconnecting the self."

Why the different language?

O'Shea's language is intended to serve both the therapist's understanding and be suitable for the client. Paulsen prefers the slightly more abstract language because there can be more than one way to achieve the function of the steps, depending on the client and the therapist's training and experience.

Prior necessary conditions

Temporal integration begins with containment and a felt sense of safety, which will likely have required practice over some time for the client to have developed those skills. Also, the resetting of the affective circuits (described in chapter 11) precedes the processing of very early trauma chronologically by time frame, which is the focus of this chapter and two subsequent chapters.

Prior necessary conditions – complex cases

For complex cases, additional prior necessary conditions before temporal integration include therapeutic rapport, sufficient two-way trust between therapist and client, basic psychoeducation and client understanding about the function of emotions in mammals, ability to tolerate affect and soma, and cooperation of the self-system, as well as stable enough environmental and living conditions, in an absence of ongoing traumatization.

Recap: Panksepp's three levels of affective processing

Those three levels are:

1) Primary affective processing, which occurs via the subcortical hardwired affective circuits (Panksepp, 1998).

2) Secondary affective processing, which occurs at the level of the amygdale and other basal ganglia, and which refers to those object relations and relationship templates acquired during the first years of life, when learning is held in implicit memory.

3) Tertiary affective processing, at the neocortical level, is all subsequent learning about emotions.

Subcortical affective circuits

Mammals, including human ones, are born with hardwired subcortical affective circuits that require no learning (Panksepp, 1998).

These early circuits provide the basic information required for attachment, fight or flight, being a social animal and obtaining nurturance and care, and the seeking of information and solutions to problems.

The capacity for smooth switching between those affective states is acquired in the period following birth, in the relationship with the primary caretaker.

Basic principles of attachment experience, affect regulation and state switching

Smooth state switching

When the child is not yet capable of regulating their own affective arousal, the presence of a loving and attentive caretaker serves to provide an externally located regulatory function(Barach, 1991; Putnam, 1988).

From such a caretaker the child learns a range of lessons that, all being well, will result in the capacity for affect regulation.

Those lessons will include, for example, that emotions come and go in waves; that one can switch smoothly between states; that emotions provide information about one's safety and well-being, leading to action behaviors, and more.

In the course of this learning, which occurs on top of the hard-wired affective circuits, fundamental lessons about relationships to others are also accrued.

Attachment learning

Infants initially do not distinguish between self and others, or at least, they don't appear to have an elaborated or developed sense of self. Over time, infants learn that others are either a source of safety or a source of danger; or perhaps that others are unreliable and not predictable, with what Winnicott called the parents' provision of "scaffolding," and we might call "containment."

More challenging is the question of whether pre-and peri-natal experience constitutes learning, and what evidence there is that such experience affects subsequent wellbeing.

History of interest in birth trauma

Freud initially agreed with Otto Rank's theory(Rank, 1929, 1959) that birth trauma was a cause of anxiety neuroses, but later rejected the idea, which caused a rift between them. Birth trauma was not studied again in earnest until Nandor Fodor, a client of Rank's, resumed inquiry in birth trauma and prenatal trauma (1949). Winnicott resumed study also of the earliest learnings of infancy (1960).

Gestational experience is contributory

In final months of gestation, babies orient to a recording of their mother's voice and prefer their mothers' voices over strangers. Other studies have found that nuances of parents' accents have been perceived in utero. French newborns and German newborns have learned to distinguish accents of parents and prefer those accents (Mampe, Friederici, Christophe, & Wermke, 2009).

Condon suggested that antenatal attachment contained the core experience of love, and could be described as a developing relationship in which the mother seeks "to know, to be with, to avoid separation or loss, to protect, and to identify and gratify the needs of her fetus." He later formally defined prenatal attachment as simply (p. 359) "the emotional tie or bond which normally develops between the pregnant parent and her unborn infant" (John T. Condon & Corkindale, 1997).

Prenatal stressors and the amygdala

Aversive prenatal stressors negatively impact the amygdala (Schore, 2003) and the emphasis is on third trimester. Schore has reviewed extensively the literature that suggests that very early experience is formative to baby's self and brain and subsequent well-being and mental health (Schore, 2009). He has stated that attachment impacts the right brain's capacity to mature, so that areas of the cortex that regulate subcortical emotional processing can be supported or impinged in terms of developmental maturity of limbic and autonomic circuits.

Ovtscharoff & Braun state that, "the dyadic interaction between the newborn and the mother serves as a regulator of the developing individual's internal homeostasis. The regulatory function of the newborn-mother interaction may be an essential promoter to ensure the normal development and maintenance of synaptic connections during the establishment of functional brain circuits (2001)."

Fetal learning is about mom

A number of creative studies have identified that fetal learning occurs in gestation. Babies in utero prefer their mother's voice over that of a stranger (A. DeCasper & Fifer, 1980), a familiar story in their mother's voice over an unfamiliar story told in their mother's voice (A. J. DeCasper & Spence, 1986; Kisilevsky et al., 2003), and their mother's native language over a foreign language (DeCasper et al., 1994). All these are important findings suggesting that learning occurs in utero, therefore, it isn't far fetched to think that attachment learning and connection might begin in utero as well.

Dirix et al. (2009) habituated fetuses to sound to assess short-and long-term memory and found that from at least 34 weeks, fetuses can store information and retrieve it four weeks later. Paternal attachment styles are also important (Condon, 1985; Weaver & Cranley, 1983), though Panksepp reports that the CARE circuit in female animals is more powerful than the male, typically (1998).

Another tantalizing finding for EMDR therapy practitioners is that during REM sleep, the fetus's eyes move back and forth just as an adult's eyes do, and many researchers believe that it is dreaming. To an EMDR therapy practitioner, lateral eye movements suggest processing of experience and learning.

Behavioral states have been described as appearing prenatally between 36 and 38 weeks of gestation. If those states are tied to Pankseppian affective circuits, then the acquisition of smooth state switching would begin in the relational context with mother, in the safety of that relationship, where she helps with down regulation (Poblano, Haro, & Arteaga, 2008).

Injuries to the self

If the parent does not provide what the child needs, the child may learn that his or her own emotions and needs are not seen or acknowledged by the other, and that only the other's emotions and needs are important. Such a child will learn to stifle their own needs, feeling and impulses early in life, and adopt the strategy of dissociation if that option is available to that child.

Children who are called, "good babies" are sometimes the ones who learned early to stifle all sounds and impulses, though other "good babies" may have been born with innately peaceful temperaments.

State switching dissociative or smooth? As each developmental time period passes, the normal developmental milestones of infancy come and go, either well or poorly navigated, depending on circumstances in baby's life, and especially, the presence or absence of a loving caretaker supporting that development. These milestones may not be navigated successfully if the infant lacks the support of caretakers or is navigating trauma as well as developmental milestones. Families that later allow frank "big T" trauma and abuse of children likely are also neglectful in infancy, in many cases.

Dissociation, therefore, is an option which allows the child the survival strategy of cutting off the experience of unbearable pain, but at the cost of not being present for the possibility of navigating developmental tasks optimally. When the foundation of a house is poorly poured, subsequent carpentry can't be straight. The effect of missed developmental milestones will reverberate for a lifetime if not repaired optimally.

If the child does not have the assistance of a loving mother to learn smooth state switching and affect regulation, cutting off of emotion is the only option. The affective circuits then are not available for normal affective information.

The cut-off affect accumulates like so much garbage thrown into the basement. Baby ends up at risk for a lifetime of affective overwhelm and dysregulation, each time the unprocessed affective material is triggered in current time by relationship or other environmental triggers, in the absence of affect regulation skills.

The task of trauma processing becomes about how to pace the work and structure it, to deal with the many dumpsters of unprocessed experience needing to be hauled out. This hauling is done by being processed to an adaptive resolution, and doing so in a way that is gentle, not overwhelming, and in which the therapist knows where s/he is and how to systematically proceed.

A Brief History of Approaches to Integration

Integration is not a new concept with the early trauma approach, having been around since the time of Janet. Specifically, two prior integration methods will be described from the hypnosis tradition: strategic integration and tactical integration.

History: strategic integration In 1984 Richard Kluft described strategic integration, whereby internal conflicts that form the basis of dissociation are resolved therapeutically, slowly decreasing the client's reliance upon dissociation. In this approach, integration occurs as a result of the strategic interventions and the dissociative structure basically collapses or resolves from within as healing occurs, little by little over time.

History: tactical integration Catherine Fine introduced the approach of tactical integrationism, (C. Fine, 1993) which leaves dissociative barriers intact, for a time, in order to protect the parts of self that function in external life domains, while the necessary and painful work is conducted behind relatively intact amnesia barriers.

Using this approach means that the part or parts of self that are most likely to present for treatment are not initially participating in EMDR therapy or explicit trauma work. Rather, that part would step aside hypnotically, the trauma work would be conducted between the therapist and other parts, and at the end of the session the front part would return, and would be allowed and encouraged to not know what had been conducted during its absence.

This takes a psychoeducational suggestion to the front part that it is in her interest to do life and not have full exposure to the disturbance while it is being detoxified. It requires a separate pitch or pitches to one or another parts behind the amnesia barrier to do the work without the involvement of the front part that does life, for a time.

History of temporal integration Paulsen coined the term "temporal integration" to explain the effect observed in the early trauma approach. The subsequent temporal integration chapters in this book describe the particulars of the method for resolving very early trauma and neglect when there are no explicit memories. First, however, a few fundamental concepts must be established.

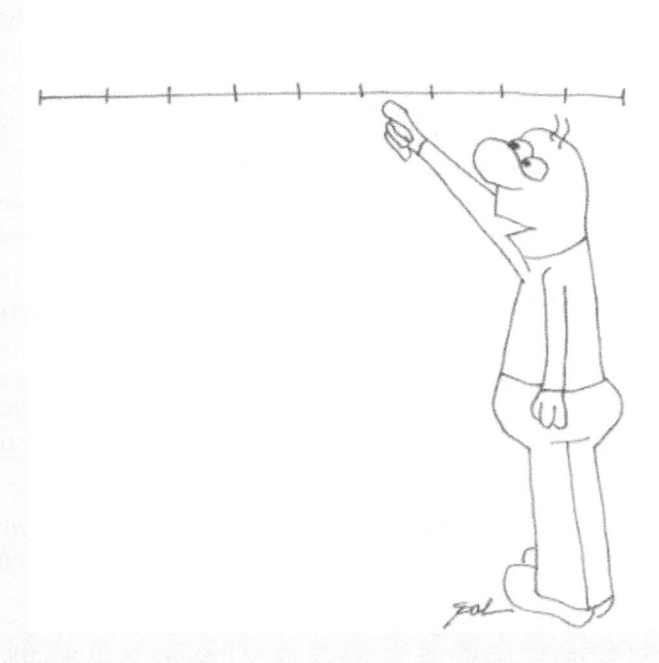

12-1 In temporal integration, the trauma from the earliest years is cleared by reviewing it by time frame from the beginning of the life time line

12-2 When the target is too large for the client's capacity, it's like trying to three-hole punch too many pages at a time, gumming up the works. Instead, we right-size the target by fractionating within the client's capacity

Problem of traditional abreactive processing

"The three hole punch theory"

Both EMDR therapy and hypnotic abreaction can be very intense and overwhelming, taking the client out of their "window of tolerance" (Siegel, 1999). The problem can be illustrated with the common three-hole punch.

If one attempts to three-hole punch 50 pages of paper at a time, one knows the likely results, namely that the holes do not punch easily or cleanly. The equipment becomes jammed and cannot be easily separated from the paper.

The person engaged in the failed punching procedure inevitably asks, "Why didn't I just punch a few pages at a time?"

In contrast, if one begins with the first pages of the stack of paper, and punches only pages one to six initially, the holes are just perfect.

Pages one to six can then be set aside or put in the three-ring binder, and then pages seven to thirteen can be similarly punched with ease and equanimity.

So it is with the early trauma approach put forward by O'Shea 2006; 2009; O'Shea & Paulsen, 2007, Paulsen, 2009).

With the earliest years punched by small time segment and laid to rest, sequentially, a new foundation is laid.

Each subsequent time frame takes its place with relative ease. There is more to it than yet described, and those vicissitudes and particulars are the subject of the remainder of this chapter.

This approach allows the work to be paced and fractionated, consistent with the counsel of Richard Kluft (e.g, Kluft, 1993, 1990).

A new understanding

A third integrationist approach is presented here called temporal integration. "Temporal Integration" (Paulsen, 2009) describes the effect of processing very *temporal integration* — early trauma by time frame when there is no explicit memory. Temporal integration as described here is based upon modification of the work of O'Shea.

The original early trauma approach, if unmodified, is not safe for use with highly dissociative clients in spite of early hopes that it might be. Paulsen modified the early trauma method for the highly dissociative client, which results in an integration that is relatively gentle and "bottom up." It may not be appropriate for every client.

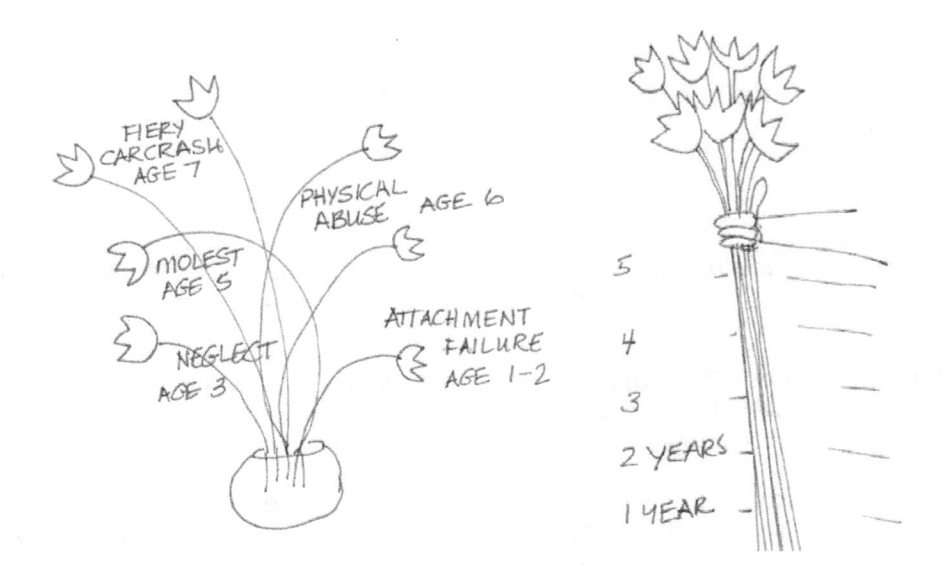

12-3 When trauma is cleared in sequential time segments from the beginning, integration occurs bottom up

When There Are No Words - Sandra Paulsen

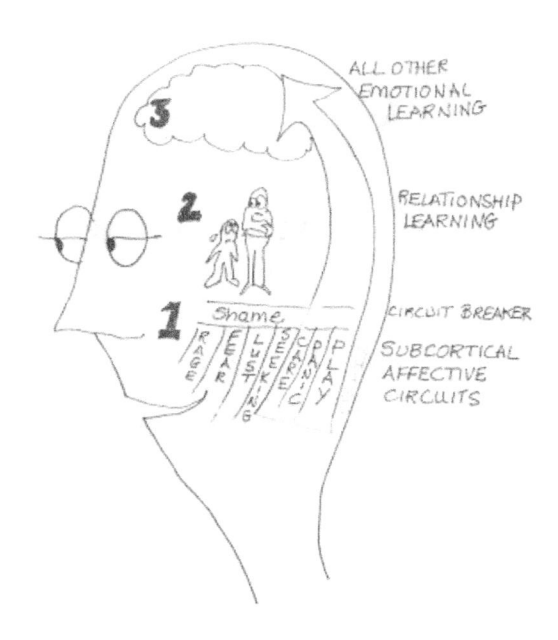

12-4 Temporal integration works directly on the deeper structures of the brain's affective processing, including the secondary affective processing level, reconfiguring object relations, in conjunction with ego state therapy, somatic therapy and EMDR therapy.

Recap of temporal integration   Temporal integration occurs "bottom up" with the early trauma approach because the intervention works directly on affective processing related to the three brain levels of affective processing, the neuro-developmental foundation of which is presented elsewhere, but is briefly summarized here.

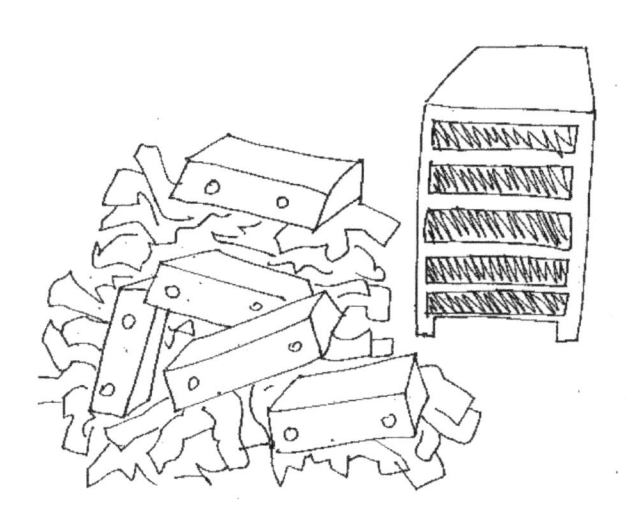

12-5 The standard protocol when applied to implicitly held trauma from infancy can produce overwhelm, if the work isn't paced or targets are too large or undefined

12-6 One of the key benefits of the early trauma approach is that it is systematic and targeting can be titrated to prevent overwhelm

Advantages of temporal integration

One of the advantages offered by the temporal integrationist approach is that by utilizing developmental phases as they unfold chronologically, integration occurs from the bottom up, that is, from the earliest years. This results in an integration process that is relatively gentle compared to attempts to process trauma abreactively at later time periods in a client's life, as in the following analogy.

Three-hole punching too many pages at once

In a brief revisit of the three-hole punch theory of trauma processing described above, in any attempt to process a trauma that occurred at age eight, all the "pages" of learning from birth to eight years old are "underneath" age eight. It follows logically that in processing the disturbing experience at age eight, there occurs a punching through of all thematically related prior learning before age eight.

For complex Cases State Switching is Often Disrupted

For individuals with complex trauma histories, this volume of traumatic learning experience may be too much to process at one time. This is especially true for those who did not acquire smooth state switching and affect regulation in infancy.

Most highly dissociative clients then have decades of unprocessed disturbance accumulated from infancy. They may also have an inability to approach the affective disturbance because of the very problem at the origin, namely, an inability to regulate affect and engage in smooth state switching. Because of this complexity, this subject will be expanded upon in a subsequent section.

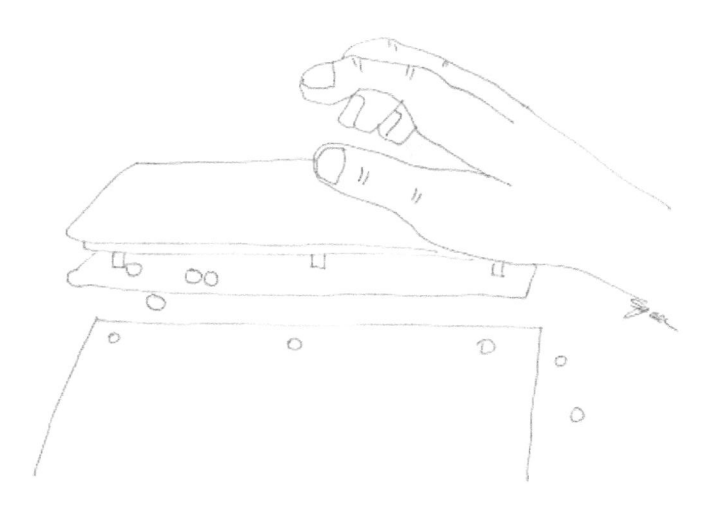

12-7 Processing very early trauma by sequential time segment is like 3-hole punching a few pages at a time instead of fifty, which gums up the works

Three hole-punching a few pages at a time

With temporal integration, instead of processing a later disturbance with all its underlying "pages," the therapist targets and processes traumatic experiences from the beginning of life.

One proceeds slowly, one small time period at a time, imaginally repairing that developmental time period in full before proceeding to the next (O'Shea, 2009).

Intense or overwhelming abreaction is much less likely and the volume of traumatic learning to process through is manageable.

Continuing with the above example, one first processes disturbance from infancy by time frame. Then when ready to process the traumatic events at age eight, those traumatic memory experiences are processed with a new foundation underneath.

While proceeding to the next phase, the client now has a new felt sense of having had his or her needs met in the prior time period. This establishes a new capacity for affect regulation and smoother state switching as one goes along.

This also makes the processing of the subsequent traumatic events much easier to process, titrate, manage and repair, because the underlying foundation has been made solid.

Before anything bad happened

It makes sense to start clearing trauma with conception or before rather than birth because then we begin before anything bad happened. Occasionally it may be preferable to begin with the client's earliest memory or primary caretaker relationships, but it may be soon evident if that will fail, because there is no good foundation to build on.

If we can find a good starting point, it tends to increase compassion for self and create a felt sense of having an okay start even if just innocent, loved by god or just having innocent DNA. This will be discussed at length later in the book.

Willful suspension of disbelief? The author suspends judgment about what the scientific basis might be for the apparent access to memory that we observe from well before birth. We simply do not know whether it is: implicit memory, neocortical constructs from present time, learnings from family stories about their infancy, personal myths, projections, schema, soul memory, psychic communication, vivid imagination, social pressure in the therapeutic relationship field (a.k.a., compliance) or some other phenomena.

Both the author and Katie O'Shea operate on the basis that acting as if the sensations were memories tends to reduce symptoms and improve functioning. Because we see that pattern over and over, reliably, we tend to think it is in some sense a memory. However, we surely can't prove that it is memory and so we suspend disbelief to do the work.

Both O'Shea and Paulsen have had clients who seem to uncover, anew, apparent memory of birth trauma or gestational trauma that it would seem they surely could not have known, who went on to confirm the events from their mother or family member.

The requirement of suspension of disbelief is also part of the cure for clients, because what is often revealed is that, apparently:

- The child or even infant had to cut off his or her own needs and feelings, in favor of adoption of the mother/caretaker's view that the child was wrong.

- One or more parts of the self carried the sequestered and forgotten painful truth of the child, and one or more parts carried the false view adopted for survival purposes, whole cloth (introjected), from the mother/caretaker.

- The false self grows up compliant but symptomatic, and comes to therapy, here early trauma therapy, for symptom reduction.

Symptom reduction is available if and only if the client can bear to hear their own "truth," by listening to the story as it is revealed not in explicit narrative memory, but in such non-verbal communications as:

- their own configuration of symptoms,

- somatic sensation of not only symptoms but what emerges in the processing, contemporaneously,

- mirror neuronal experience of the therapist,

- affect emerging during the processing,

- enactments in the relationship field,

- dreamscape imagery emerging during processing, and

- hypothesis testing during the work.

The author has come to see these types of information as communications from the infant, or one could say, the story itself. Because it is not amenable to direct recall, it can only telegraph itself into the ether and emerge as enactments this way.

To return to the premise that the client must sometimes suspend disbelief to affect the cure, the front or adult part of the client typically is the false self, the one that signed the invisible contract to see themselves and the world through the perpetrator or mother/caretaker's eyes. Therefore, to receive and embrace their own <u>true</u> story requires suspending the introjected and skeptical view point and consider the untold story as revealed in the list above.

- In fact, it is still a hypothesis-testing model, because if the true story is heard and received, it follows that the symptoms will remit, and we see that they very often do remit. If they do not remit, something is not right in the hearing of the story. Either:

    - it is altogether wrong and false, and should be abandoned,

    - an introject is still clinging to the introjected viewpoint for survival, perceived or real, as if a life-threatening danger is still present, <u>or</u>

    - a nuance of the story has not been perceived correctly.

Of the three options described above, it makes sense to try:

- to ask to speak to the part of the self holding the parent/caretaker/perpetrator's introjected viewpoint (appreciating its protective function, orienting to present circumstances, and mediating and problem solving, getting it a new job, all of which have been described elsewhere, (e.g., Paulsen, 2009; Paulsen, 2007; Paulsen & Golston, 2014).

- To attempt to discern that nuance which has not yet been heard, which the client and therapist collaboratively consider.

This experience has tended to support our belief that often these may be some kinds of memory, but again, does not prove it and does not prove it in each case, even if it proves it in one case.

Readers are encouraged to read the recent work suggesting that infants are affected by gestational experience, described elsewhere in this book, and beyond.

This author is guided by the understanding that on some level, the findings are emotionally true for the client, and therefore, listening and honoring that story is the necessary path to "catching and releasing" the symptoms.

12-8 When infants are exposed to high levels of stress early in life, they can be primed for chronic high levels of arousal, dissociation, and endogenous opioids

When There Are No Words - Sandra Paulsen

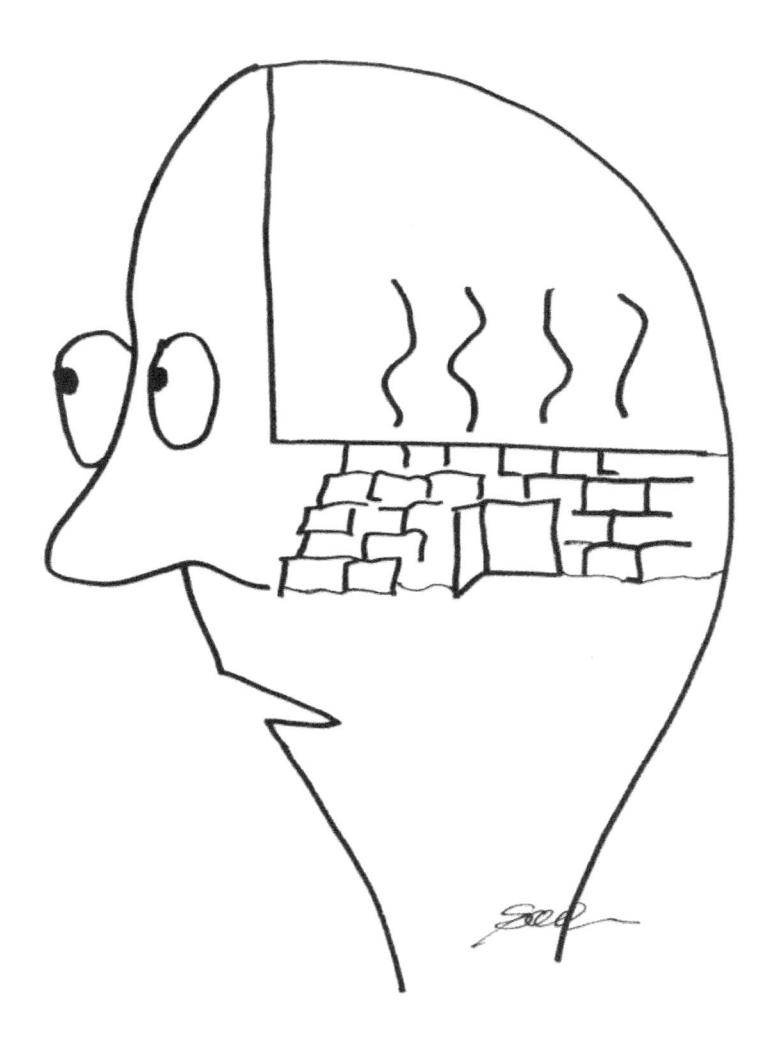

12-9 When working in implicit memory, maintaining dual-attention awareness of the "then" and the "now" is challenging because there is no picture or narrative as there would be when processing an explicit memory. Traumatic transference or reenactments emerge in the relationship field to tell the untold story.

Is it part of the memory? The term "traumatic transference" may be useful for some clients, but the author is more likely to refer to it as "vapors leaking up from King Tut's tomb," a metaphor that captures the subtlety of early memory that leaks into present time and the ancientness of the material.

12-10 The therapist's mirror neurons and clinical intuition can apperceive information in the energy/relationship field to hear the story in the non-verbal

Emotional flashback Some individuals will benefit by the simple instruction that it is a "flashback," and that flashbacks and memories don't have be visual. They can be emotional, bodily, or include other sensory channels such as smell and taste. This subject will be more fully explored in the procedures sections.

The fundamental task of the work is to help the client to hear his or her own story with curiosity as it emerges in the narrative but also in the non-verbal communications represented in affect, soma, reenactments, mirror neurons, and more. This transforms the client's symptoms into communications from the depths of the self, to be heard, honored and only then resolved and released, as part of what the author calls a "catch-and-release" program.

*Confusing
then and now*

*What if it's
part of a long
lost memory*

*Baby's
sad story*

12-11 Very commonly, people think their present mood is from present matters, but often, it's really from unprocessed memories, leaking up from implicit memory and wrongly associated with a current trigger

12-12 As first the therapist and then the client hear the baby's unspoken story through the non-verbals, the symptoms, which are shrines to that story, remit. This is the "catch-and-release program."

13 Temporal Integration: Basic Procedures

This is the bare bones of doing EMDR therapy on trauma and neglect occurring in infancy.

This section will discuss the basic procedures for temporal integration to clear trauma held in implicit memory by time frame. Because targeting is quickly followed by desensitization in this work, and because negative and positive cognitions emerge out of the processing instead of before the processing, these topics tend to merge in discussion. However, the following overarching topics will be covered below:

- EMDR therapy phase III targeting
- EMDR therapy phase IV desensitization and phase V–installation
- Dual attention awareness and hearing the story in the non-verbals
- EMDR therapy phases VI through VIII–body scan, debriefing and re-evaluation

13-1--The primary task is for the therapist to hear the story as it's told in the non-verbals, for the first time ever, so the symptoms can finally remit.

EMDR Therapy Phase III–Targeting

Targeting in the standard EMDR therapy

In the standard EMDR therapy approach, phase III refers to the targeting work of selecting the memory that will be worked upon and selecting a picture that represents the most disturbing aspect of that memory.

Targeting further involves articulating both a negative cognition that reflects the words that bespeak the client's negative belief about themselves now when they think about the memory; and a positive cognition that reflects the goal of what the client wishes to believe instead of the negative cognition.

Targeting also involves determining a VOC rating which reflects the validity of the positive cognition on a seven-point scale where 1 represents completely false and 7 represents completely true.

Finally, targeting also involves asking the client to hold the picture and the negative cognition in mind and identify what the feeling or emotion is in present time, where that disturbance is felt in the client's body, and how disturbing it is.

Disturbance is measured as a SUD number (subjective units of distress scale) from 0 (no disturbance) to 10 (the most disturbance imaginable).

EMDR therapy targeting in implicit memory

It is not possible to target in the standard EMDR therapy protocol described above when using the early trauma approach because there is no explicit memory to target via images and cognitions, or known narrative in many cases.

Rather, one targets a time frame. The therapist turns the client's attention to the time frame, beginning at or before conception initially, and asks the client to just notice whatever is there.

At first, clients may say there is nothing there, because they are expecting conventional memory with images to appear, which of course is impossible for this time frame. With repeated explanation, the client comes to understand that all that is needed is to attend to the felt sense in the body and just notice. This act of focused attention to the nuances of the felt sense initiates phase IV–desensitization.

Early trauma approach targeting

The standard EMDR therapy approach typically targets an explicit memory with its concomitant imagery, negative cognition, affect and body sensation.

Since there is no explicit memory and likely no explicit image or overt cognitions, the target in the early trauma approach is merely the time frame from the first years, beginning at the beginning. Additional targeting material may or may not emerge during the processing. For the layperson, a memory, by definition, refers to a picture or image of a past event.

However, in the early trauma processing the target is a time frame for which there is likely no image, no explicit memory, and therefore no possible negative or positive cognitions initially. Only the felt sense is being processed but other material may emerge.

Specifically, the therapist should be alert to any self-referencing cognitions that emerge, and capture negative and positive cognitions as they occur spontaneously in the course of the work.

For example, a client may start with a felt sense of doom or unsafety, with no context, and then say that it seems as if she hears arguing, for example.

The therapist will support a suspension of disbelief and a stance of curiosity to enable the client to process through whatever the disturbance is, without stating a certainty that the therapist knows what the nature of the disturbance is.

If during the processing the client states a vague sense of believing, "I'm so bad," the therapist should note this as a captured negative cognition "I'm bad" and ensure that an appropriate positive cognition such as "I'm fine," is installed using bilateral stimulation before work is complete on that time frame.

The infant's early world is experiential, not particularly cognitive in the verbal sense, and focused on developmental milestones.

Therefore, the work of repairing trauma from infancy revolves around several tasks, namely: specific developmental tasks associated with the given time frame in question; baby's awareness of physical growth, emotional growth, and relationship tasks.

The relational and attachment tasks are associated with the secondary processing level of brain development (Panksepp, 1998; Schore, 2001, 2003), which includes: the I-and-thou of inter-subjectivity (Trevarthen, 1979); and the infant's earliest learnings about relationship with others (Fonagy et al., 2002; Fonagy, 2001; Fonagy et al., 2005). These contributors emphasize the importance to the infant's burgeoning self and ability to regulate self of being seen, honored, having an effect on others, and coming into coherence in that relationship, (Siegel, 2015; Schore, 2001, 2003).

Fractionating targets In listening to the unfolding of baby's story for themes such as the above, the targeting of time frames is important to consider.

Typically, the therapist may target time frames of the following sizes, as one example. These time frames are not a forced march. The clinician should use good clinical judgment to determine the right size for time frames for a given client. A client whose life was apparently good before the car crash at age 3 will tolerate bigger time frames, most likely, than the client who had two surgeries and the death of a twin in the first months of life.

For the latter, very small time frames might be required. As another example, a client who describes wonderful loving parents and a picture perfect infancy, with trauma beginning later in childhood with lengthy hospitalization, will move through the early years rapidly, and it will be acceptable to use time periods of three, six or even twelve months.

However, a client who reports hospitalization and two surgeries in the first weeks and months of life will perhaps benefit from targeting a month at a time or even smaller time segments to titrate the intensity of the experience.

If a time period produces overwhelm, it might be broken down into smaller segments for better pacing (Kluft, 1989) and fractionation (Kluft, 1990). The size of the time periods to target are variable depending upon what is known about trauma complexity for the client in that time period.

All things being equal, a therapist might start with a heuristic of time frames similar to this one, modifying as required by circumstances of the history.

Right-sizing the time frames Typically, the therapist may target time frames of the following sizes, as an example. These time frames are not a forced march. The clinician should use good clinical judgment to determine the right size for time frames.

Once the work has gone beyond the formative first two years, thereafter the processing may go by year unless historical information indicates otherwise.

Once the person has access to explicit memory, it makes sense to switch to an unmodified standard EMDR therapy which targets explicit memory of disturbing events.

An example of typical time frames: but not a cookie cutter

- pre-conception
- conception
- first trimester of gestation
- second trimester
- third trimester
- birth, first week of life
- first three months after birth

- three to six months
- six to 9 months
- 9-12 months
- 12-15 months
- 15-18 months
- 18-24 months
- 24-30 months
- 30-36 months

Smaller time frames if more trauma Some individuals may require smaller time periods if, for example, there were known traumas such as premature delivery, illness or surgery, or other events within specific time periods. Right-sizing the fractionation helps pace the work in a way tailored to the needs of the client.

Some clients may sense that little occurred within any given time period and move through larger segments of time until they get to a hot spot where there is disturbance to process. The therapist shouldn't be too willing to assume there is nothing there just because a client reports there is nothing there, if the client also evidences alexithymia or an inability to sense and track body sensations. Such clients will require somatic work to first connect and attune so they can do this work.

Some individuals will report feeling nothing, and this may be a sign that there is no disturbance to process. However, when the work is subsequently checked in another session, sometimes it is revealed that a layer has been peeled open that was previously inaccessible.

Targeting is not a cookie cutter, and time frames will vary depending upon the facts of the case. However, if the time available is brief, skating quickly across time periods will not likely produce good results for many clients, and slowly dropping down into the felt sense will produce better results even if only a small foundational piece can be achieved.

Continuing targeting by time frame through life or through age 5

Some clients wish to continue targeting by time frame throughout life, but after about age 3 or 5 years of age explicit memory kicks in, though the age for this shift is variable for different clients. Once the client has explicit memories for childhood experience, the unmodified EMDR therapy approach is better to use because there is research on its use.

Future templates are not typically employed in this work until the early years are repaired in full.

However, there may be some exceptions where the particular early traumas are so discretely formulated that it makes sense to target the future with future templates.

For example, if the client is repairing their desperately neglected first years of life using imaginary parents, once the client has a clear felt sense of having been well loved, the therapist may ask the client to imagine what it would be like tomorrow or next week to go through life feeling loved.

For the dissociative client, this may or may not work, depending on how many subsequent memories need clearing and repairing first.

Why include pre-conception

In the example of fictitious client Hope, her very conception occurred in rape. Throughout her life, she'd heard how much her mother hated her father for raping her on their first and only date, and how Hope, by her physical resemblance to him, reminded her mother of that much-despised father.

Beginning trauma processing at the beginning of Hope's life was to begin with a very bad start in which baby Hope was herself despised, unwanted and begotten of violence.

However, when the writer asked Hope where she was before she was conceived, she answered with softness, "In God's heart." Using pre-conception as a starting point, that powerful resource of being held in the heart of God was, in and of itself, a transformative construct to contemplate.

As the therapist and Hope installed the awareness of having been in God's heart before conception, her visage changed and a new foundation was laid that made subsequent processing much easier.

From that day forward, she never again felt like a hated mistake, but rather, that she was cherished and loved by God. She believes she was planned before the beginning of time, according to Psalm 139, and had learned this truth years before, but had not had the felt sense of this beginning in love until the ET procedure. This new foundation enabled the therapy to move forward in time and process through a sequence of very terrible early experiences without affective overwhelm.

Conception, gestation and beyond Again, the writer does not take the position that clients can remember events from their gestation, although in later gestational periods it certainly sometimes appears to be the case that learning has already begun for babies (see for example, DeCasper & Fifer, (1980), DeCasper & Spence (1986).

The debate of what it possible to remember is outside the purpose of this chapter. Rather, interest lies in transforming the felt sense associated with that time frame, no matter what the actual source of that felt sense may be.

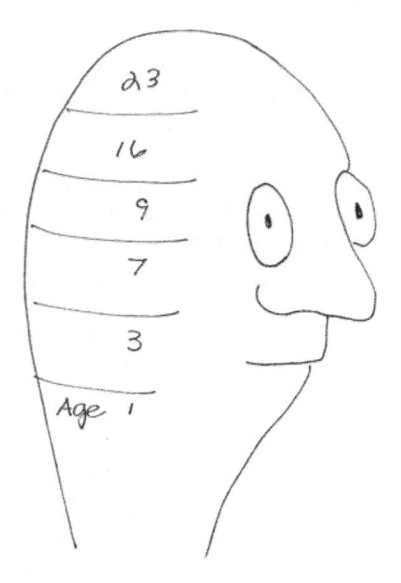

13-2 EMDR therapy targeting in the early trauma approach involves selecting time segments of the right size or "bite size" and digestible by the client's capacity to process

Example As an example, let's assume the memory targeted in a session is, say, the fiery car crash at age 24 when the client was rear ended. If the client is especially vigilant on the road and checking the rearview mirror, they may well realize this is because the memory is opened up and near the surface.

Implicit memory misperceived as being about present time In doing early trauma work, however, there is no picture, and the memory is vague or even merely a felt sense. For example, when the client's attention is turned to the time from six to nine months, she may access a sense of emotional hurt with pain in the chest around the heart, without awareness of what the memory is that is associated with the hurt. The client may say, "I feel hopeless, sad but I don't know why, it's very big though….no, I don't know what's going on. I think I'm no good at this EMDR business, I'll never get the hang of it. You must think I'm stupid. I hope you don't hate me."

The therapist might say with curiosity, "Is it possible that the feeling of hopelessness, being no good, not being able to figure it out feeling rejected, is part of the memory?" The client will typically say, "oh, yes, I bet you're right" or just nod.

Similarly, and this is the direct comparison with the fiery car crash example, the client may notice between sessions that they are feeling especially blue at work, convinced that learning the new software is hopeless, feeling stupid and that the boss hates her.

Even if the therapist has alerted the client to this possibility, typically the client will have forgotten. If there is a regular session or a phone check-in between sessions, the client may report how they have been feeling and attribute it to the therapy or not, but without understanding that it is baby-state's feelings leaking up into present time.

Once reoriented to this possibility, the client will have a better time at work, or handling the feelings between sessions. This issue is the same dual attention awareness that has always been critical for conducting EMDR therapy, but extended to the time between sessions.

Inoculate to the probability of transference

The therapist should mention this matter before early trauma work as part of the informed consent, during the work to keep them from attributing the dynamics to the therapeutic relationship, and between sessions to minimize the risk of erroneously attributing the emotions to their present life.

Emerging nuances during processing

What emerges in the course of processing by time frame is awareness, often very subtle, of possible dynamics or circumstances related to attachment and child development.

For example, in the third trimester of gestation, a client may report feeling that there was arguing and violence in the family that affected the client's felt sense of safety.

There may be a felt sense of helplessness and depression, or a discernment that the moods belonged first to the mother, and that baby took on those feelings.

There may be a sense of being unwanted, or wanted but in circumstances that were overwhelming, etc. Again, without worrying as to whether the thoughts are veridical, the approach is "review, release and repair," described below.

Capturing NCs and PCs during the processing

It is not possible to articulate a target from explicit memory and therefore it isn't possible to formulate negative and positive cognitions. However, it is important to retain fidelity to the standard EMDR therapy approach.

Both negative and positive cognitions are keenly important to articulate before considering the work complete, as measurements of progress and to enlist and generalize to adult resources. Therefore, both negative and positive cognitions for each time period are still captured as the work unfolds. This is a key step in ensuring that the ET approach cleaves closely to the standard approach, and is still EMDR therapy.

13-3 Because the target memory is implicitly held without narrative or picture, the negative and positive cognitions are captured as they emerge in the processing

Example of captured cognitions

For example, while working on the time period from three to six months after birth, neither therapist nor client will know what to expect. The client reports a feeling of irritability and loneliness, with an emerging sense of stillness and silence. The therapist makes notes in the client's file, "NC: I am alone," and "I must be silent."

As the processing continues and the disturbance clears, the therapist asks what the client would have needed to have a different outcome. The client answers, "to be held," and subsequently "to be able to cry out for what I need."

The therapist notes these as PCs in the form "I deserve to be held," and "I can ask for what I need." When the client has vividly imagined having those needs met, the therapist offers the verbalizations of the PCs and whether that wording fits or if other words fit better.

Those PCs or their improvements are then installed while the client envisions getting what they needed on their own terms for that time period. The time period is then checked again for further disturbance. If it feels clear and resolved, the work proceeds to the next time period.

If further disturbance appears or persists for the same time period, the work stays in that time period with the therapist again capturing NCs as they emerge or are implied in the work, while capturing likely PCs for use in the repair phase for that time period.

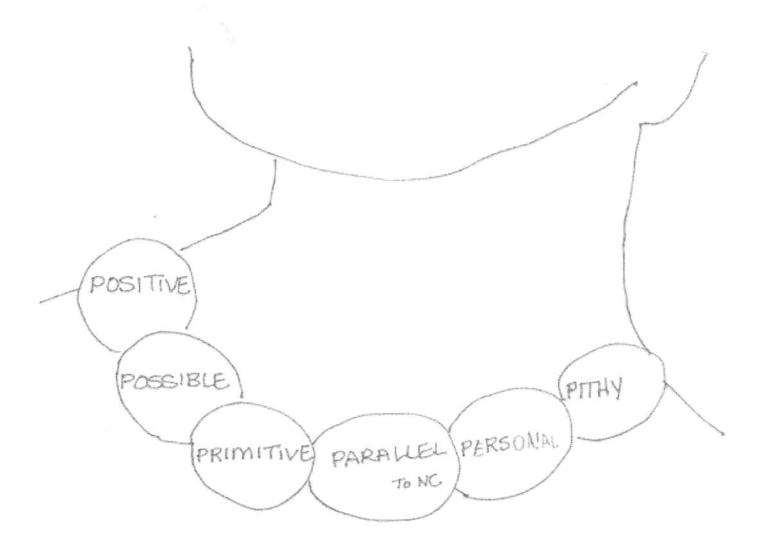

13-4-Six p-p-p-pearls that characterize good positive cognitions

Capturing positive cognitions and the six pearls for positive cognitions

Paulsen has long espoused "six pearls" for positive cognitions. Positive cognitions should be:

- P for positive (should have no negative words in it, such as "no", "not," "never", etc),

- P for possible (that is, "I am the Holy Virgin Mary" is likely not possible to achieve, so is not a suitable positive cognition),

- P for primitive (similar to the point about pithiness, but slightly different) (The statement, "As I approach my dotage, I find that I am well worth love and honoring as is any sentient being," is less useful a PC than the more primitive and viscerally felt, "I'm fine.") They should be true to a voice more characteristic of the emotional and simple valence of the right hemisphere than of the heady verbal nature of the left hemisphere. This tone difference is more evident in the inverse, with the negative cognition, where the primitiveness quality really is salient. A potent NC sounds like, "I'm bad," or better but hard to evoke, "Me bad," bespeaking the child's primitive thinking. The converse PC then, "I'm good," or "I'm fine," is, though more mature, still keeping the primitive simple nature and is therefore more useful as a PC, and is likely to achieve more pervasive generalization than a more esoteric and intellectualized PC.

- P for parallel (that is, the negative and positive cognitions should be bookends of each other, as in, "I'm unworthy," and "I'm worthy.")

- P for personal. With only the rarest of exceptions, positive cognitions are self-referential, not about the other.

- P for pithy ("I am a sentient, exceptional human being, loved by God and cherished by those most important to me, with few exceptions," is not a good PC, because it is wordy. "I am lovable," is far better.)

"Review, release, repair" The sequence of "review, release, and repair" is integral to the early trauma approach (O'Shea, 2009b) and the language is O'Shea's. O'Shea subsequently went on to describe the sequence as "review, release, relearn and repair." This author, however, cleaves to the original "review, release, and repair," because all therapeutic change involves relearning, new associative linkages, and isn't a separate step as the other three are.

Review The review phase involves just noticing, with a curious and mindful stance that is attuned and present to the felt sense in the body in current time. This ability to tolerate the felt sense will have been established earlier in the containment and stabilization phase, and as part of the somatic resourcing addressed prior to embarking upon the processing of early trauma. The disturbance may or may not shift spontaneously or it may stay stuck or be unresolved.

Release In the release phase, there may be spontaneous releasing or letting go, or it may be necessary to evoke a release by asking a pertinent question such as "what would you have needed to have a different outcome?"

This typically evokes a thoughtful imagining of a different outcome, which accompanies a shift in the felt sense, including a release of whatever the processing is stuck on.

Processing is often poignant, heart-felt and tearful, especially when related to attachment needs for love and connection, and vividly imagining a fulfillment of those needs.

Repair In the repair phase, spontaneous positive imagery may emerge, or the therapist may need to suggest repair by asking if there is anything else the client would have wanted to have had their needs met on their own terms, using such language as offered by O'Shea, 2009:

- "what would you have needed or needed to do," or
- "imagine getting what you needed, the way you needed it to be"

This is repeated for each time frame until that time period is completely repaired with no residual disturbance on inquiry, however slight. Then, and only then, is there readiness to move to the next time frame.

It is a mistake to proceed to the next time frame while any residual disturbance remains, no matter how subtle.

Experiential interweaves: canine or natural

Experiential interweaves are those which require the client to be engaged with something in the environment to produce a needed insight or shift.

Paulsen will frequently utilize actual dogs, horses, trees, sage, or other resources in nature to produce shifts. For example, it is enormously powerful if a client is recalling an infant state of abject loneliness and despair, and at just the right moment, a delicate poodle kiss is gently administered by a canine assistant, where welcome and appropriate.

This tends to produce spontaneous, in many clients, shifts of felt sense and insight such as, "I did survive," "I am loveable," "I can connect," etc.

13-5 Tiny shoes, wordlessly presented, will confront the client with the truth that s/he was an innocent child

Experiential interweaves: tiny shoes

Another experiential interweave that is helpful with any client who is unforgiving in harshness with their own infant state's needs was suggested by Debra Wesselmann (2010). In that intervention, the therapist produces an actual pair of tiny baby shoes to illustrate the tininess of the child. In a variation of this method, the tiny shoes can be held next to the therapist's own adult shoe for greater contrast. This experiential method and what the author calls the "Pocatello interweave" (also called "neocortical objectivity" by the author) both produce object cathexis where the subjective primacy of shame would otherwise prevail. The Pocatello intervention is described elsewhere in this book.

"Known or unknown, inside or outside, asleep or awake, alive or dead."

Speaking to all parts of the self...

13-6 All-points bulletin to the far corners of the self-system

Ego state interweaves: asking to speak to whatever part can help us understand

When early trauma processing is stuck or looping and the therapist is at a loss to understand why, and the client is not able to provide needed information, it is often quick and efficient to simply ask,

"I'd like to invite whatever part of the self comes up next, or whatever part of the self can help us understand what's happening here, to come fill us in, at this time."

Then the relevant ego state/alter can either switch or provide information through another alter. Or the client may associate to a later memory, which, by prior agreement, is permitted to inform just such a situation.

Once the later memory is pondered to identify the thematic dynamic germane to the infant's experience, the later memory is again set aside and the client and therapist return their attention to the baby's stuck process, now informed by the theme gleaned from the later memory.

Cognitive interweaves in early trauma processing for dissociative clients

Interweaves in the standard approach of EMDR therapy are used when processing is stuck or "looping," and are often cognitive in nature. However, in the early trauma approach, interweaves to resolve stuck processing may be imaginal, experiential, or relational, instead of cognitive. They may also be ego state interweaves or somatic interweaves.

With DID clients, ego state interweaves are frequent and essential. All the other interweaves here may also be appropriate for complex trauma/DID as well.

The processing occurs relatively in the dark, making it quite mysterious and subtle and more difficult to discern whether the processing is actually stuck, or just continuing in a subtle way.

Many clients require specific instruction regarding this point, such as, "I hear that it's 'about the same' so I'm wondering if it is exactly the same or a tiny bit different somehow? Because if it is even a little different, that means it is not stuck and we can let it continue. If it is exactly the same, it is stuck, and I need to do something to get it restarted. Does that make sense?" That will be enough for the majority of clients. In rare cases, that same psycho-educational piece must be repeated multiple times. The following are examples of several types of interweaves.

Imaginal interweaves Imaginal interweaves, as defined by O'Shea, consist of language such as, "What would you have needed,--or needed to do--to have had a different outcome?" The client vividly imagines that outcome. Another important cognitive interweave wording, as per O'Shea (2011, personal communication), is to say, "Imagine what would have happened if everything had been the way you needed it to be."

13-7 Imaginal repair with DAS/BLS

"Getting what you needed, the way you needed it to be" The client may have needed to have been loved or rescued, or to have fought back, or to have been born to a different family altogether. There is no limit to what can be imagined.

It is best if the solution imagined comes directly from the client, because it is the client's perceptions of unmet needs that are the key. At the same time, some people, especially the severely dissociative, have little capacity to imagine what they might have received because of a paucity of exposure to optimal parenting, or because of the interference of beliefs about being too needy, etc.

If the client appears to be unable to envision optimal parenting or is inhibited from articulating normal needs, the therapist prompts them by saying "there is no limit! We can bring in angels or superheroes or clone your mother or whatever you want. We aren't limited to a 'dry crust of bread.'"

This vivid imagining of better outcomes tends to produce a profound shift and resolution. If the client resists, saying, "but that's not what happened, that's just pretending," the therapist explains that the brain doesn't distinguish between what's real and what's imagined, that it has been waiting a long time to have the felt sense of being loved (or whatever the developmental milestone requires).

The author likes to say to the client that the use of imagination allows the brain to be "marinated" in the very biochemicals it has needed all these years.

Imaginal repair of attachment nurturing

Where touch is legal and not otherwise contraindicated, it should, of course, be boundaried touch, with no effort on the part of the therapist to re-mother in the form of acting out of client urges or misguided therapist urges.

If the client requests to be held or rocked, the therapist would ask the client to notice the yearning to be held and rocked, saying, "Baby, we" (adult client and therapist) "hear you, you wanted so very much to be held, and rocked and loved. So sorry, baby, that you weren't held and rocked. Notice that." The subsequent repair should vividly provide the holding and rocking in imagination, and without too long a delay, lest the client be left "twisting in the wind."

Imaginal repair in the client's mind's eye, utilizing either the image of the biological mother, or any other real or imagined figure, providing loving and holding and nurturing, is suggested kindly instead of actually attempting to hold or rock the client. If the client becomes angry that the therapist won't provide that holding, the therapist would then say, "I'm wondering if baby was really, really mad when no one came to hold her and rock her. Did I get that right or wrong? Notice that. Baby is <u>really, really mad</u>!!"

It is important to recognize that the somewhat regressive nature of this work is not a permanent emphasis, but rather a deliberate and temporary focus, necessary to review, release and repair unprocessed very early trauma.

This emphasis is quite different from the standard approach of EMDR therapy. The therapist should take extra care to ensure that the client does not leave in the midst of a lancing a boil of despair or longing, without also having offered a good portion of imaginal repair, complete with verbalization of nurturance, and the visualization of a kind caretaker's loving eyes and smile.

Closed-ended questions for facilitating imaginal repair

If a highly-injured client continues to exhibit an impoverishment of ability to imagine improved possible outcomes, the therapist may suggest imaginative interweaves. Samples, from O'Shea, include these:

"Did you get picked up when you needed to be?"
"Did you get enough to eat, and as often as you needed?"
"Did you get what you needed from your dad?"
"Was your birth easy?"

Expect "emotional flashbacks" between ET processing sessions	For the early trauma work, the most common between-session symptoms are emotional or bodily or even simply a felt sense described in terms like, "not unhappy, just sort of inert." This can be addressed by saying, "is it possible that's part of baby's memory, of just sort of being there, like, 'I'm here, what's next?'" The term "somatic flashback" might also be helpful. Either term conveys that a flashback need not be a "picture memory," as many people expect it to be.
Incomplete sessions	An additional point regarding informed consent here. In addition to the usual EMDR therapy informed consent process, for the early trauma approach incomplete sessions need to be closed taking into account the following and alerting the client to the possibilities as appropriate.
Client's attributions & implicit memory	When a client is processing a fiery car crash with the standard EMDR therapy approach, and after an incomplete EMDR therapy session they have a startle response when they hear brakes screech, they likely know it's a memory because the car crash is held in explicit memory with visual images and auditory sounds.
Attributing flashback emotion to present time	In contrast, when a client is processing longstanding emotional neglect in implicit memory, and they feel abandoned by the therapist when the therapist turns to switch off the ringing phone in the middle of the session, they are less likely to realize the feeling of being abandoned is part of the diffuse memory currently being processed.
Repeat, repeat, repeat: "Could it be part of the memory?"	It is critical that the therapist continuously reorient to the possibility that whatever is disturbing to the client either between sessions as they go through daily life or in session in the therapeutic relationship may be part of the memory being processed. Raising this possibility as frequently as necessary, in combination with grounding and orienting to present time, is needed also during processing in order to prevent overwhelm during ET processing.

When There Are No Words - Sandra Paulsen

13-8 Orienting to present circumstances

Transference material is an emotional flashback from implicit memory

With a traumatic or neglectful experience from the first years of life, reenactment or memory of the experience is like a flashback, albeit a different kind of flashback.

The experience is held in implicit memory in the right hemisphere (Schore, 2009) and so there is no picture or cognition per se.

Rather, the person is likely to experience just an emotion or felt sense or thought or focal or general somatic sensations.

Because these memories are diffuse and not specific, it is common for clients to not realize that what they are experiencing is a memory.

Specifically, they think it is happening now, and may attribute their sensations or emotions to what is happening in present time.

They can be overwhelmed in present time, because they don't realize it is a memory. Therefore, re-orienting the person to present circumstances with some frequency is often necessary.

14 Advanced Temporal Integration for Dissociative Clients

14-1 Expect the unexpected

Overview This section is organized into several subsections:

- Introduction to temporal integration with dissociative clients
- Assessment
- Ego state preparations
- Somatic preparations
- Targeting–bite size
- Interweaves
- Final concepts

Basic Concepts for Temporal Integration with Dissociative Clients

A summary of key points

Four things to take into account in complex trauma are stated here as summary; they will also emerge in the discussion below in more detail.

1) Ego state therapy is necessary to enlist the client's self-system in the work. Without ego state therapy, EMDR therapy will loop, as loyalty to the aggressor interferes with processing. This is always true with EMDR therapy, but especially with early trauma processing, where loyalty to the parent's point of view was baby's bread and butter.

2) Somatic therapy is very often necessary to hook up disconnected dash board wires. Tracking in a moment-to-moment way, oscillating between trauma and resource prepares clients for EMDR therapy processing by nibbling around the edges of the disturbance and teaching them that they can survive addressing affect.

3) This remedy works because in the first years of life, infants learn that there is a crescendo and a decrescendo of affect, if they are held in Mom's loving arms. If not, they crescendo and, having no downward regulation ability in mom's arms, they truncate or dissociate at the apex of the disturbance, probably at the thalamus, flipping the circuit breaker. They shut down. So when we use somatic therapy to hook them back up gently, they learn there is not only a crescendo but a decrescendo.

4) Working with perpetrator introjects addresses the defenses that are the dragons protecting the castle. At the moment of trauma it was necessary to look through the perpetrator's eyes to survive. There was no choice. The narcissist's point of view and needs and feelings were all that mattered; the child did not matter. The child <u>must</u> put aside their own needs and feelings to survive.

5) Orienting, appreciating the perpetrator introjects and mediating internal conflicts, negotiating experiments, are all important to soften perpetrator introjects and get them off their spots to permit the work.

6) Each and every session that addresses remote ego states requires a closure or "tucking in" procedure the same way a surgical intervention isn't complete until the incision is closed and stitched up. Failure to close and tuck in a deep session will result in decompensation in many cases.

7) The story tells itself in the reenactments in the relationship field in the office, and in the client's present life. This manifests also amidst EMDR therapy, e.g., "I'm doing this wrong aren't I? You must hate me!" is less about the present moment (in many cases) and more about the story held in implicit memory, incorrectly attributed to the present time.

14-2 Every session using ego state maneuvers should end with a closure or "tucking in" procedure to prevent overwhelm and enhance safety post session

Terminology: "complex trauma" and "dissociative"

This section describes the modifications of the basic early trauma approach that are needed to use the procedure with complex or highly dissociative clients. Those terms, "complex trauma," and "highly dissociative," are used nearly interchangeably here but there is an exception to that heuristic.

The exception is that there are some clients who are not structurally dissociative but are somatically dissociative and/or alexithymic from trauma and neglect in the first years of life who will need considerable somatic work in order to be able to do the early trauma processing. For those clients, ego state work will not be as important as somatic work. For structurally dissociative clients, however, ego state work will be key, as described below.

Temporal integration and the bouquet of tulips

The systematic clearing and repair by time period, beginning at or before conception, serves to titrate the intensity of early trauma which is typically experienced without access to adult resources, but with the felt sense of baby's meager emotional resources.

The result is dramatically less abreactive overwhelm, even with dissociative clients. Additionally, for dissociative clients, there is a phenomenon of integrating from the base, which causes less overwhelm overall.

That is to say, as the work progresses, the alters/ego states come together from the base, so that all subsequent processing is made that much easier by the trending toward integration of states.

To illustrate this temporal integration from the beginning of life, consider a bouquet of tulips. If they are held by one hand from the base of the tulips' stems, the heads of the tulips will splay outward with space between them. This is comparable to the dissociated alter personalities.

If while still holding the tulips from the base, one moves the other hand up the stems, the heads of the tulips come together.

They are still separate tulips, comparable to separate ego states, but they are more integrated and less disparate because as the hand moved up the steps the hand pulled the tulip heads together.

The bouquet of alters The tulips metaphor conveys, somewhat, what we see in using the early trauma approach with dissociative clients. The dissociative client initially is less integrated, with alters less aware of each other, less working together as a team. However as the early trauma work proceeds, beginning from the beginning of life, the alters spontaneously integrate bottom up, and become more a smooth functioning system or team. Wth dissociative clients, it is necessary to use the early trauma approach in conjunction with somatic work to increase resourcing and soma tolerance and ego state work at each phase to enable the system to permit the integration.

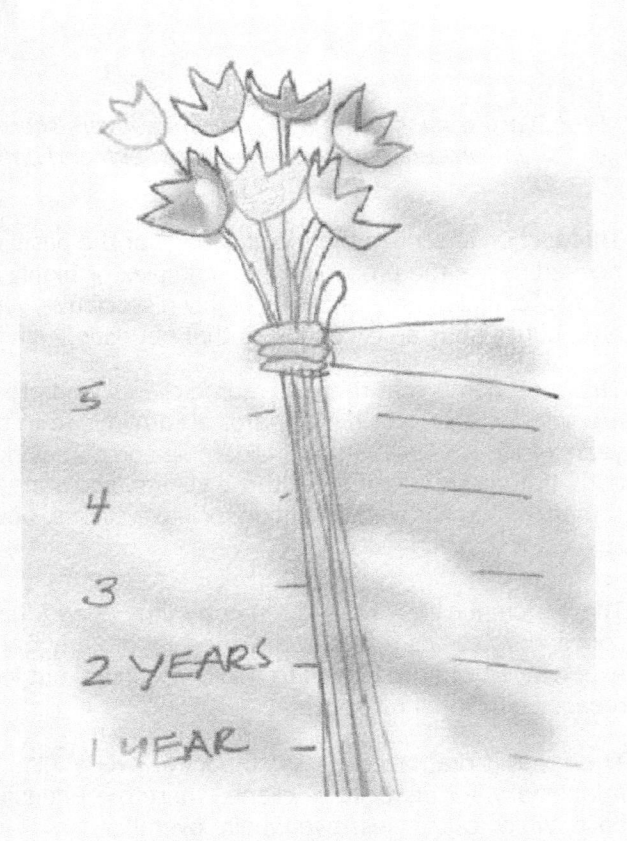

14-3 Tulips coming together bottom up

First year of life is seminal for many dissociative clients in   For DID clients, the amount of trauma held in the early time frames can be daunting. The time and cost of the intensive work, even using the early trauma approach, can be prohibitive. However, spending the time intensively on even the first year of life for a DID client will produce tremendous, though partial, integration that will make any form of subsequent therapy far more time efficient.

how their self-system is organized

This is a better use of that same time than it would be to skate quickly over the top, for a greater number of time-periods, with less deep resolution.

The first year of life is profoundly important to repair because of the seminal nature of developmental milestones in that period.

Dissociative clients

Dissociative clients may not be ready to undergo early trauma treatment for some time, but as soon as it can be safely conducted, it enables profound integration and clarity to occur without abreactive overwhelm.

This makes subsequent trauma processing much easier to conduct. As a result, the trauma processing phase of treatment for DID clients goes much more manageably and smoothly. The systematic nature makes it easier to conduct.

In short, for dissociative clients, however much of the early trauma approach can be conducted, the work, if properly carried out, will lay a new foundation which will profoundly change the substrate, character tapestry, resources, degree of integration and co-consciousness, and internal cooperation.

This will make a significant improvement in not only subsequent therapeutic efforts but in the experience of life itself.

Dissociative clients who have undergone this early trauma procedure to any degree, even if resources did not permit complete processing in an intensive format, will find subsequent therapeutic work of any kind to go easier.

Repair challenges: loyalty to the aggressor

A cautionary statement here is that if baby's annihilation terror and despair is accessed but not resolved, the client may stay in this state for some weeks or months.

Therefore, it is imperative that an imaginal repair be offered to the client in the form of an improved imaginal parent or caretaker providing what baby needed, the way baby needed it to be.

Parental introjects may not have the wherewithal to provide this nurturance even if they want to, as they don't know their lines, and may have never seen or heard true infant nurturance before.

For that reason, the therapist should be available to provide the necessary language to assist the client in imagining that an ideal or improved parent provides the full and lavish nurturance that one would want for the client or for any child.

No "dry crust of bread" approach will do here as the client needs to imagine nurturance in its fullness.

Parental introjects may interfere even if they were brought on board with the process ahead of time and even if the therapist carefully obtained their consent ahead of time.

Still allied with and attached to the external perpetrating (or neglectful) parents, the therapist should be prepared to reorient introjects to present time and place and the fact that they are in the client's body and are decidedly not the external parent.

The pivotal point in this intervention is the compassionate understanding by the therapist that the internal parent is not really an adult but a child part of self that had to "look through the parent's eyes" as a condition of survival.

Once this is acknowledged with great appreciation and compassion, the introject may then again allow the therapist to work with the baby part.

Finally, the parental introject itself may be a baby part, and is deserving of the very same nurturance offered to the baby part identified with self.

14-4 Lavishly providing what the brain has been waiting for all these years

14-5 I don't need much …. Just a dry crust of bread….

Processing infancy For many complex trauma or severely neglected clients, accessing the first year of life may evoke acute annihilation terror associated with being left alone far too long, unhelped and unheld at, for example, four or six months. For this reason, the system should be informed ahead of time that if this does occur, it will be a memory and not something that is happening in the present moment.

Resource states Parts of the client's self-system may need to be designated ahead of time to sit with the baby and help the baby feel safe during processing. The acuity of the pain of this experience cannot be underestimated, and the therapist must continuously reorient and reground the client to the fact that it is not currently happening and that the annihilation feeling is part of the memory.

Similarly, the client may come to feel utterly hopeless and despaired and say that the procedure isn't working and that nothing will help them.

Although, of course, the client retains the right to stop the procedure, the therapist should ask if it is possible that "baby felt utterly hopeless and despaired."

After the client nods and says, "yes," the therapist can then say, "we hear you baby, it was utterly hopeless and desperate, as if you were nothing and no one would come and help you. Is that right or wrong?" The client will typically say this is right. The therapist's job is to help transform the felt sense and the behavioral enactment in the room and in the relationship field into words, a narrative which accurately represents the baby's story.

Clearing by time frame for dissociative clients

For dissociative clients, the clearing of trauma by time frame is made complicated by a myriad of internal distractions, conflicts, double binds, and defenses.

The three preparation steps of the ET approach (O'Shea, 2009; O'Shea and Paulsen, 2007; Paulsen, 2009) will have been adjusted to accommodate a dissociative self-system. To review those alterations:

In the containment step, parts may have individualized containers or may share an image of a container, for example. In the safe state step, parts may have individualized imagery that they associate with safety, and some may be highly reluctant to believe that safety is possible.

In the resetting affective circuits step, it may be necessary to first reset basic safety systems related to fight, flight, freeze and connect responses.

For some states, extensive psycho-education about the normal role of emotions, and about freeze, fight, flight, and connection may be necessary.

See the stabilization chapters for more information, and especially Chapter 11 on the affective circuits.

Assessing the Degree of Dissociation, Affect, and Soma Tolerance

Assess the self-system

Assessing for dissociation and affect/soma tolerance

A therapist might assess for structural dissociation early in the work using dissociation diagnostic measures such as the MID, the SCID-D, the SDQ-20 or SDQ-5, or screening with the DES-II, or other suitable device, as has been described elsewhere (e.g, Frankel, 2009; International Society for the Study of Trauma and Dissociation, 2011)

A therapist might assess for soma tolerance early in the work by inviting the client to discern where in their body they feel sensations either comfortable or uncomfortable.

Limits of discernment of degree and type of dissociation

However, there can be false negatives and false positives on both alexithymia and structural dissociation early in the work, and the client's actual relationship to body and affect and the client's actual structure of their self-system is likely to be subsequently revealed in the course of the early trauma work itself.

Alexythymia, both positive and negative affect and soma intolerance often co-occur with structural dissociation, but not necessarily.

For those reasons, the author has not made a clear bright line between these definitions.

Further assistance

D. Michael Coy and the author are collaborating on a structured decision process for assessing not only history and presenting problems, but also to determine which preparation steps might be indicated for complex cases to determine readiness for early trauma or other EMDR therapy processing (U. Lanius, Paulsen, & Coy, April 2-4, 2016). That is, some will need, in addition to the three preparation steps described by O'Shea:

- Somatic work to connect dash board wires
- Ego state work to shift loyalty to the aggressor, deconflictualize the self-system and enlist the self-system in the work for maximal results,
- Hypnotic interventions for various purposes
- Additional steps as needed (see, e.g., Paulsen & Golston, 2014)

Ego State Preparations for Temporal Integration in Dissociation

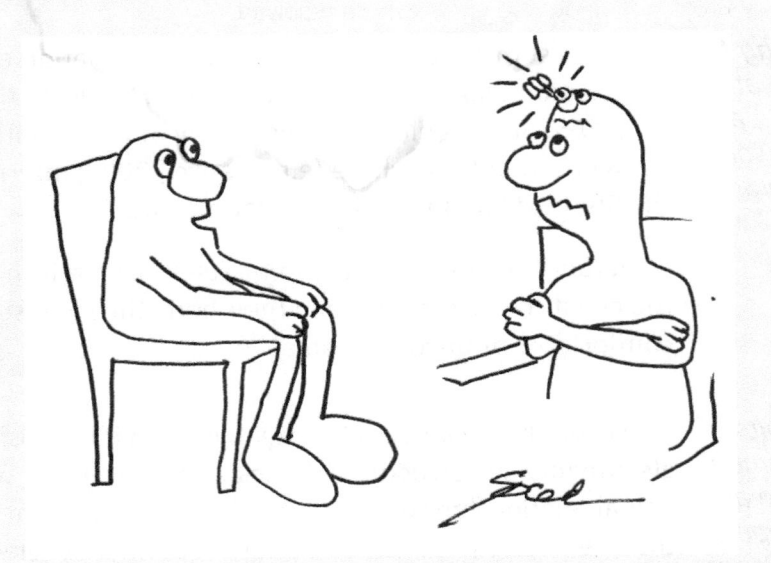

Engage the self-system

14-6 The emergence of a headache is a signal of approach/avoidance or a conflicted self. Usually the remedy is to address the "honchos", often perpetrator introjects, which keep the perpetrator's secrets for survival but are disoriented to present circumstances

(Figure originally appears in Paulsen, 2009, "Looking Through the Eyes")

Consent of the self-system

The therapist doing early trauma work on dissociative clients should studiously attempt to get internal consent from the client's self-system before doing processing by timeframe.

While this will have been occurring right along in the therapy, by the frequent use of ego state therapy, and more specifically via the three preparation steps, the goal is to get the system, including any cranky and protective parts of self, to agree to allow the infant states to be helped by the therapist. In preparation for temporal integration –clearing trauma by timeframe, the therapist will have explained the process, and specifically asked for questions or concerns from older parts of the self.

The therapist's instruction will specifically include asking the older states to sit on standby, or on bleachers (or other suitable imagery if bleachers are triggering), and allow the infant to be helped.

Curiously, even cranky older parts and perpetrator introjects who are oriented to present circumstances, will often allow the therapist to help the baby, even when not allowing the same therapist to help in other ways.

The therapist asks them to hold their own later memories aside in containers until "the time is right."

One exception, which the therapist names up front, is that if states see that the therapist and client are stuck in the processing for an infant state--baffled by a particularly resistant or mysterious dynamic that isn't resolving--an older state may bring in a theme from a later memory if it informs the work on the early memory, so the latter can be resolved.

Once the theme has been received and applied to the stuck infant state processing, the older memory goes back into the container and the older state goes back to the bleachers, so the infant's work can continue.

14-7 We ask the older parts of self to hold aside their memories until the time is right, but we will take the <u>theme</u> and see if it applies to baby's story.

Additional steps for dissociative clients

Additional steps needed to conduct temporal integration--clearing trauma by time frame for highly dissociative clients include:

- Getting permission from the "honchos" to help the baby

- Addressing any concerns addressed by honchos

- Inviting alters to be co-conscious ("watch from the bleachers")

- Educating that later memories will need to stay contained, except for thematic information

When There Are No Words - Sandra Paulsen

14-8 Doing EMDR therapy without permission from the "honchos" that guard the core of self, the baby, is inviting trouble and decompensation. However, when asked if the therapist can help the baby, the honchos will often stand aside

Permission to help the baby from the honchos

Getting final permission from the self-system "honchos" to help the baby, which they are likely to allow even though they may not overall be amenable to the treatment.

As mentioned in the prior chapter, this effort often produces extraordinary results, because even introjects or other cranky defensive alters will often stand down to a great extent if the therapist asks for permission to help the baby, even if no baby alter has been met.

Infant states are typically not true alters with extensive learning histories but either:

1) brief learning histories acquired on top of Panksepp's hardwired emotional circuits, or

2) states related to Panksepp's secondary brain processing associated with object relations or relationship templates.

As previously mentioned, failed attachment experiences in infancy results in a failure of horizontal linkages between affective circuits which would have resulted in smooth state switching. It also results in somatic dissociation because the baby has no choice but to shut down when soma or affect is more intense than baby's meager resources are able to accommodate, if there is insufficient help from a loving attentive caretaker or frank abuse.

By beginning prior to conception, any ego investedness in separateness, conflicts, double binds that gnarl later learning (and the alters that hold them) part like the Red Sea. This permits profound, deep integration to occur on primary and secondary levels of brain processing.

When There Are No Words - Sandra Paulsen

"I'd like to speak to the highest ranking honchos. I don't want to do this without your permission... what concerns do you have?"

> Is it OK if I go help the baby? Please speak up if you have concerns!! Watch every move I make!

> Let's Not

> Let's do EMDR now!

14-9 It is key for the therapist to get the introjects on board with the work before and during processing to reduce resistance, especially loyalty to the aggressor

Watching from the bleachers/ seats in co-consciousness

It is necessary to establish a mechanism via imagery whereby alters will allow their own later traumas to be set aside in containers while they watch or otherwise allow the work with the baby states. This tends to cause enormous shifts and the birth of compassion and understanding throughout the self-system.

It is through this watching and allowing that the system's compassion and understanding for self occurs.

There is a poignancy to this step in working with a dissociative client that is reminiscent of the magical air associated with the Nativity scene, or as captured in such a Christmas hymn as "It came upon a midnight clear" when kings from disparate countries, shepherds, animals, angels all gathered wordlessly with awe to watch the sacred child. In the early trauma approach, all babies are sacred, to be regarded with great awe and compassion, and with a little help even formerly fierce protective alters will soften with compassion and love for self.

Leaving later stories contained

By prior arrangement, the client's self-system will need to agree in theory that the one exception to their leaving their own stories aside while the baby is helped is if the alters see that the therapist is floundering, or the work is stuck, and there is no ability to understand the baby's story. In this situation, an alter personality may insert an associate from later life (from their stories) that informs the processing being done with the infant states.

When the therapist and client have extracted the requisite insight from the later memory to inform the theme of the infant memory, the alter personality is asked to set aside their later memory again, until the time is right.

At that point, the processing returns to the infant informed by the theme that was revealed from the later memory.

Select a target

Targeting in Temporal Integration for Dissociative and Complex Clients

ET targeting for dissociative clients

Some of the following discussion has been interspersed elsewhere, but is repeated here because of its importance and sequence in the TI process. As previously established, it is necessary to conduct the preparatory steps with something resembling the entire dissociative self-system and not only with the presenting front part of the self. One never knows if one has the whole system, and it shouldn't be a forced march, but rather an invitation and discussion with the known system.

In fact, it is never the "entire system;" realistically, one may never get to know the ego state that swims or makes coleslaw competitively, but that won't affect the outcome of the therapy. Here, when we say "entire system," the reader might understand that we are intending to mean a "critical mass" of the system, including the "honchos" powerful enough to derail the work if they are not on board, most especially perpetrator introjects.

It is important to educate the entire system that they will be asked to sit on the sidelines, or in bleachers, in the mind's eye, while the therapist helps the baby (or babies), and they will keep their own traumatic memories held aside in containers of their own until their turn comes up in sequence.

If the other parts are older child states, their traumatic material may be addressed using the standard EMDR therapy approach, once the material held in implicit memory prior to about age 3 has been addressed. It is especially key to get the approval of the head honchos in the self-system, especially any perpetrator introjects.

Time segments may need to be smaller for dissociative clients

There is no fixed rule about how long a time segment should be for early trauma processing. For non-DID clients, the authors often use a structure as follows: the time before conception, conception, first trimester, second trimester, third trimester, birth, first three months of life, second three months, and so on by three month time periods. This structure is no more a cookie cutter than is EMDR therapy's standard approach, and the size of time segments chosen should be driven by what is clinically manageable.

As mentioned, when there is knowledge of trauma, one might target those time frames in smaller pieces.

Additionally, for dissociative clients, when it seems likely that gestation, birth, or the first year of life might have been highly traumatic, it is often necessary to use smaller —even much smaller--time frames as well to prevent overwhelm or flooding.

Desensitization in Temporal Integration with Dissociative Clients

Desensitize time frame

The importance of somatic nuances

With highly dissociative clients, it is important in early trauma processing to pay close attention to experiences of dissociation, especially somatic. The therapist must hear and honor those early experiences where states of mind and body were overwhelmed and could not be internally regulated from a time when baby had insufficient help, or if the primary caretaker(s) were also perpetrators.

The therapist acknowledges out loud, with words, and hears every nuance of baby's story. Only then will there be, for the first time, an integration of those baby states into the client's fund of knowledge and somatic sense.

It cannot be said too often, that if some of the symptoms fail to remit that this is evidence of one or more nuances in the story having not yet been heard. That is to say, any residual or stuck symptoms are signs that some part of the story hasn't been heard.

The symptom is keeping the score, to take liberty with van der Kolk's classic line, "the body keeps the score." Conversely, when all the elements and their nuances of the infant's story have been heard sufficiently, the systems will remit, the time period will be clear, the repair will take and hold, and the work can move on to the next chosen time period in infancy.

Captured NC/PCs

As with non-dissociative clients, with dissociative clients the therapist will need to capture NCs and PCs as they emerge in the processing.

Captured PCs are made complex in the work with DID clients because, if attempted prematurely, they can evoke a cascade of self-blame or self-loathing. The therapist will need to use clinical judgment to identify both when the client is ready to attempt a PC, or find a modified PC that is less ambitious.

So, for example, trying to install the PC "I'm lovable," after just a few repairs in infancy, when there are years of profound abuse ahead to address, will result in failure, quite often, because of the weight of self-loathing carried by older ego states whose burdens of shame haven't been addressed. Instead, "today, we've begun the loving acceptance of baby," may be more likely to stick.

Ego State Interweaves in Stuck Processing in Temporal Integration for Dissociative Clients

Interweave if stuck

Asking to speak to the mother (or father or other) part of the self

Stuck processing often occurs because the material that is in line to be processed next is part of an approach/avoidance conflict. One alter represents the child's point of view and another represents the point of view required by circumstances. The child cannot reconcile the conflict and so dissociates one, then the other point of view. In the processing, then, very often, but not always, the alter causing stuck processing is an introject of a parent or perpetrator, because the external parent or perpetrator's point of view was deemed more important than the child's at the time of the trauma by that parent or perpetrator, which viewpoint was taken in whole by the child. This loyalty to the aggressor requires frequent addressing in treatment, and is not a one-time intervention.

Additionally, the client often does not spontaneously report the presence of an introject of an external parent or perpetrator and it is incumbent upon the therapist to know that theoretically and dynamically such an introject is likely there, go looking for it without leading, and orient it to present person place and time.

The therapist should never confuse such introject with the external parent. That is, unless the client's actual physical parent or perpetrator is in the therapist's office with the client, any presence claiming to be the parent or perpetrator is an alter personality and more specifically, is an introject.

This introject and other alters or ego states in the client are likely to be confused regarding this point and feel the introject is the very parent or perpetrator.

The therapist must demonstrate empirically that the introject is in the client's body with other aspects of self, using a mirror or pointing to the client's clothes and placement in the office, to persuade the introject and other alters that they are all parts of the client. See Paulsen (2009) for elaboration on this method. This work will have been undertaken in advance of the early trauma approach, but may need to be repeated in the middle of an early trauma session.

Additionally, even if an introject has been oriented to present circumstances outside of the early trauma approach, additional introjects of the same external person for a different age in the client's life may be encountered during the early trauma approach. In that case, the same measures should be undertaken to orient the introject and bring it on board with the treatment even though similar measures have already been taken with other introjects.

14-10 Adding ego energy by speaking directly to a part adds a spotlight of focus and energy to the aspect in question, a powerful tool in the therapeutic armamentarium

Adding ego energy to give voice to a forsaken aspect of self

Other alter personalities may also require ego state therapy in the course of the early trauma work. This is required when processing is stuck by asking who can inform about the nature of the stuckness, who has concerns, and those concerns are addressed.

Paulsen is a proponent of speaking directly to the alter, which adds ego energy to it, a far more incisive and profound way to work than requiring that another part of the client do all the internal communications with an alter personality.

Additionally, many dissociative clients cannot initially talk through another part because of insufficient coconsciousness. Such individuals may not be suited to early trauma processing until some co-consciousness and system consent is achieved because of the difficulty of communicating across impermeable amnesia barriers.

Internal communications are important, but nothing produces shifts as profound as the addition of ego energy by directly speaking to a part. If need be, internal communications may also be conducted, and the addition of object energy is its own important intervention, useful for evoking insight and compassion as in the Pocatello intervention described below. See Chapter 1 under the History discussion and chapter 5 under Stabilization and ego state work for a more extensive discussion of ego and object energy.

14-11 "Imagine a family we don't know, not your family, in Pocatello," for neo-cortical objectivity

Adding object energy: the Pocatello intervention, aka neocortical objectivity interweave

If the client continues to blame the child self for being "demanding" or "bad" for having normal developmental needs, the therapist will need to work additionally with parental introjects to shift the loyalty to the client's point of view and away from the parent's point of view.

This may be accomplished by inviting a viewing in a crystal ball or on a movie screen of a hypothetical child in Pocatello or Bemidji or Tuscaloosa or Talkeetna (a nearby town where the client doesn't know anyone well), who is crying to be fed or longing to be held. If the introject part of the client, or whatever part of the client is interfering with the repair, views the hypothetical child in the third person objective stance (that is, with object awareness or in object cathexis (Federn, 1952; Watkins &Watkins, 1997, (Paulsen & Watkins, 2005), and bilateral stimulation is added, there will often be a poignant shift.

Paulsen calls this the Pocatello interweave for convenience and vividness, and to remind practitioners to pick a memorable nearby town at optimal distance from the client's subjective locus. In fact, a more scholarly name, which she hereby assigns it, is that it is a neo-cortical objectivity interweave.

This is important because it is often almost impossible to dislodge clients from the subjective ravages of shame, which occur deep in the lower brain structures, as a cutting off from the felt sense of emotions and body sensations, forsaken as required by the mother, caretaker or perpetrator's requirements for the child's survival. Only with the objectivity afforded by the neo-cortical perspective of looking <u>at</u> (not being) a child in similar circumstances can the client associatively link to adaptive neural networks that hold the decisive awareness that the child did <u>nothing</u> wrong by having needs, feeling, longing for love, yearnings to be seen, and dependency requirements. <u>Nothing</u>! That insight is only available to the shame ensconced with sufficient doses of neo-cortical objectivity, and a child we don't know in a nearby town is a great device for achieving that perspective, and enabling a shift from shame to compassion for self.

Somatic Interweaves Somatic interweaves are simple and straightforward. The therapist may ask the client, "what do you notice in your body at this time?" or "is there an impulse in the body at this time?" and just notice it or accommodate in slow motion any impulse to kick or thrash or cry out or bite, etc.

Known as micro-movements in the somatic tradition, this enables the release of pent up fight or flight responses associated with sympathetic arousal.

Clients often want to do the movement rapidly, but it is necessary to allow expression in slow motion.

14-12 The therapist should use somatic micro-movements for DID clients cautiously and only after obtaining agreement from the honchos for client empowerment

Micro-movements for DID

Dissociative clients may not be able to do micro-movements without inducing heightened inner conflict from introjected aggressors' points of view about whether the client deserves to be empowered.

Somatic work, including micro-movements, should be introduced outside of EMDR therapy ET processing, and touch only used where appropriate, and sometimes with the buffer of a pillow for the pushing or other micro-movements interventions. Therapists should be trained in somatic procedures and <u>certainly</u> with this population.

Tracking somatic signs e.g., of thwarted sympathetic arousal

Often, the segue to a somatic interweave is for the therapist to observe the body of the client with curiosity and empathy, and wonder aloud,

"what does that (clenched) fist want to do?" adding,

"just notice, and allow that impulse to be expressed ever so slowly, that's it, slowly, comically slowly." The judicious use of the word "comically" may correct for the client's impatient wish to express the movement rapidly.

14-13 Somatic micro-movements can allow thwarted sympathetic arousal (fight/flight) to be released, facilitated with attenuated resistance, where appropriate

14-14 Clients often stop micro-movements prematurely, but the release generally occurs with full extension, and a time of holding the full power position

14-15 For many highly dissociative clients, touch is clinically contraindicated. But a therapist can sit on a footstool for resistance, so the client can push with the feet, when able to tolerate the felt sense of sympathetic arousal (after the introjects are on board).

Orientational interweaves More so with DID clients, but also with less dissociative clients, among the first interweaves tried should be, "hi (ego state's name or function), "are you remembering that it is (present year), s/he is in (present location) and you are all in the same body?"

"And the bad things aren't happening now?" if the latter is true. Adding bilateral stimulation to these orientational interweaves, while grounding to the present circumstances, e.g., using canine assistance, or features of the office, etc, can produce profound shifts.

When one returns to the very early time frame, then, it is with acuity of awareness that the baby lived, or deserves the love of a poodle, or has the adult self present in the present year, to bring adult resources to the infant states or alters.

For the DID client, the system may agree to mobilize around the baby and provide that which should have been provided.

If parts are unwilling to assist, they might be asked to step back so that other parts will provide what is needed to the infant states. Interestingly, in DID clients, even the crankiest parts will often permit ministration to the infant self. On some level, the client does understand that she was an innocent child deserving of love.

Micro movements for dissociative clients When appropriate and indicated, micro-movements can be important for DID clients. Paulsen invites "the kids," (ambiguously enough) to be in the arm, for example, if pushing away to release trapped unprocessed adrenaline in a thwarted fight response being processed as part of early trauma processing. This sounds like, "Kids in the arm, pushing away, kids in the arm," and if the client (or parts of the client) are too frightened to engage in the procedure, invite the subject alters to look through the eyes to see where they are, "just you, me and the poodle," orients the client every time, because the client invariably looks at and/or touches the sleeping canine assistant. Once oriented, the micro-movements can continue with the child alter executive or at least present in the arm. Paulsen feels the energy as it releases, so can discern if the intervention is successful. Otherwise, the therapist will rely on the self-report of a client, and compliance may cause the client to report a satisfactory result whether or not it has succeeded in releasing the trapped fight energy.

Temporal interweaves As previously described, the therapist can gently prompt the client to realize that the present sense is part of the memory. If processing has stopped because the client says, "I don't think I can trust you," referring to the therapist, the therapist should first check to see if s/he has done anything to evoke a feeling of mistrust, and if so, deal with it appropriately.

If not, the therapist can use a temporal interweave, by saying, "I wonder if baby you felt it wasn't safe to trust," or "I wonder if that feeling is new just now? Or part of the memory for baby. Just notice that."

Repair: Getting to Adaptive Resolution and Repair with Dissociative Clients

Positive cognitions and assignment of appropriate responsibility

With any of these five types of interweaves, the therapist may, after the initial interweave has been made, offer positive cognitions to accompany the shift, especially if none have occurred spontaneously. These should then be recorded. Then, before that time period is left, the PC should be checked with a validity of cognition taken, to ensure complete processing. O'Shea emphasizes that it is especially critical that the therapist be sure that responsibility is appropriately assigned before going on.

Clients often deeply disbelieve the important notion that a child is never responsible for his or her abuse, and that an adult caretaker always had the responsibility for the outcome for the child, no matter what the caretaker believed or said or did.

The classic interweave, "Whose responsibility was it?" may need supplementation with others as described above, especially using object awareness to increase compassion for the child's size and age, ego state therapy to work with parental and/or perpetrator introjects, and others.

Compared to the typical EMDR therapy approach, O'Shea and Paulsen both observe that there are fewer spontaneous shifts to the positive, and more stuck looping, so it is more likely that an interweave will be needed, or many interweaves needed, in order to get a shift.

14-16 When stuck, the therapist asks the older alters what she is missing in hearing baby's story

A final point about interweaves in this work is that, unlike the standard approach of EMDR therapy, a great deal of jumpstarting by the therapist is typically required, in order to get the client to tap into an adaptive neural network because the infant states have so little in the way of resources. As a reminder, O'Shea's "review, release, repair" heuristic should guide the therapist. That is, the therapist will review the time period, there will be a release either spontaneously or via interweave, and repair imaginally to build the new foundation.

14-17 Review, release and repair; review, release, repair; review, release, repair

Review, release, repair

O'Shea concisely described the sequence of ET processing as involving "review, release and repair," in that order.

First, the processing reviews the nuances of implicit memory, gleaning whatever aspects of the story can be gleaned, which enables the energetic and traumatic holdings to be released.

If they don't release spontaneously they are shifted by use of interweave, as described above.

Finally, the developmental period and its unmet milestones are repaired imaginally for the processing to be complete. Once the milestone is repaired, the time period is completed and the work can move to the next time frame, with the new and solid foundation just completed.

For completeness, any captured positive cognitions that emerged in the course of processing should be installed either at the end of each bit of processing, the end of a 90-minute session where appropriate, or by the end of a day of processing. If no PC's have emerged spontaneously from the client, or if no PC's have been captured by the therapist's intuition in the course of processing, the therapist should ask, "do any words come to mind that reflect what you now believe about yourself?"

Assuming the words meet criteria for a conventional positive cognition, then those words become the new PC for installation for the early time segment, processing segment, or session.

When There Are No Words - Sandra Paulsen

Close the session ## Closure Procedure for Incomplete Processing with Dissociative Clients

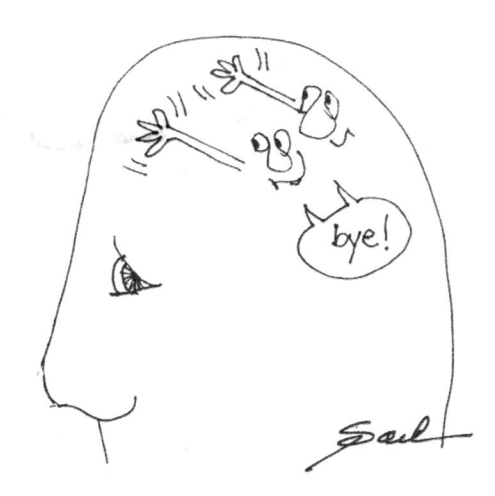

14-18 Tucking in alters who processed or helped includes appreciating them and acknowledging that work is progressing even when incomplete.

Incomplete processing and the two step tucking in process for dissociative clients: 1) containment and 2) tucking in ego states

With a non-DID client, step 1 and 2 is repeated at the beginning of each intensive session.

With a DID client, the same is true, but the form may be different. Containment may involve using different containers for each alter, though they may choose to share containers as well. Additionally, the use of a bleacher or amphitheater of bean bag chairs enables older child states to sit on standby and observe processing where indicated and preferred. Again, the therapist must sleuth out any reluctant ego states before processing begins, and check again if processing is stuck.

With the use of EMDR therapy for later memories for DID clients, Paulsen recommends tucking in those states who don't need to be there for a given memory (2009a, b). However, for the ET approach, all ego states are older states than the infant. The infant's well-being is of interest to all the states, and typically they will all watch amicably, though warring groups may need separate bleachers.

Body scan where appropriate

For non-dissociative clients at the end of a day of ET processing, a final body scan should be conducted, if only to check to see if more "tucking in" and containment is needed to have the client leave fully grounded.

For dissociative clients, this step is overly ambitious, and simple containment is more likely to be a successful goal. For all clients, containment steps may include whatever language has been typically employed for this client, over the time of prior therapy, for ending a session. Because the step 1 from the early trauma approach involves use of container imagery, that imagery should be utilized at the end of the session in the form of "let whatever is left go into your container now, and let me know when that is complete."

175

For a dissociative client, the language may sound more like, "thank you to each part of the self that helped today by allowing their memories to be held separately, and now gathering up any fragments of memories for any part of the self, and for baby, and allowing those memory fragments to go into the container or containers, that's right, and putting the containers on the shelves, and with appreciation, I'll fluff up the cloud pillows for any who want it, and tuck you in with cloud blankets, and I'll wave good bye as your clouds pull away and take you deep inside for a deep healing sleep, deeper and deeper still," or other such end-of-session language.

The Paulsen two step for closure

The above offered language has the advantage of being two-step (Paulsen, 2009), with one step for the non-egotized memory fragments, and one step for the ego states or alters involved. This provides a system-wide meta-cognition that assists with grounding, pacing and stabilization.

A third step is sometimes needed if the first two have not completed a safe tucking in. That third step is to interview the part of self not tucking in about its concerns, and to negotiate an acceptable and safe outcome with that part. Language such as, "Hi, whoever is still there, I bet there is a good reason why you don't want to go, and I know better than to argue with you about that, because I know who would win that argument," (recalcitrant protective state typically appears pleased) "but in case you get tired, there is a ranger station on the horizon, with a comfortable cot, because your burden is very great, and binoculars so you can keep an eye on things," then to the executive part of self, "how is he doing now?" Client typically says, "he's gone."

14-19 The therapist avoids "bossing around" the honchos/perpetrator introjects, but kindly points out that there is a ranger station on the horizon and a comfortable cot and binoculars, in case they are weary from their burden

Debriefing at end of session Certainly when there is residual disturbance, but even if there is not, the client should be alerted to the possibility of continued processing and/or disturbed sleep.

Also different from the debriefing instructions for typical EMDR therapy is that the client should be alerted to the possibility that the baby's story may "leak" into present relationship.

The therapist should instruct the client that, for example, if the work had to stop in the middle of a piece involving helplessness that was not able to resolve, the client may be in a state of helplessness until the work can continue in some form.

The client may feel helpless at work or in her marriage, etc. but chances are that the feeling is fueled by the work with the baby state.

The client is very likely to forget this instruction, and the therapist should use some means of reminder of this likelihood. At a minimum, at the next session, when the client reports her status, the therapist should listen careful for indications that the client is in the midst of a state fueled by the early work.

In case of emergency Dissociative clients will need a prearranged strategy in case their "boat is rocked" by the substantive nature of this work. The client and therapist will already have, over the months or years, established a procedure and understanding for handling emergencies. Whatever that practice is, this work may call upon it. Paulsen applies downward pressure to emergency calls and instills in clients a practice of trying numerous things to cope before calling; however, after this work, a phone call is sometimes necessary. There are apps available for smart phones that enable clients to have an armamentarium of coping strategies in case of emergency.

Modifications for dissociative clients The reevaluation for dissociative clients may involve ego state work so that alters can synthesize what they have learned. They may have concerns or questions that require psycho-educational elements as part of the synthesis, or skills training to help remediate a developmental milestone once the traumatic impediments have resolved.

A very common dynamic is that, even though ego state work may have already have been conducted to get introjects on board before doing the trauma work, an introject may feel sorely pressed to remain loyal to the perpetrator and/or parent's point of view.

This needs to be untangled and the loyalty to the aggressor shifted. Ego state therapy or EMDR therapy for the introject targeting their love or loyalty to the perpetrator, will often move the introject from their spot. There may also be a need to allow for time to process grief, as a cherished but harmful relationship is let go, or changed.

A checklist for points to cover to lessen client attachment to a perpetrator introjected point of view is included in Paulsen (2009). There can be tremendous requirements for grieving as the client's self-system integrates and the whole picture begins to become clearer and the enormity of the client's losses are revealed. EMDR therapy is a very helpful way to facilitate this grieving process.

First year of life is seminal for many dissociative clients

For DID clients, the amount of trauma held in the early time frames can be daunting. The time and cost of the intensive work, even using the early trauma approach, can be prohibitive.

However, spending the time intensively on the at least the first year of life for a DID client will produce tremendous integration that will make any form of subsequent therapy far more time efficient. This is a better use of that same time than it would be to skate quickly over the top for a greater number of time periods, with less deep resolution. The first year of life is profoundly important to repair because of the seminal nature of developmental milestones in that period.

Conclusion

This chapter has described the modifications of the Early Trauma approach required when applying it to highly dissociative clients. One final caution is to remember that the approach is not a cookie cutter, not every complex case will fit this method.

If using the method causes a problem, the therapist should stop using it for that client after a reasonable attempt to debug the problem, or get consultation. Used well, the early trauma approach of EMDR therapy can produce great progress in a dissociative client, by creating temporal integration beginning before the beginning.

Complex Case

There had been a non-life threatening accident that shook up the client and the parts of her, and the therapist had used a brief bit of EMDR therapy to get the disturbance back down to baseline for the client, without uncovering prior trauma, but rather, re-containing it.

The therapist spoke to Greta Lynn about doing very early trauma work, not only to the front part of the self which went by the name Greta, but also the honchos.

The therapist said to father part of the self, first, because he was the highest ranking honcho in the internal system, "Father part, I would like your permission to go help the baby. What do you think?"

"Well, I hope <u>someone</u> could help her, what would you be doing?"

The therapist answered, "Remember the only time we have done EMDR therapy so far was after that car accident? We did the eye movement thing to get you guys back to a reasonably stable state. This is similar but different. With the car accident there was a picture and we knew what we were targeting to desensitize and process. But when we go to help the baby, we will instead target by time frame."

"Here, we'll be repairing by time frame beginning before the beginning. I'd ask all of you to stand by, you can watch if you like, unless that's overwhelming, and then I'd ask some to sleep until the time is right. I'll ask you all to hold your later memories aside, with one exception.

If you see I'm struggling to understand baby's story, you can bring up a later memory and we'll see if the theme from the later memory helps us understand baby's story. Does anyone have concerns?" Some time was necessary to explain, reassure and get consent from a sufficiency of the self-system, especially the honchos, namely, parental introjects, an angry teen and an ashamed child.

As the work progressed, it was common for the introjects to "grow back," that is, to lose their orientation and need reminding. "Father part, are you remembering you aren't the outside father, and the outside father is now dead or very old, and can't hurt you? and the girl is 43, and you're here with me and my tiny poodles? Would it be okay if we continue to help the baby?"

For some of the work, very small time segments were required. At some points it was impossible to constrain the associations and the work was "kidnapped" to a Big T later trauma, requiring clearing, before we could return to repair baby's story.

Without question, with Greta and many others, the pivotal piece is getting the shift in the loyalty to the aggressor by orienting the introjects to the work. Much of the work is commonly done with the client mute, so the therapist's capacity to tolerate abreaction and discern meaning and nuance in the relationship and energy field is critical.

Though the early trauma work is quite gentle, it can still be overdone, and so with Greta, there would be some weeks on and some weeks off in doing early trauma processing.

Mechanics See an Appendix B to this document for suggestions for mechanics of the work with complex trauma clients.

When There Are No Words - Sandra Paulsen

15 Final Remarks

Summary This book has described an approach to repairing very early trauma in the attachment period, originated by Katie O'Shea, refined in collaboration with this author, and extended by this author to apply to complex trauma and dissociative clients.

Undertaken with judicious care, this approach can alleviate a considerable portion of a client's symptoms related to affect dysregulation, dissociation, attachment injury, and maladaptive schema learned early in life and resulting in characterological injuries. If a client is getting worse, not better, the therapist should a) stop doing what they are doing, b) seek consultation, and/or c) do something different.

Cautions To repeat several of the most important cautions that have been mentioned throughout the book:

- If individuals are not getting better, something has been overlooked, and the approach should be suspended at least until consultation can be obtained.

- If the intensive approach is used to structure sessions, the full range of protections should be in place for safe and effective work as described in the appendix.

- Dissociation can be highly covert, outside of the client's awareness, and unnoticed by even an astute clinician.

- If a client has trouble in the middle of or after an early trauma session, the therapist should consider not only whether the disturbance is related to present time, but also whether the disturbance is the affective or somatic expression of baby's story, emerging into the present circumstances and relationship field, without the client's awareness. (E.g., if the client feels dysphoric, abandoned, betrayed, alone, panicky, irritable, etc., it may be because the neural network activated in the trauma work is discharging unresolved elements of the trauma story and it only seems to be about present time.)

- Challenges, obstacles and defenses evident in the work are always there for a reason, and that reason is part of baby's story. Characterological features that challenge the work can be heard as necessary adaptations the client made to navigate developmental milestones and relationship challenges in the first years.

The therapist should remember at all times that what is being repaired is nothing less than the infant's attachment experience and sense of self as being either alone in a world with no people, or connected to another with hope and caring.

When There Are No Words - Sandra Paulsen

15-1 Baby was alone in a world with no people. Once we hear the story, with resonant attunement, the symptoms will remit. This time, baby is not alone.

Intensive work for clinicians   The author's practice is almost entirely comprised of doing early trauma work with other mental health professionals who come to her office for several full days of intensive work. The structure and logistics of this work is described at www.bainbridgepsychology.com. An Appendix to this book includes descriptions on considerations in making sure that intensive clinical work is ethical, safe, and effective.

References

Barach, P. (1991). Multiple personality disorder as an attachment disorder. *Dissociation, 4*(3), 117–23.

Bausch, S. & Stingl, M. (2011). Alexithymia and script-driven emotional imagery in healthy female subjects: no support for deficiencies in imagination. *Scandinavian Scandinavian Journal of Psychology, 52*(2), 179–184.

Bowlby, J. (1969). *Attachment: Attachment and loss (vol. 1)*. London: Hogarth.

Bowlby, J. (1973). *Attachment and loss: Vol. 2. Separation anxiety and anger*. New York: Basic Books.

Condon, J. T. (1985). The parental-foetal relationship-a comparison of male and female expectant parents. *Journal of Psychosomatic Obstetrics & Gynecology, 4*(4), 271–284.

Condon, J. T., & Corkindale, C. (1997). The correlates of antenatal attachment in pregnant women. *British Journal of Medical Psychology, 70*(4), 359–372.

Costa, V., Lang, P., Sabatinelli, D., Versace, F., & Bradley, M. M. (2010). Emotional imagery: assessing pleasure and arousal in the brain's reward circuitry. *Human Brain Mapping, 31*(9), 1446–1457.

D'Argembeau, A., Feyers, D., Majerus, S., Collette, F., Van der Linden, M., Maquet, P., & Salmon, E. (2008). Self-reflection across time: cortical midline structures differentiate between present and past selves. *Social Cognitive and Affective Neuroscience, 3*(3), 244–52.

DeCasper, A., & Fifer, W. (1980). Of human bonding: newborns prefer their mothers' voices. *Science, 208*(4448), 1174–1176.

DeCasper, A. J., Lecanuet, J.-P., Busnel, M.-C., Granier-Deferre, C., & Maugeais, R. (1994). Fetal reactions to recurrent maternal speech. *Infant Behavior and Development, 17*(2), 159–164.

DeCasper, A. J., & Spence, M. J. (1986). Prenatal maternal speech influences newborns' perception of speech sounds. *Infant Behavior and Development, 9*(2), 133–150.

Dirix, C. E. H., Nijhuis, J. G., Jongsma, H. W., & Hornstra, G. (2009). Aspects of fetal learning and memory. *Child Development, 80*(4), 1251–1258.

Doan, H. M. P., & Zimerman, A. M. (2003). Conceptualizing Prenatal Attachment: Toward a Multidimensional View. *Journal of Prenatal & Perinatal Psychology & Health, 18*(2), 109.

Egan, K. (1991). *Imagination in Teaching and Learning: The Middle School Years.* Chicago: University of Chicago Press.

Federn, E. (1952). *Ego psychology and the psychoses.* New York: Basic Books.

Fine, C. (1993). Clinical perspectives on multiple personality disorder. In R. P. Kluft (Ed.), *Clinical perspectives on multiple personality disorder* (pp. 135–153). Washington, DC: American Psychiatric Press.

Fine, C. G., & Berkowitz, A. S. (2001). The Wreathing Protocol: The Imbrication of Hypnosis and EMDR in the Treatment of Dissociative Identity Disorder and other Dissociative Responses. *American Journal of Clinical Hypnosis, 43*(3–4), 275–290.

Fonagy, P. (2001). *Attachment Theory and Psychoanalysis.* New York: Other Press.

Fonagy, P., Gergely, G., Jurist, E. L., & Target, M. (2002). *Affect Regulation, Mentalization and the Development of the Self.* New York: Other Press.

Fonagy, P., Roth, A., & Higgitt, A. (2005). Psychodynamic psychotherapies: evidence-based practice and clinical wisdom. *Bulletin of the Menninger Clinic, 69*(1), 1–58.

Fosha, D. (2000). *The Transforming Power of Affect: A Model for Accelerated Change.* New York: Basic Books.

Frankel, S. (2009). Dissociation and dissociative disorders: Clinical and forensic assessment with adults. In P. F. Dell & J. A. O'Neil (Eds.), *Dissociation and the Dissociative Disorders: DSM-V and Beyond.* (pp. 571–584). New York: Routledge.

Fraser, G. A. (1991). The Dissociative Table Technique: A strategy for working with ego states in dissociative disorders and ego-state therapy. *Dissociation: Progress in the Dissociative Disorders, 4*(4), 205–213.

Fraser, G. A. (2001). Fraser's "Dissociative Table Technique" Revisited, Revised: A Strategy for Working with Ego States in Dissociative Disorders and Ego-State Therapy. *Journal of Trauma & Dissociation, 4*(4), 5–28.

International Society for the Study of Trauma and Dissociation. (2011). Guidelines for treating dissociative identity disorder in adults, third revision. *Journal of Trauma & Dissociation: The Official Journal of the International Society for the Study of Dissociation (ISSD), 12*(2), 115–87.

Jarero, I., Artigas, L., & Hartung, J. (2006). EMDR integrative group treatment protocol: A postdisaster trauma intervention for children and adults. *Traumatology, 12*(2), 121–129.

Jurist, E. L. (2005). Mentalized Affectivity. *Psychoanalytic Psychology, 22*(3), 426–444.

Keil, A., Müller, M. M., Gruber, T., Wienbruch, C., Stolarova, M., & Elbert, T. (2001). Effects of emotional arousal in the cerebral hemispheres: a study of oscillatory brain activity and event-related potentials. *Clinical Neurophysiology, 112*(11), 2057–2068.

Kim, S.-E., Kim, J.-W., Kim, J.-J., Jeong, B. S., Choi, E. A., Jeong, Y.-G., … Ki, S. W. (2007). The neural mechanism of imagining facial affective expression. *Brain Research, 1145*, 128–37.

Kisilevsky, B. S., Hains, S. M. J., Lee, K., Xie, X., Huang, H., Ye, H. H., … Wang, Z. (2003). Effects of Experience on Fetal Voice Recognition. *Psychological Science, 14*(3), 220–224.

Kitchur, M. (2009). The strategic developmental model for EMDR. In *EMDR solutions: Pathways to healing* (pp. 8–56). New York: Norton.

Klaus, M., & Klaus, P. (2000). *Your amazing newborn*. Da Capo Press.

Kluft, R. (1990). The fractionated abreaction technique. In C. D. Hammond (Ed.), *Handbook of hypnotic suggestions* (pp. 527–528). New York: Norton.

Kluft, R. (2013). *Shelter from the storm: Processing the traumatic memories of DID/DDNOS patients with the fractionated abreaction technique*. Charleston, South Carolina: CreateSpace.

Kluft, R. P. (1984). Treatment of multiple personality disorder: A study of 33 cases. *Psychiatric Clinics of North America, 7*(1), 9–29.

Kluft, R. P. (1989). Playing for time: temporizing techniques in the treatment of multiple personality disorder. *The American Journal of Clinical Hypnosis, 32*(2), 90–8.

Kluft, R. P. (1993). *Clinical Perspectives on Multiple Personality Disorder* (1st ed.). American Psychiatric Pub.

Kolk, B. Van Der. (2014). *The body keeps the score: Brain, mind, and body in the healing of trauma*. New York: Penguin Publishing Group.

Lanius, U. F., Paulsen, S. L., & Corrigan, F. M. (2014). Neurobiology and Treatment of Traumatic Dissociation: Towards an Embodied Self. In U. Lanius, S. L. Paulsen, & F. Corrigan (Eds.), *Neurobiology and Treatment of Trauma and Dissociation: Toward An Embodied Self* (p. 536). New York: Springer Publishing Company.

Lanius, U., Paulsen, S., & Corrigan, F. (2014). *Neurobiology and Treatment of Traumatic Dissociation: Towards an Embodied Self*. New York: Springer Publishing Company.

Lanius, U., Paulsen, S., & Coy, D. M. (n.d.). The Neurobiology of Traumatic Dissociation - Facilitating Treatment Outcomes. In *International Society for the Study of Trauma and Dissociation*. San Francisco.

Levine, P. (1997). *Waking the tiger: Healing trauma: The innate capacity to transform overwhelming experiences*. California: North Atlantic Books.

Levine, P. A. (2010). *In an Unspoken Voice: How the Body Releases Trauma and Restores Goodness*. California: North Atlantic Books.

Lovett, J. (2007). *Small Wonders: Healing Childhood Trauma With EMDR*. Berkeley: Free Press.

Luria, A. (1973). *The working brain*. London: Panguin Books.

Mampe, B., Friederici, A. D., Christophe, A., & Wermke, K. (2009). Newborns' cry melody is shaped by their native language. *Current Biology : CB*, *19*(23), 1994–7.

Mason, J., Wang, S., Yehuda, R., Riney, S., Charney, D. S., & Southwick, S. M. (2001). Psychogenic lowering of urinary cortisol levels linked to increased emotional numbing and a shame-depressive syndrome in combat-related posttraumatic stress. *Psychosomatic Medicine*, *63*(3), 387–401.

McCabe, C. S., Haigh, R. C., Ring, E. F. J., Halligan, P. W., Wall, P. D., & Blake, D. R. (2002). A controlled pilot study of the utility of mirror visual feedback in the treatment of complex regional pain syndrome (type 1). *Rheumatology*, *42*(1), 97–101.

Moncher, F. J. (1996). The Relationship of Maternal Adult Attachment Style and Risk of Physical Child Abuse. *Journal of Interpersonal Violence*, *11*(3), 335–350.

Moseley, G. L. (2004). Graded motor imagery is effective for long-standing complex regional pain syndrome: a randomised controlled trial. *Pain*, *108*(1–2), 192–8.

Nathanson, D. (1992). *Shame and pride: Affect, sex, and the birth of the self*. W W Norton & Company.

O'Shea, K., & Paulsen, S. (2007). A protocol for increasing affect regulation and clearing early trauma. In *annual meeting of the Eye Movement Desensitization & Reprocessing International Association Conference, Dallas, TX*. Dallas, TX.

O'Shea, M. (2003a). Accessing and repairing preverbal trauma and neglect. In *EMDRIA Conference. Denver, CO. EMDR Europe Conference*. Istanbul, Turkey.

O'Shea, M. (2003b). Reinstalling innate emotional resources. In *EMDR Europe. Rome, Italy*. Rome, Italy.

O'Shea, M. (2006). Accessing and repairing preverbal trauma and neglect. In *Paper presented at EMDR Europe Conference, Istanbul, Turkey*.

O'Shea, M. K. (2001). Accessing and repairing preverbal trauma and neglect. In *EMDR Canada Conference, Vancouver, British Columbia, Canada*.

O'Shea, M. K. (2009). The early EMDR trauma protocol. In R. Shapiro (Ed.), *EMDR solutions II. For depression, eating disorders, performance and more* (pp. 313–334). Norton.

Ogden, P., & Fisher, J. (2014). Integrating body and mind: Sensorimotor psychotherapy and treatment of dissociation, defence and dysregulation. In U. Lanius, S. Paulsen, & F. Corrigan (Eds.), *Neurobiology and Treatment of Trauma and Dissociation: Toward An Embodied Self* (pp. 399–422). New York: Springer Publishing Company.

Ovtscharoff, W., & Braun, K. (2001). Maternal separation and social isolation modulate the postnatal development of synaptic composition in the infralimbic cortex of Octodon degus. *Neuroscience*, *104*(1), 33–40.

Panksepp, J. (1986). The psychobiology of prosocial behaviors: Separation distress, play, and altruism. In *Altruism and Aggression, Biological and Social Origins* (pp. 19–57). Cambridge: Cambridge University Press.

Panksepp, J. (1998). *Affective Neuroscience: The Foundations of Human and Animal Emotions*. New York: Oxford University Press.

Panksepp, J., & Biven, L. (2012). *The archaeology of mind: neuroevolutionary origins of human emotions (Norton series on interpersonal neurobiology)*. New York: W W Norton & Company.

Paulsen, S. (1995). Eye movement desensitization and reprocessing: Its cautious use in the dissociative disorders. *Dissociation: Progress in the Dissociative Disorders, 8*(1), 32–44.

Paulsen, S. (2009a). Act-as-if and architects approaches to EMDR treatment of DID. In M. Luber (Ed.), *EMDR scripted protocols: Special populations*. New York: W W Norton & Company.

Paulsen, S. (2009b). *Looking through the eyes of trauma and dissociation: An illustrated guide for EMDR clinicians and clients*. Charleston, NC: Booksurge. Charleston, NC: Booksurge.

Paulsen, S. (2014). Temporal Integration. In U. Lanius, S. L. Paulsen, & F. Corrigan (Eds.), *Neurobiology and Treatment of Trauma and Dissociation: Toward An Embodied Self*. New York: Springer.

Paulsen, S., & Golston, J. (2014). Stabilization basics. In U. F. Lanius, S. L. Paulsen, & F. M. Corrigan (Eds.), *Neurobiology and Treatment of Traumatic Dissociation: Towards an Embodied Self* (pp. 289–320). New York: Springer Publishing Company.

Paulsen, S., & Golston, J. (2014). Stabilizing the relationship among self-states. In F. Lanius, S. L. Paulsen, & F. M. Corrigan (Eds.), *Neurobiology and Treatment of Trauma and Dissociation: Toward An Embodied Self2* (pp. 321–340). New York: Springer Publishing Company.

Paulsen, S. L., O'Shea, K., & Lanius, U. F. (2014). Alexithymia, affective dysregulation, and the imaginal: Resetting the subcortical affective circuits. In *Neurobiology and Treatment of Traumatic Dissociation: Towards an Embodied Self* (p. 510). New York: Springer Publishing Company.

Paulsen, S., & Lanius, U. (2009). Embodied self: Integrating EMDR with somatic and ego state interventions. In *EMDR solutions II: Depression, eating disorders, performance, and more*. New York: W W Norton & Company.

Paulsen, S., O'Shea, K., & Lanius, U. (2014). Dissociation - Cortical Deafferentation and the Loss of Self. In U. F. Lanius, S. L. Paulsen, & F. Corrigan (Eds.), *Neurobiology and Treatment of Trauma and Dissociation: Toward An Embodied Self* (pp. 5–28). New York: Springer Publishing Company.

Paulsen, S., & Watkins, J. (2005). Best techniques from the armamentarium of hypnoanalytic, EMDR, somatic psychotherapy and cognitive behavioral methods. In *Workshop presented at the Fall Conference of the International Society for the Study of Dissociation, Toronto, Ontario, Canada*. Chicago.

Peelen, M. V, Atkinson, A. P., & Vuilleumier, P. (2010). Supramodal representations of perceived emotions in the human brain. *The Journal of Neuroscience: The Official Journal of the Society for Neuroscience, 30*(30), 10127–34.

Phan, K. L., Britton, J. C., Taylor, S. F., Fig, L. M., & Liberzon, I. (2006). Corticolimbic blood flow during nontraumatic emotional processing in posttraumatic stress disorder. *Archives of General Psychiatry, 63*(2), 184–92.

Phillips, M., & Frederick, C. (1995). *Healing the divided self: Clinical and Ericksonian hypnotherapy for post-traumatic and dissociative conditions*. New York: W W Norton & Company.

Poblano, A., Haro, R., & Arteaga, C. (2008). Neurophysiologic measurement of continuity in the sleep of fetuses during the last week of pregnancy and in newborns. *International Journal of Biological Sciences, 4*(1), 23–8.

Porges, S. (2011). *The Polyvagal Theory: Neurophysiological Foundations of Emotions, Attachment, Communication, and Self-regulation (Norton Series on Interpersonal*. New York: W W Norton & Company.

Putnam, F. (1988). The switch process in multiple personality disorder and other state-change disorders. *Dissociation: Progress in the Dissociative Disorders, 1*, 24–32.

Ramachandran, V., Blakeslee, S., & Sacks, O. (1998). *Phantoms in the brain: Probing the mysteries of the human mind.* New York: William Morrow.

Rank, O. (1929). *The trauma of birth.* New York: Courier Corporation.

Rank, O. (1959). *The myth of the birth of the hero, and other writings.* New York: Random House Incorporated.

Rubin, R. (1975). Maternal tasks in pregnancy. *Maternal-Child Nursing Journal, 4*(3), 143–53.

Sabatinelli, D., Lang, P. J., Bradley, M. M., & Flaisch, T. (2006). The neural basis of narrative imagery: emotion and action. *Progress in Brain Research, 156*, 93–103.

Scaer, R. (2014). *The Body Bears the Burden: Trauma, Dissociation, and Disease.* New York: Routledge.

Schore, A. (2001). Effects of a secure attachment relationship on right brain development, affect regulation, and infant mental health. *Infant Mental Health Journal, 22*(1–2), 7–66.

Schore, A. (2003). *Affect dysregulation and the repair of the self.* New York & London: WW Norton. New York: W W Norton & Company.

Schore, A. (2009). The paradigm shift: The right brain and the relational unconscious. Invited plenary address to the American Psychological Association 2009 Convention.

Schore, A. N. (2001). Contributions from the decade of the brain to infant mental health: An overview. *Infant Mental Health Journal, 22*(1–2), 1–6.

Shapiro, F. (2001). *Eye Movement Desensitization and Reprocessing: Basic Principles, Protocols, and Procedures.* New York: Guilford Press.

Siegel, D. J. (1999). *The Developing Mind: Toward a Neurobiology of Interpersonal Experience.* New York: Guilford Press.

Siegel, D. J. (2015). *The Developing Mind: How Relationships and the Brain Interact to Shape Who We Are* (2nd ed.). New York: Guilford Publications.

Steele, K., van der Hart, O., & Nijenhuis, E. R. S. (2005). Phase-oriented treatment of structural dissociation in complex traumatization: overcoming trauma-related phobias. *Journal of Trauma & Dissociation : The Official Journal of the International Society for the Study of Dissociation (ISSD), 6*(3), 11–53.

Sutton-Smith, B. (1997). *The Ambiguity of Play.* London: Harvard University Press.

Tomkins, S. S. (1963). *Affect Imagery Consciousness: Volume II, The Negative Affects.* New York: Springer Publishing.

Trevarthen, C. (1979). Communication and cooperation in early infancy: A description of primary intersubjectivity. In *Before speech: The beginning of interpersonal ...* (pp. 321–347). Cambridge: Cambridge University Press.

Twombly, J. (2009a). Height orientation. In *EMDR scripted protocols: Special populations* (p. 249). New York: Springer Publishing Company.

Twombly, J. (2009b). Installation and transmission of current time and life orientation. In *EMDR scripted protocols: Special populations* (p. 243). New York: Springer Publishing Company.

Watkins, J., & Paulsen, S. (2003). Ego state therapy: EMDR and hypnoanalytic techniques. In *Workshop at the Society for Clinical and Experimental Hypnosis, Chicago.* Chicago.

Watkins, J., & Watkins, H. (1997). *Ego states: Theory and therapy.* New York: W W Norton & Company.

Weaver, R., & Cranley, M. (1983). An exploration of paternal-fetal attachment behavior. *Nursing Research, 32*(2), 68–72.

Wildwind, L. (1992). Treating chronic depression. In *First Annual EMDR Conference, San Jose, CA.*

Winnicott, D. (1960). *The theory of the parent—infant relationship. In The Maturational Processes and the Facilitating Environment.* New York: International Universities Press.

Appendix A Working in the Intensive Format

Intensive format Both Paulsen and O'Shea do considerable amounts of work in an intensive format, where someone comes for several days of intensive work, sometimes more than once.

Advantages Advantages of the intensive format are that:

- In the conventional therapy structure, it is customary, in a 45- or 50-minute appointment, to have 10-15 minutes to drop into the deep work and 10-15 minutes to wrap up the session and prepare the client to leave the office (Kluft's Rule of Thirds). In the intensive format, there are a few minutes to drop into the work but then the work remains in the subjective, somatic, and deep level for some time. Although Paulsen never works without at least 15 minute breaks every 90 to 120 minutes, the work goes all day, sometimes for several days, enabling efficient deep work without it being disorganizing.

- It is the depth of the work that contraindicates the intensive format for most DID clients. Imagine someone who was, say, held captive in a basement for days, now being "held captive," in a painful intense treatment approach, where the client who was trained to be compliant, feels they can't say, "enough!" and change gears or leave.

- Another advantage of the intensive format is that a client can seek out someone at a distance who may be able to provide the work that their usual therapist may not yet be trained to do (only with the referral of that therapist however).

Draw-backs of the intensive format The therapist might have an inflated idea of what they are capable of, incurring considerable expense on the part of the client, setting aside days of time which cost thousands of dollars, producing negligible results.

In Paulsen's experience--where she has seen cases where other therapists did ET therapy on undiagnosed dissociative clients without the necessary modifications-- the problem turns on a failure get the caretaker/perpetrator introjects on board, squandering time and money and antagonizing the self-system's primary protectors. This can cause, beyond waste, decompensation and other serious clinical risks.

The therapist has a burden of assessing, sometimes by phone, whether the client is appropriate for the intensive format, necessitating the following assessments:

- Intake interview as usual
- Assessment of degree of dissociation (not based on assumptions or on client self-report of degree of dissociation)
- Assessing whether the client's self-system, including any perpetrator or parental introjects, are amenable to the ET treatment
- Assessment of degree of internal resources and capacity to tolerate affect and soma
- Assessment of degree of external resources to determine whether the client is aware of the cost of the treatment and has a local therapist in place to receive

the client on their return to their home city.

- In no case should a therapist conducting intensive work abandon the client or fail to assist in transition after the intensive work.

- The intensive format is not without precedent in the clinical tradition, but it is also not the usual structure, so the therapist may be incurring risks not normally encountered in a conventional therapy practice.

DID and intensives Most highly dissociative clients are not appropriate for the intensive format. Only those who are well along in their work, returning to care with an informed and supportive therapist, psychologically minded and resourced, are suitable for intensive work. Otherwise either the work or the travel involved, if any, can be destabilizing. Some dissociative mental health professionals and a few other hardy individuals have good containment, good resourcing, good insights, and are suitable for intensive work.

Although the author has for decades treated DID clients in a conventional format, she typically does not work with DID clients in the intensive format, except in a half day (or two consecutive-day half-days) structure, lest there be a risk of destabilization. On rare occasion, a DID client is both so resourced and so far along in treatment, having done so much work over the years, that an exception can be made. It is much more likely, however, that an exception would be an error, so readers are cautioned against assuming an exception is warranted.

It would be a serious risk of traumatization and destabilization for a therapist to fail to assess for dissociation, agree to work in the intensive format with someone who shouldn't, proceed to work intensively for days including with EMDR therapy, causing dissociative barriers to fail with resulting decompensation and suicidal crisis, and then have the client return to their home locale with no therapist in place. Therefore, therapists are urged to not adopt the intensive format unless all these considerations are well in hand. An informed consent process should surely advise the client about relevant risks and structures and the need for follow up care.

Post-intensive status updates
- When working within the intensive format, it is wise for the therapist to ask for a phone or other communication of brief status update within 2-3 days, to know if the client is doing well. Because it is gentle, the procedure rarely is disorganizing, but occasionally the implications of the work cause some disturbance upon reentry to everyday life.

- A second update at 2-3 weeks later is useful because by then most will know if their symptoms have remitted, and what remains and what is gone.

- Under no circumstances should the client be left without follow up care if they need it. If the intensives therapist is not able to provide follow up care, they must provide continuity of care and appropriate referrals to ensure the client is supported. Otherwise it is at risk to be a reenactment of early abandonment scenarios.

- Paulsen ensures that clients likely to need ongoing care have a therapist at the ready to receive the client after treatment.

- Paulsen does not undertake intensive treatment with someone who has an extant therapist without the referral information, support and commitment to ongoing care from that other therapist

Appendix B The Mechanics

Source Most of these mechanics are from O'Shea's original contribution, modified by Paulsen to take complex dissociation into account.

Mechanical tips Several mechanical and ergonomic factors make processing easier, especially when the work is being conducted in intensive sessions of several hours of length.

What is different from the standard approach is that eye movements in particular are too cognitive, too adult, and too hard to attenuate for the nuanced sensory information to be easily apperceived.

Therefore, somatic bilateral stimulation is best as it is consistent with the somatic emphasis of infantile development.

Touch where appropriate, or physical proximity is key in the baby state Where appropriate, bilateral tactile stimulation should be in the form of touch, if clinically appropriate and legally permitted, on the client's ankles, knees or wrists, rather than tactile probes, especially for the first year of life.

Auditory tones may be suitable for some clients but the presence of headphones is less compatible with the infant states accessed than is simple human touch.

Highly Dissociative Clients Where touch isn't appropriate, which is likely with many DID clients, the therapist's physical proximity may be very important, even while tactile probes or auditory tones are used with appropriate EMDR equipment.

Clients with torture or electrocution histories may not be able to tolerate tactile equipment without undue triggering. If all else fails, the therapist can sit at an appropriate distance while the client touches or taps his/her own body bilaterally.

Recliner chair and rolling chair for therapist ergonomics For ergonomic support, the therapist may wish the client to be reclined in a recliner chair with the footrest extended, so the therapist can easily tap on the client's ankles, where appropriate and acceptable.

Some dissociative clients will not do well in a reclined or horizontal state, and need to keep their feet squarely grounded on the floor.

Paulsen has at times used speakers built into an overstuffed chair for bilateral auditory stimulation without requiring earphones, touch, eye movements or tactile equipment.

Extended session length

Extended sessions are ideal for this work, but only for non-dissociative clients in nearly all cases.

A standard therapy session is difficult to utilize well for early trauma processing, because it takes some time to get into the felt sense, time to process and then time to wrap up the session.

For that reason, one or several consecutive 90-minute sessions are ideal. The author often conducts several days with four 90-minute sessions, adjusted to accommodate the requirements of processing.

Note that this format would be unsuitable and contraindicated with the standard EMDR for most people, certainly for DID clients and is explicitly not recommended here.

However, with the ET approach, the work proceeds gently and is nuanced and restorative, not abreactive typically, and so extended sessions may be safely accommodated for optimal results.

The structure of 90 minutes (to 120 minutes) with a break, repeated several times in a day, is necessary to keep containment and structure of the work, provide breaks for both therapist and client, and ensure that the client doesn't feel overwhelmed by what might otherwise seem to be an infinite expanse of unstructured time.

B-1 ISST&D treatment guidelines caution against long sessions except, rarely, for special procedures

Problems of extended sessions for dissociative clients

Some dissociative clients were kept in captivity for long extensions of time, so 90 minute sessions may be the maximum. The ISST&D Treatment Guidelines–3rd Edition (2011) state that sessions longer than 90 minutes are generally contraindicated except for very special procedures.

This procedure certainly qualifies as a very special procedure, but maintaining the structure and boundaries of the work and relationship are still critical to prevent decompensation or inadvertent reenacting of traumatic circumstances which the client may not readily be able to verbally decline.

Open or closed eyes

Many clients will perceive the nuances of body sensation, affect and subtle awareness most readily if they close their eyes. If they do so, especially for DID clients, the therapist may occasionally need to ask them to peek to see where they are, orienting them to the room and to the present time. The question of whether or not it is best for the client to close their eyes is a complex one.

In general, DID clients will often require keeping their eyes open and frequent reorienting to the room and continuous efforts by the therapist to maintain dual attention awareness, including such frequent utterances as, "I'm right here with you," "it's a memory, not happening now," and "touch the poodle to remind yourself you are here in the room with me and the dogs," etc.

B-2 To orient to body, ask a part to peek through the eyes, and say "whose hands are those? the girl's? the mothers?"

Therapist demeanor

Even if touch is contraindicated, as it may be for many DID clients, the therapist should use a comforting, gentle and warm voice and demeanor. Eye contact at the right moments will be especially important for some clients as they work through the absence of eye contact with a primary caretaker.

Appendix C Working with Perpetrator Introjects to Reduce Loyalty to the Aggressor

History & terminology

A checklist for shifting loyalty to the aggressor to loyalty to the self was originally published by Paulsen (2009), and is reprinted, modified, here. In can't be stated too often that ego state work to address loyalty to the aggressor is key not only with highly dissociative clients, but with many clients who are not especially structurally dissociative.

There are a number of ways that therapists can appreciate the survival function of a perpetrator introject; a part that identifies with the perpetrator, and whom the other parts of self variously fear, loathe, or love. The following is a checklist for making sure the important points have been made, so the introject can shift loyalty to client's self, away from the perpetrator.

The terms "perpetrator' or "aggressor" are used interchangeably here, but in fact, many of those who seek early trauma work are best served by the term "parental introject." This is because the parents perhaps were not big T perpetrators, but rather, were doing the best they could with their own inadequacies or trauma histories.

Additionally, at the beginning, the use of the term perpetrator may alienate the client and cause them to defend their parents, increasing loyalty to those parents. As the work continues, the client may well come to the realization that no matter how well intended the parents were or weren't, the baby's needs were not met on baby's terms.

C-1 Clients typically experience perpetrator introjects as "monstrous," though they may not appear in the mind's eye as a monster, per se.

Orient the introject	• Orient the introject to the face they are in the client's body, the present time and the present location. If the perpetrator is dead or far away, make that clear. Utilize magazines, calendars, newspapers, maps, mirrors, to orient.
	• "If I'm right that you are an internal holographic likeness of the external perpetrator but not the actual external perpetrator, there are significant implications."
	• It is absolutely critical for the therapist to remain clear that the introject is NOT the external perpetrator, but rather a part of the client's self. So we don't say, for example, "father" but, rather, we say, "father-part-of-the-self."
Appreciate the introject	• Thank you for identifying with the external's power, so the self didn't ONLY feel helpless; at least one part of you felt there was some power.
	• Thank you for keeping her under your thumb, because that kept things under control, so there wasn't only chaos. You may have saved her life (if true).
	• Thank you for holding the perpetrator energy, so it didn't spread all over her. Like a cyst encapsulates pus, the introject kept the toxic energy from spreading, when the toxic energy was "injected" at the moment of trauma. Thanks for holding the toxin; that's a tough job.
	• Thanks for maintaining the attachment to the father. Kids will do anything to preserve whatever crumbs of love they can find or imagine. You have been very loyal to the father, and that preserved the little bit of love she had from him.
Create a vision of a different future	• Don't worry about being out of a job; we have lots for you to do.
	• When the energy you hold is freed to empower the self, that's a powerful battery, anything is possible then. That's an important new role for you.
	• You can help her envision a future of being, for example, a fair-minded conscience, reasonable, and without double binds, enabling compassion.
	• You can always revert to fierceness to protect self if needed.
	• You can allow the toxin to be released so she can heal, very heroic of you.
	• If you turn your loyalty away from the father and to the self, she can heal and move forward.
Summary: what the introject needs	• Understanding and appreciation from the therapist and the self (inner applause).
	• Holding and nurturing from another source in the mind's eye to experience nurturing internally, so he could have been a better father to her.
	• Acknowledge their great fatigue, how nice to free the energy in a healing sleep.
	• The improved introject, or if impossible another borrowed nurturing source, may be able to provide to the younger states.

- In later phases, for some clients, bilateral stimulation may be added to this intervention. For some, trauma work must be conducted first to get this shift.

About the therapeutic relationship

- The therapeutic relationship serves to provide expert methods, strategies and tactics, techniques and procedures.
- It must never be forgotten that the strength of the therapeutic relationship is the best predictor of therapeutic outcome after half a century of treatment outcome studies.
- In the early trauma approach, the relationship picks up where mother left off in infancy, hearing the non-verbal yearnings of a wordless child, in the most ancient sacred form, that of mother and child.
- We are not re-parenting, but we are hearing what should have been heard in the first place. With this catch and release, the body can settle the score, and lay down its arms, and be at peace.
- Words are part of it, but the resonant attunement and the effort to hear in the non-verbal communication is the bulk of it.

When There Are No Words - Sandra Paulsen

Appendix D Containment for Closing Sessions with Complex or Dissociative Clients

Purpose The purpose of containment imagery and scripting is providing a means to wrap up any session in which ego state work has been conducted. Many therapeutic misadventures are the direct result of therapists failing to take the step of properly closing the session down. Ego state therapy can be conducted with or without formal trance induction. However, even when no formal trance induction is employed, highly dissociative clients are often inadvertently in trance, either as a result of the ego state intervention (which may not have been intended as hypnotic) or because they are dissociative by the use of self-hypnosis over a life time. That is, self-hypnosis maintains the structure of the self-system. For these reasons, it is imperative that any session which has employed ego state maneuvers also employ a procedure for closing down the session. To fail to do so is like doing hypnotic induction without bring the person out of trance, or, more dramatically, like making a surgical incision without closing the wound.

There can be many ways to end a session (e.g., the light stream approach is but one), but this sample language is intended to work with parts of self directly, and to address common issues evoked in ending an ego state session. Other metaphors and methods may also work but they should address the same elements to cover the same ground as the following script.

Paulsen two-step This technique has the moniker of the Paulsen two-step, so named by the author's colleague Joan Golston. It has a sometimes needed third step, as follows:

Step One Containing Elements of the Memory

"I'd like to invite those who are willing to help to gather up any fragments of memory that have been pulled forward by our work today, gathering them up, and putting them in (container/jar/box/vault), not forever, just until the time is right, that's it, gathering them up, gathering up and putting away. Good."

Step Two Tucking in the Parts

Appreciating "I want to thank all the parts of the self that helped today by talking and listening and allowing the work." (Optional: "I especially want to thank [Part X], who has an especially thankless job/great burden/great courage today]."

Paradoxically suggesting they will be leaving "….. and I'm wondering if there is something that simply must be said before we tuck things in and close things down?" (pause to see if there is a response, something such as, "thanks," or "don't forget about us," etc.).

Offer a means of conveyance "There's a beautiful fluffy white cloud waiting with it's motor running" (or birch bark canoe, or mountain bike, or buffalo, or magic carpet, or any other method of transportation), "….and you can climb on board your cloud, or clouds, as some may want to go together and some may want to go separately, and that's fine….and I'll wave goodbye as the cloud pulls away and takes you deep inside, deeper and deeper, deeper and deeper still… that's it….. so long, see you later, bye bye ….. "

Check for grounding "…… (Name of front part) …is that you? Are you all the way back and road worthy? Please check the conference room please. Occupied or empty?"

Step Three Problem Solving

If conference room is not empty
"Ask who is visible in the conference room. If the answer is (Part Y), say, "Hi, I bet there is a good reason you are still here. Is there a concern we need to address?" Address any concern. Often the part simply didn't know it was time to leave.

If the part is unseen or unidentifiable
"Check under the table and in the corners and see if someone is hiding there, and address as in prior paragraph. T

If the part does not want to leave and has the appearance of a child in the conference room
"I understand that you don't want to leave, and I'm very glad we found you too." The part may wish to play, explore, or just have control of the body). "and I'll be happy to hear what needs to be heard when the time is right. But here's the thing. If you stay forward when she leaves and drives, since you're little, I'm afraid for your safety while driving. And, if you are forward and she can feel your pain, which is very great, I'm afraid she won't want to bring the body back. And since you are all in the same body, it seems to me, then how can I hear your story?... and I do want to hear your story. So, I'm sorry to say, little one, that I need to ask you to wait a bit longer until the time is right, even though you have waited so long already. And if you tuck in now, she'll feel great after the session, and then she'll let us speak again. Okay?" Occasionally, one needs to negotiate a deal with the front part to give the other part some air time, e.g., coloring, or skating, or dancing, or listening to music if it is a child or teen part. This is especially likely in a client who doesn't get much time off of work or down time for relaxation or self-care. Then say, "I agree with you, she does need more down time. I will talk to her about the importance of this, and see what I can arrange for you. Are you willing to step back now and I'll arrange that if I can? Thank you." Then the therapist must explain the converse to the front part of the self who may or may not have amnesia for the discussion about play. Say to the front part, upon her return to executive control of the body, "Look, I cut you a deal, there is a part that did not want to go, and only did because I said I'd negotiate a deal with you, and now my credibility is on the line with that part. If you don't let that part (color/play/dance/listen to music, or whatever safe and legal behavior was asked for), I'm afraid that she's not going to cooperate in the future, and then your (name troublesome symptom) will be worse, because that one has the power to make your symptoms better or worse.

If there is a headache	On occasion, it can be beneficial or necessary to demonstrate to a recalcitrant or disbelieving front part that another part of self has the power to bring on a symptom like a headache. Say, while the front part is executive, "Part (Y), if you're listening, can you show her how you can make her headache come or get worse?" "well, (to the front part) how is it?" Typically the front part is incredulous, and says, "it's worse!" Then say, "Part (Y), now show her you're <u>really</u> powerful enough to make the headache better." Then inquire, "how is it now?" Usually, the front part says, "it's better! How did you do that." Explain, "I did it by acknowledging the power and importance of that part. Do you see why it is in your interest if we work with that part and take <u>her</u> needs into account too? I think you need to take some time to (color/play/dance/listen to music, and so on).
If the part has the appearance of a parent and/or perpetrator	In this example, the part will have the appearance of dad, and believes himself to be the client's dad, who is dead. See the prior discussion of orienting and appreciating perpetrator introjects, as that discussion will need to have happened already, prior to the containment step. "Hi, dad part, I bet there is a good reason why you are here. Are you concerned about something or you just want to keep an eye on things?" Ask the front part of the client how the introject is responding. They will typically say, "he's not pleased," or "his arms are crossed," or "I don't think he's going anywhere." Say, "I know better than to argue with you about <u>that</u>, because I know who would win <u>that</u> argument! And it wouldn't be me, because you are very powerful." Ask, "How is that going over?" The client will typically answer, "he looks pleased," or "damn straight," etc.
Join the defense	Since the introject is there as a measure of loyalty to the aggressor which was necessary for survival historically, joining the defense is a better strategy than trying to strip the client of the defense. Say, "Dad Part, it makes sense to me that you want to keep control of the situation, and I'm not going to challenge you on that. I will point out, however, that there is a ranger station on the horizon, if you find yourself feeling very weary, because your burden is very great. And it has a pleasant soft (hammock/cot) and binoculars, so you can get some much needed rest, and still keep an eye on things. Thanks, Dad Part, see you later." Then check with the front part, "what's happening?" Typically they will say, "he's gone." Because any such ego state work will initially rock the boat, there might be initial upset to the system in the first weeks. This means repetition is needed to get the introject's loyalty shifted to the self. See Appendix C.
More than one front part	There is often more than one front part, for example, one has the job of doing life and not knowing anything about the internal world, behind an amnesia barrier, and one that may be able to do life and know the internal world. Just because a front part speaks about the conference room contents does not mean it is necessarily the same part that drives home and writes the check. Any amnesia barrier should be preserved for the early portions of the treatment, consistent with the tactical integrationist approach described elsewhere (Fine, 1993). When the front part, whose job it is to not know, returns for the drive home, we allow ambiguity about what has transpired, lest the dissociative barrier be prematurely compromised.
Check the conference room	"So take a glance in the conference room, occupied or empty? Lights out? Okay, we'll see you next week, then!"

Repetition After a few weeks of repetition of the tucking in procedure or its variations, the client's self-system will develop a conditioned response and take a cue when it's time to wrap up the session. It gets easier over time.

Initial Attempts The first time or times the tucking in is employed, there may be upheaval in the system, just as the first time any ego state maneuver is employed may cause upheaval. The initial attempts may require therapist availability by phone to re-tuck in parts that may be reluctant or concerned that secrets will be told or they will be eliminated. The therapist should provide reassurance that we don't "get rid of parts," but help them get up-to-date jobs and that we won't tell any secrets if silence is needed for safety. It may be necessary on the phone to repeat the orienting procedure to remind the perpetrator identified part that he is not the external perpetrator, but is internal, that it is the present year, present age, present location, and present circumstances. Like blackberry bushes, the forgetting grows back but gets easier over time.

When There Are No Words - Sandra Paulsen

Appendix E Original Worksheets by O'Shea and Paulsen

History The following pages are intended for clinical use in conducting the early trauma approach. They were developed from Katie O'Shea's original material, then created jointly by Sandra Paulsen and Katie O'Shea to accompany the workshop they each taught separately.

Purpose The original worksheets (steps one through four) are intended for use with the basic early trauma approach and do not have all the information one needs for using the early trauma approach with complex trauma and dissociation.

The intended use of the worksheets are:

Summary Page To summarize the progress of all steps on one page.

1 Container For the containment step, using O'Shea's original scripting.

2 Safe state For the safe state step, using O'Shea's original scripting.

3 Reinstalling innate emotional resources This worksheet is for use with the step that Paulsen described as resetting the affecting circuits. O'Shea's original sample scripting. "Reinstalling innate emotional resources" is O'Shea's original language.

4 Trauma clearing This worksheet is for the trauma clearing step, which Paulsen calls temporal integration.

When There Are No Words - Sandra Paulsen

WORKSHEET FOR CLIENT: _____

1. CONTAINER (to ensure client has the capacity to titrate affect & fractionate trauma)	DATE:

Choose at least one strategy:
- ☐ **Container** (see script)   Cue Word is: _____
- ☐ Rheostat (imaginal dimmer switch they can feel under their hand to turn down intensity)
- ☐ Screen (to view disturbing material at a distance)
- ☐ Waiting Room (to hold material or states not the subject or "star" of today's work)
- ☐ Other:

2. SAFE STATE (to ensure client is in an empowered state to increase processing capacity)	DATE:

Choose one:
- ☐ **Safe state (how you feel when nothing bad is happening)** (see script) Cue Word is: _____
- ☐ Resourced state (imagine how it would look and feel to have that attribute)
- ☐ Somatic resource (how it feels in your body when you think about your favorite place)
- ☐ Safe place (a place where you feel calm and safe)
- ☐ Other:

3. REINSTALLING INNATE EMOTIONAL RESOURCES (so emotional system is free to work and transmit) DATE:

Having resourced client (in 1 above) and set up a titration procedure (2 above), Instruct client that we are making sure their dashboard wires are hooked up, that we aren't working on their feelings about anything, but just checking to make sure the wires work.   What does (name emotion) look like?
- ☐ Shame (not a Pankseppian circuit found in rats, but perhaps a circuit in humans)

BASIC CIRCUITS (Subcortical, hardwired, not learned)
- ☐ RAGE (irritation to rage)
- ☐ FEAR (concern to terror)
- ☐ PANIC/SAD (you may wish to do this as two, first panic when can't get help then sadness at not getting help) ☐ CARE (nurturance, caretaking, love)
- ☐ LUST (desire)
- ☐ SEEKing (curiosity, initiation, motivation)
- ☐ PLAY

OTHER EMOTIONS TO CONSIDER CLEARING
- ☐ If needed, additional protective/life preserving emotions: such as hurt, betrayal, abandonment, self-pity
- ☐ If needed, additional life enhancing (such as happiness, joy, pleasure, connectedness)
- ☐ Other such as: pain, disgust, hunger, touch, as needed
- ☐ If client can't do above without felt sense of emotion, target safety systems first

Alarm/Fight/Flight/Freeze

4. TRAUMA CLEARING (to clear early trauma by time frame in fractionated dosages)	DATE:

To "clear the desktop", start every session saying, **"Let everything that still needs to be reviewed go into your** (container cue word) **and say to yourself** (resource cue word or phrase)." Pause, and when they are ready, say: **"Now let's take out anything that needs to be reviewed during** (targeted time frame)" and add DAS/BLS. If you know there were early traumas, break the time frames into smaller fractions, e.g. half a year, months or even the next important experience to titrate the intensity. Use a separate sheet to record the time frames used. A common size for time frames might be 3 months, but there is great variability.

CAPTURED NCs/PCs:

STEP 1 – CONTAINER

SAMPLE SCRIPT

""We know there is a lot of material that needs to be reviewed, so we need to have a way to set it aside until we can take it out a piece at a time and review it. Our right hemisphere stores experiences, knowledge and information until we can give them our full attention and learn all that we need to learn. We can help our right hemisphere set things aside when we're not working on them, by having an image of a place or container to put them in. What comes to mind as a place where whatever you still need to review can be stored until you can give it your full attention? It can be an image in your mind, or you can leave it with me in my container."

Pause and when they are ready, say: *"Now, just focus on the (container), and let whatever still needs to be reviewed go into the container in whatever form it takes. Tell me when it is all in, or if you are having trouble."* (pause until they indicate it is all in their container) *"I'd like you to begin practicing using your container between now and the next appointment, and you'll get better and better at using it. If the container changes, that's fine."*

Additional Notes:
1: Container should not be one they see frequently in day to day life, or it may be triggering, because the material is so ready to be cleared,
2. Container should have a lock or lid or a method to keep material inside it.
3: Ego states should NOT be placed in a container, but may be "tucked in" in a nurturing fashion, Paulsen (2009).

TYPICAL PROBLEM	SAMPLE SOLUTION
If client can't think of anything, problem may be performance anxiety or trying	*"Trying is the biggest problem, just think of needing to have a place and see what comes to mind"* (or in conference room or on internal TV screen). Or, say, *"It's like watching the Containment Channel on television. You don't have to do anything, just watch, as your brain knows how to do it, so we just let it do what it knows how to do."*
If client says it won't go in the container	*"Are you TRYING to make it go in, or just looking at it, easily and effortlessly, to see what happen,"* or, *"Ask yourself what's the danger of just letting it go in"* *"Ask yourself what's keeping it from going in"*
If most material is in container but some pieces are still out	*"Ask yourself what's keeping these pieces from going in?"*
If it doesn't feel safe to set troubling material aside	*"Everything you need is always available. What's being set aside is only what hasn't yet been reviewed. You've already learned a lot from your experiences and anything you need is always available."*
If there is an urgency about the material	*"Something in your system is ready to be reprocessed, so you are REALLY ready to review it. It is important for us to pace the work so you stay comfortable. Together we can decide when is the best time to target it, now, next session or later."*
FOR HIGHER LEVELS OF DISSOCATION	(Note: We never put ego states in a container, but rather "tuck them in" in a nurturing fashion, until the time is right. Paulsen, 2009, 2014

STEP 2 – SAFE STATE

SAMPLE SCRIPT

For Safe State (one type of resourced state):   *"Sometimes we may stay on guard even when we are actually safe. Our amygdala is on duty 24/7, asleep or awake, scanning every aspect of our environment, internal and external, with the ability to respond in half a millisecond, so we don't need to be consciously vigilant. That's exhausting and makes us less able to respond to danger when we need to. So, would it be okay to FEEL safe when you ARE safe, when nothing bad is happening? In order to feel safe when we are safe, we need to be sure that everything that still needs to be reviewed/sorted through is in our container. Just focus on the image of your* (container cue word) *and let anything that needs to be set aside go in.* (When they confirm, continue). *Your body already knows what to do, so let's rely on it ….and just notice, easily and effortlessly… with curiosity… how your body feels. I'll add some right/left stimulation to accelerate the process and we'll just see what happens. Is it okay if I tap your knees?"…"Just notice."*

Continue DAS/BLS, checking in periodically, until they reach a state of relaxed awareness, our natural state when no danger is present. Say, *"As you focus on what you're feeling now, what word or words come to mind? I want you to have a way to quickly call back this feeling, so hold that word (or words) in mind while you focus on the feeling, and I'll add BLS."* Tap for about 30 seconds, then ask, *"Did those words stay or change?"* If it stayed, ask them to practice it in order to get in the habit of feeling safe when they are safe. If it changed, add DAS/BLS until it appears to be set.

Note: May also use instead: safe place or other highly resourced state. We want them in a ventral vagal state so that 1) they feel strong enough to withstand any disturbance that arises in subsequent steps and 2) so that they have a relatively clear backdrop against which to notice any disturbance that arises in subsequent steps.

"It takes about 2 weeks of practice for your system to get out of the habit of being in an on-going distressed and fragmented mode and into a healthy, natural, relaxed, aware mode. You'll respond very rapidly if there is danger present. Your amygdala is on duty 24/7 like a fire alarm, so we don't need to be vigilant". Instruct them to **Contain and Resource: b**efore sleep, upon awakening, and when they change activities.

PROBLEM	SOLUTION
Emotional distress comes up	*"Let that go in (container) for now. We'll come back to it."*
Disturbance comes back repeatedly	*"There is something that you are really ready to review, let's decide together whether to target it today or next week, or later."* Use clinical judgment to determine whether it's a readiness to proceed or a dissociative incapacity to distance from felt sense
If the client speaks of never relaxing, always being on alert:	*"That's exhausting and makes us less able to respond to danger when we need to. So, would it be okay to FEEL safe when you ARE safe, when nothing bad is happening? If so, we need to be sure that everything that still needs to be reviewed or sorted through is in our container."*
Client still is unable to experience a good, comfortable, or safe feeling	May have overlooked a dissociative disorder; use an ego state approach. CAUTION: Do not use this procedure with a highly dissociative client unless you are trained and experienced with treating dissociative disorders.
Client says, "It's stupid to ever feel safe" etc	Do extensive education on amygdala and safety systems of fight, flight, freeze. Consider using animal examples. Spend considerable time on animals' states of social connection, caring, other ventral vagal states, then human states of safe connection.

STEP 3 – REINSTALLING INNATE EMOTIONAL RESOURCES

SAMPLE SCRIPT

"Before we begin reviewing your early experiences, we need to make sure your emotions are working the way they were intended to work – as sources of important information to help us learn what's dangerous, what's unfair, what's connected, and more. They are there at the beginning of our lives. No one has to teach a newborn baby how to feel. Many people have been taught to ignore feelings, and may even have learned that it's not OK to feel some feelings, so they disconnect from their feelings. That's like clipping the dash board wires in our car, just because we get uncomfortable when we see a red light that says the engine is overheating! When that happens there is often shame present about having other emotions"

For individuals who need basic education about the role of common emotions as information, give or read to them the Client Handout about emotions. Ensure sufficient education about the function of emotions before proceeding with the following. Some can proceed directly, and some need much education.

"First, let everything unresolved in your system go into your (container) and remind yourself it's ok to feel safe when you are safe, with your (cue word from Step 2 – Resource state) (Pause long enough for them to do that). *"With your permission, I'll provide bilateral stimulation by tapping on your knees (or ankles), and you can close your eyes if you want and notice the pictures that come. We'll take one emotion at a time, and all you need to do is notice what the feeling looks like, and watch with curiosity, to see if the picture is changing or staying the same. When the picture stops changing, that means the emotion will be ready whenever you need it, and not when you don't need it. We'll clear the protective emotions first, because they need to be working well before we can fully experience the regenerating, life enhancing emotions. Let's begin with 'shame.' What does 'shame' look like?* "(They report what they see) **"Notice that"** and **"What does shame look like now?"** It's okay if it transforms, is symbolic, a story, or shows a thwarted response. Do tapping sets until the picture stops changing. It may become positive, neutral, or just stop changing. Do for each emotion.

SHAME → RAGE → FEAR → PANIC/SAD → CARE → LUST → SEEKing → PLAY

Some may benefit from resetting learned emotions or the safety circuits themselves. If high levels of dissociation are present, use a formal ego state approach (e.g., Paulsen 2009). Do not use this procedure with highly dissociative clients unless you are trained and experienced in treating dissociative disorders.

PROBLEM	SOLUTION
The client sees no image.	Usually is trying, remind them to just allow an image to be there, **"Just notice while I read what this emotion does, tell me when an image comes to mind"**
The image doesn't stop changing	Go to the next emotion, and come back to this one later. Go through them as many times as necessary, until the essence becomes neutral and stops changing
They have made many connections	Periodically bring them back to an image, saying, **"what does __ look like now?"** and continue until it stops changing.
They can't observe from a distance and slide into the felt sense	Teach the difference between being in an emotion and looking at an emotion. If needed, use a "prosthesis" like a cartoon of an emotion. If they still slide in after two tries, they may need to reset *fight look like"* and *"flight"* and *"freeze."*
If they still can't observe an emotion from a distance	They may need more work using ego state therapy or somatic resourcing before they can do this step. Must see with objectivity, rather than "sliding in," to work

STEP 4 – CLEARING EARLY TRAUMA BY TIME FRAME

SAMPLE SCRIPT

"Now we'll review the time" (name an appropriately sized time period, e.g., 'second trimester,' 'your birth,' '12 to 15 months," to be sure that any trapped energy is released and conflicting information is cleared up. All you need to do is notice what happens, just like you're viewing a video." The following shows the natural sequence of processing that occurs for many people. It is included below to help the clinician be aware of phase completeness, and adaptive resolution. Incompleteness at one phase will result in inability to completely process subsequent phases.

Contain & Resource
- *First, let everything that still needs to be reviewed, go into your (container)* and say (resource cue word) *to return to feeling relaxed and ready* (or *"to help your amygdala"*). (Pause until they accomplish that.)

Review
- *"Now, just let your focus go to the time ('before you were born' or 'of your birth' or 'from (age) to (age), while I tap, to see if there's anything left that needs to be reviewed, released or repaired.* We don't emphasize verbalization, which may interfere with the felt sense of subtle shifts associated with right hemisphere processing."

Release
- If emotions loop, say, **"imagine what you need or need to do."** If physical sensations loop, say, **"Imagine it (physical sensation) happening."**

Relearn & Repair
- If the following doesn't happen spontaneously, say, *"Imagine getting everything you needed"*, or *"Imagine your parents being /doing what they couldn't be/do back then,"* or *"imagine everything being the way you needed it to be."*

Install
- *"Is there a positive statement (thought) that comes to mind when you focus on the (time frame).* If so, install that and say *"I'm also going to add some thoughts that came to me, so let whatever feels OK stick and whatever doesn't, just slide off."* Complete Standard Installation.

Body Scan & Close
- If session is complete, *"Hold the thought(s) with the (time frame),"* tap until they are in a resourced state. Whether complete or not, say *"Let everything else that still needs to be reviewed, go into (container),* and say *(resource cue word). We'll continue at our next session"*

PROBLEM SOLVING FOR STEP 4 – CLEARING EARLY TRAUMA	
TYPICAL PROBLEM	**SAMPLE SOLUTION**
They don't think they can recall anything from before a certain age.	*Explain that most people don't have conscious memory before about age 3, but that we seem to have the ability to remember more than we think we do. What we learned early we learned so well that we don't realize it, and it is now automatic. Our brain works a lot like the internet and we just need to "Google" it (give it our attention) and our brain also will help us check on what still needs to be reviewed, or find the information that's in conflict with what we know now.*
Client doesn't get anything.	*They are probably trying. Suggest they **"just notice how your body feels."** Let them know it usually takes people a while to get used to not trying. Or, say, **"what's dangerous about reviewing this?"** Depending on what they say, decide whether to re-explain the process or add more safety measures.*
They get overwhelmed with distress, and If it is memory from the time you focused on that is overwhelming them: If it is memory from a later time that is overwhelming them:	*If saying **"Imagine what you need or need or need to do" doesn't work, consider:** Break the time period into small increments.* *Have the client consciously set it aside for later reprocessing, using their container.* *Remind them that the overwhelm is part of the baby's story, it actually isn't about the PRESENT MOMENT. (Felt Flashback)*
If you are trained and experienced in treating dissociative disorders and this client is dissociative, and if the client switches to another ego state before you can finish the reprocessing:	*Be sure you have cooperation of their system and have developed a treatment plan based on their degree and type of dissociation,* *Go back to earlier time frame to ensure earliest trauma is resolved, so the system can come together at the base of experience to work on these experiences without overwhelm. Do not continue to use this procedure if it causes destabilization for any dissociative client.*
IF THERE IS SIGNIFICANT KNOWN EARLY TRAUMA	*For teens and adults, fractionate the information by time and severity. Depending on the amount of trauma, you may need to break the time period down into months, weeks or "moving forward to the next trauma" within the time period. Use knee taps if possible (with a heartbeat cadence for before birth and birth), monitoring their physiology and supporting them in just noticing whatever they notice. Set length often varies greatly.*
KEY CAUTION	*Do not attempt to treat a highly dissociative (dissociative identity disordered) client with this protocol unless you are trained and experienced in the treatment of dissociative disorders. The procedure is different for dissociative clients, requiring more extensive preparation and ego state work. Ignoring this caution could result in harm to your client if flooding occurs or dissociative barriers are prematurely taken down, or if key ego states are not on board*

Appendix F Modified Worksheets by Paulsen

History The following pages are intended for clinical use in conducting the early trauma approach instead of the original ones offered in Appendix D. Paulsen modified the worksheets to reflect how her own suggested scripting came to be over time.

Purpose The original worksheets (steps one through four) are intended for use with the basic early trauma approach. The original worksheets did not attempt to address using the early trauma approach with complex trauma and dissociation.

Scope Paulsen added comments to each worksheet to take into account some of the things to address in complex or dissociative clients. Additionally, she created an additional worksheet to suggest some of the additional preparation steps commonly needed for complex trauma and dissociative cases. The worksheet is not intended to be inclusive for all complex cases. Clinician judgment must determine how much preparation is needed, and when trauma processing just be suspended while resourcing, grounding or other preparation steps are revisited or while synthesis and consolidation of gains occurs.

Troubleshooting Many of the troubleshooting tips are O'Shea's original suggestions, and some have been added by Paulsen for complex cases.

About The Worksheets

1-Containment Paulsen uses the general term containment instead of O'Shea's specific word container, to remind the clinician that there are numerous containment strategies available from the hypnosis tradition. She often uses the phrase "containment for fractionation" in this step to help clients understand that we contain material in order to address it later by fraction.

2 Resourced state Paulsen uses the general term resourced state instead of O'Shea's specific term safe state, to remind the clinician that there are many ways to activate the client's ventral vagal nervous system. The important thing is that the client feel safe and resourced enough to do the work in present time.

3 Resetting the affective circuits Paulsen uses the phrase "resetting the affective circuits," instead of O'Shea's "reinstalling innate emotional resources," because it is helpful to instruct clients that these emotional circuits have been experimentally demonstrated to exist in mammals, that they are there from birth and require no learning. This normalizes the range of emotions and educates clients that we are supposed to have them.

4 Temporal integration Paulsen uses the term "temporal integration," rather than O'Shea's "clearing trauma," because processing this way is highly integrative. Also, the phrase points out that the approach is a third integration approach, following strategic integration (Kluft, 1984) and tactical integration (Fine, 1991).

STEP 1 – CONTAINMENT FOR FRACTIONATION

SAMPLE SCRIPT

"Have you ever done beadwork or detail work? If so, you know you need a clear space to work in, or you will lose the details in the clutter. Working with early experience is like that. Because the material we will process may be very subtle, it's easy to miss if we have a cluttered mind. So we will set everything aside to create that clear workspace. Each of you can have your own container if you like, or you can share a container.

Your brain already knows how to do this, so we are just allowing your brain to do what it knows-- to set things aside until we can turn attention to it when the time is right. Please bring to mind a container of your choice, something with a lid. May I know what that is? Good, now just watch as everything that needs review or might distract goes into the container, easily and effortlessly. You may not even know WHAT is going into the container, and might just see movement. Take your time, and let me know when it is complete or if there is difficulty. Wait until the client says that it is complete. Or if there is difficulty, see trouble shooting tips. If there is still difficulty, a dissociative disorder may have been overlooked. Then say, *"I'd like you to practice this daily or better, several times a day, until we meet again. It is helpful in doing the early trauma work, but also in daily life, to set things aside until we can turn our attention to them."*

Later in our work, we can pull forward the material for a time frame as we are ready for it, much like we can take just one tissue out of a box, then another, and then another, each in turn, as needed. So we'll just take out a fraction of material at a time, and that will make it much easier to do work, even difficult work."

Additional Notes:
1: Dissociative clients often can readily distance from a memory by switching, here we do it deliberately.
2. Container should have a lock or lid or a method to keep material inside it and should have a cue word.
3: Ego states should NOT be placed in a container, but may be "tucked in" in a nurturing fashion, Paulsen (2009).

TYPICAL PROBLEM	SAMPLE SOLUTION
If client can't think of anything, problem may be performance anxiety or trying	*"Trying is the biggest problem, just be curious and see what comes to mind"* (or in conference room or on internal TV screen). Or, say, *"It's like watching the Containment Channel on television. You don't have to do anything, just watch, as your brain knows how to do it, so we just let it do what it knows how to do."*
If client says it won't go in the container	*"Are you TRYING to make it go in, or just looking at it, easily and effortlessly, to see what happens"* or, *"Ask yourself what's the danger of just letting it go in"* *"Ask yourself what's keeping it from going in"*
If some is not contained	*"Ask yourself what's keeping these pieces from going in?"*
If it doesn't feel safe to set troubling material aside	*"Everything you need is always available. What's being set aside is only what hasn't yet been reviewed. You've already learned a lot from your experiences and anything you need is always available."*
If there is an urgency about the material	*"Something in your system is ready to be reprocessed, so you are REALLY ready to review it. It is important for us to pace the work so you stay comfortable. We can decide when is the best time to target it, now, next session or later."*
For Dissociative Clients	We never put ego states in a container, but rather "tuck them in" in a nurturing fashion, until the time is right. Paulsen, 2009, 2014, see Appendix. If there is difficulty, check that introjects approve the step or if any other alter has concerns.

STEP 2 – STRENGTHEN A RESOURCED STATE

SAMPLE SCRIPT

For Safe State (one type of resourced state): *"Would it be ok to feel safe when you ARE safe? Sometimes people brace in readiness for trouble even when safe. Our amygdala, though, would go off like a fire alarm when there is ACTUAL danger, in a fraction of a second. We can TRUST our amygdala that way. Like a car alarm that's too sensitive or not sensitive at all, we need an alarm that's set just right, to go off only when there really is trouble. So first we'll set things aside in your container* (use cue word), (add DAS/BLS, with permission. In this moment, in this place, is there sufficient safety to allow the work? Invite concerned alters to peek through the eyes... to see where and when they are presently, maybe it's safe enough to do the work.

With highly dissociative clients, safety may be out of reach. Use another resourced state like awareness of nature, or a beloved animal, or anything life enhancing that allows them to tolerate doing the work even in a state of some vigilance. We want them in a ventral vagal state so that 1) they feel strong enough to withstand any disturbance that arises in subsequent steps and 2) so that they have a relatively clear backdrop against which to notice any disturbance that arises in subsequent steps. Ask parts to peek through the eyes and see where they are, the bad stuff isn't now, look how tall the body can reach on the door frame. Never again a helpless child.

"It takes about 2 weeks of practice for your system to get out of the habit of being in an on-going distressed and fragmented mode and into a more healthy, natural, relaxed, aware mode. You can count on your amygdala still though to respond instantly if danger is present. Invite them to Contain and Resource: before sleep, upon awakening, and when they change activities.

PROBLEM	SOLUTION
Emotional distress comes up	*"Hi, whoever is concerned, what's bothering? Do you see where you are?"*
Disturbance comes back repeatedly	*"There is something that you are really ready to review, let's decide together whether to target it today or next week, or later."* Use clinical judgment to determine whether it's a readiness to proceed or a an internal conflict sabotaging. If the latter, orient, appreciate, mediate, negotiate a solution.
If the client speaks of never relaxing, always being on alert:	*"I understand that you may feel a need to always be vigilant or if anything bad happens, it might be very dangerous or perhaps you'll feel responsible. But you're here in THIS place, and you're (age) years old, and the bad stuff isn't happening even though it sometimes feels like it* (if that's true) ... *so maybe there is enough safety to do an experiment to see if we can heal this?"*
Client still is unable to experience a good, comfortable, or safe feeling	Continue to use ego state maneuvers to ascertain the dynamics behind the unsafety. Are parts disoriented? Are perpetrator introjects sabotaging or sadistic? Or child parts expect reenactments from the therapist? *"Who can help me understand what's bothering? I don't want to ignore your concerns."*
Client says, "It's stupid to ever feel safe" etc	Do extensive education on amygdala and safety systems of fight, flight, freeze. Consider using animal examples. Spend considerable time on animals states of social connection, caring, other ventral vagal states, then human states of safe connection. Use animal photos to normalize if needed.
Strengthen resource state in dissociative clients	There may be resource alters willing to step forward on request, already deputized as part of a "resource team" (Paulsen, 2009) to evoke a safe state.

STEP 3 – RESETTING THE AFFECTIVE CIRCUITS

SAMPLE SCRIPT

"All mammals are born with hardwired emotional circuits that are present from birth and require no learning. Emotions are like dashboard gauges, there to tell us if something is wrong or needs attention. But many people learned early in life that they had to clip their dashboard wires completely, or learned to get used to all the red lights being continuously on. You wouldn't clip your dashboard wires in your car, would you? or ignore a red light on the dashboard? Why not? That's right, we need that information to stay safe and keep the car functioning. Same with our emotions. They are there for a reason. But we want to make sure they are in good working order. If your car gauges were out of order you might have to take it to the mechanic and they'd put it up on a rack to adjust it. You couldn't expect the mechanic to repair it while the car is rolling down the road! Similarly, we want to take your emotions off line while we make sure the gauges work well. We will do that by having you not FEEL each of several emotions, but rather, just LOOK at each one with objectivity. All but the first, shame, has been proven experimentally to exist at birth in mammals.

For individuals who need basic education about the role of common emotions as information, give or read to them the Client Handout about emotions. Ensure sufficient education about the function of emotions before proceeding with the following. Some can proceed directly, and some need much education.

"First, let everything unresolved in your system go into your (container) and remind yourself it's ok to feel safe when you are safe, with your (cue word from Step 2 – Resource state) (Pause long enough for them to do that). *"With your permission, I'll provide bilateral stimulation by tapping on your knees (or ankles), and you can close your eyes if you want and notice the pictures that come. We'll take one emotion at a time, and all you need to do is notice what that emotion LOOKS LIKE (not feels like), LOOKS LIKE... and watch with curiosity, to see if the picture is changing or staying the same. We'll let it process until it stops changing.*

Let me know if you start sliding in to the FELT sense of the emotion, because I can help you with that. You might see people or animals or something abstract or a color – it doesn't matter as long as you aren't feeling the emotion. If you see people, let it be people you don't know. If I hear you are seeing people from your life, such as your father, I'll say, "let it be a (father you don't know). If I hear you are seeing yourself in the scene, I'll have you watch someone you don't know in the scene instead. You can't flunk, and know that I'll help you if you have trouble. The people who have trouble often benefit the most when we finally get these emotions processed with objectivity. We'll start with one that is unique to humans, and that is shame, that we THINK might be a circuit, though it hasn't been proven, because it's hard to do experiments with people.

What does 'shame' look like? "(They report what they see) **"Notice that"** and **"What does shame look like now?"** It's okay if it transforms, is symbolic, a story, or shows a thwarted response. Do tapping sets until the picture stops changing. It may become positive, neutral, or just stop changing. Do for each emotion.

SHAME → RAGE → FEAR → PANIC/SAD → CARE → LUST → SEEKing → PLAY

Some may benefit from resetting learned emotions or the safety circuits themselves (fight, flight, freeze, connection, or the amygdala). Do not use this procedure with highly dissociative clients unless you are trained and experienced in treating dissociative disorders because system consent is required for these steps.

| PROBLEM | SOLUTION |

The client sees no image.	Usually is trying too hard, instead of just noticing, ask them to just allow an image, *"Just notice while I say what this emotion does, tell me when an image comes to mind, and just watch it, as it may change as we go."*
	Encourage them to *"Just notice,"* if needed explain that their stance is not one or trying or working or effort, but, *"noticing with curiosity,"* and use a light-hearted, nearly lyrical tone of voice to convey this curious spirit, as if *"easy does it."*
The image doesn't stop changing	Go to the next emotion, and come back to this one later. Go through them as many times as necessary, until it becomes neutral and stops changing
They have made many connections	Periodically bring them back to an image, saying, *"what does __ look like now?"* and continue until it stops changing.
They can't observe from a distance and slide into the felt sense	Teach them the difference between being in an emotion and looking at an emotion. If needed, use a "prosthesis" like a cartoon of an emotion. If they still slide in after two tries, they may need to reset *"what does fight look like"* and *"flight," "freeze,"* and *"connect,"* first, THEN return to the hardwired circuits. Or you can have them try to achieve objectivity by watching the emotion on a TV channel, or a black and white TV through the neighbor's window, or it can be cartoon people on TV, or even paper clip people that exhibit what the emotion looks like.
If they still can't observe an emotion from a distance	They may need more work using ego state therapy or somatic resourcing before they can do this step. Must see with objectivity, rather than "sliding in," to work
If they appear to slide in to the felt sense but don't tell you	They may be reenacting their first year of life, when they had no help with a difficult emotional task. In spite of having instructed them to tell you if they slide in, they might not, so you can remind them that you'll help them (e.g., with the objectivity devices suggested above).
If they feel as if they are failing because they are sliding in	Remind them that they cannot fail, saying, *"if this is hard for you then we are right where we need to be. Your life will be different after we get this cleared up, so let's take our time, and I'll help you. This time you aren't alone. You can't flunk this. I'm the only one here who can flunk and I have no intention of it."*
If they are tense or worried about the process	The author uses humor, and uses her poodle as a "straight man," as she does asides to the poodle, such as, *"I'm not sure how to convince (client's name) that she can't fail! I'll help her with this!"*
	"It's like being on the bank of a river. We want to watch the leaves float by, but not slide in…so hang onto that birch tree and just watch without sliding in."
	If all the client STILL cannot watch with objectivity, say, *"We just learned some important and useful information. You will benefit, I'm sure, from practice and taking a mindfulness class…."* However, the above procedures suffice with nearly everyone.
Dissociative Clients	Make sure introjects agree to allow this step. Some alters may be named after single emotions, so the task requires having part(s) of the system LOOK AT those emotions or, perhaps unavoidably, the emotionally-named alters with objectivity, and NOT have those alters executive or "looking through the eyes" during the processing.
	Ask them to imagine the scene, NOT from their own life, from a TV character they don't know, on a black and white TV screen. If that doesn't work, ask them to envision

When There Are No Words - Sandra Paulsen

	the vignette as a cartoon show on the TV. If that doesn't work, ask them to imagine that the cartoon show is about paper clip people. If they say they are STILL feeling it, express surprise that they are sliding in to the feelings of an imaginary paper clip person we just made up this minute. Use kind humor to keep them in present orientation.
	If that fails, ask them to imagine a vignette played out between circles and cubes of different colors. Eventually they'll be able to imagine with objectivity. If progress is slow, tell them that it is STILL progress and with time they'll get better and better at viewing with objectivity.
	Go back if needed and reexplain about the normal adaptive and mammalian functions of emotions. If you work with therapy animals, demonstrate the role of emotions in animals everyday life. There is no shame to having emotions – we all need them.
	Introjects will sometimes reenact traumatic memories in this step, by demonstrating that the work is impossible to achieve. If the therapist feels despaired or hopeless, or without solutions, consider that despair and hopelessness and no solutions is part of the client's story. In that case, ask them to imagine THAT vignette, paper clip people that no matter WHAT they try, they can't win, they can only despair. Ask them to watch with objectivity. Try again over time until this becomes more possible.

STEP 4 – TEMPORAL INTEGRATION

SAMPLE SCRIPT

"Now we'll review the time" (name an appropriately sized time period, e.g., 'second trimester,' 'your birth,' '12 to 15 months," to be sure that any trapped energy is released and conflicting information is cleared up. All you need to do is notice what happens, just like you're viewing a video." The following shows the natural sequence of processing that occurs for many people. It is included below to help the clinician be aware of phase completeness, and adaptive resolution. Incompleteness at one phase will result in inability to completely process subsequent phases. Begin at or before conception, working through gestation, birth and beyond.

Contain & Resource
- First, let everything that still needs to be reviewed, go into your (container) and say (resource cue word) *to return to feeling relaxed and ready* (or *"to help your amygdala"*). *(Pause until they accomplish that.)*

Review
- *"Now, just let your focus go to the time ('before you were born' or 'of your birth' or 'from (age) to (age), while I tap, to see if there's anything left that needs to be reviewed, released or repaired.* We don't emphasize verbalization, which may interfere with the felt sense of subtle shifts associated with right hemisphere processing in implicit memory."

Release
- If emotions loop, say, **"imagine what you need or need to do."** If physical sensations loop, say, **"Imagine it (the urge or physical sensation) happening, to completion."**

Relearn & Repair
- If the following doesn't happen spontaneously, say, *"Imagine getting everything you needed"*, or *"Imagine your parents being /doing what they couldn't be/do back then,"* or *"imagine everything being the way you needed it to be."*

Install
- *"Is there a positive statement (thought) that comes to mind when you focus on the* (time frame). If so, install that and say *"I'm also going to add some thoughts that came to me, so let whatever feels OK stick and whatever doesn't, just slide off."* Complete Standard Installation.

Body Scan & Close
- If session is complete, *"Hold the thought(s) with the (time frame),"* tap until they are in a resourced state. Whether complete or not, say *"Let everything else that still needs to be reviewed, go into* (container), **and say** (resource cue word). *We'll continue at our next session"*

REVIEW/REPAIR	TROUBLE SHOOTING DESENSITIZATION OF IMPLICIT MEMORIES
If they don't believe they can remember that early	Reassure that although we don't have explicit memories or "picture memories" from very early life, we seem to be able to know in our bodies more than we think we can, just by listening to the body and to the "dust bunnies" that emerge in the felt sense.
If the client gets nothing	They might be trying too hard, might be expecting pictures or narrative (which rarely comes), in which case they need instruction that if anything is noticeable it might be subtle "dust bunnies" without much shape or form, nuances of emotion, symbolic images, or body sensation.
	They might be alexythymic, unable to identify that they are feeling or what they are feeling, or find words for what they are feeling.
	They might be somatically dissociated, in which case they may need somatic therapy prior to doing ET work, though some can be more quickly trained than others to drop down into the felt sense of the body.
To attain greater specificity	The therapist might say, *"Babies of this age are often working on x, y and z milestones. How might that have gone in your family?"*
If the therapist picks up sensation in her/his mirror neurons that isn't the therapists own feelings	Consider whether it might be the patients unacknowledged feelings that the therapist is discerning. After seeing if conventional methods will enable processing to occur, the therapist might say, for example, *"Is there something in the throat?"* or *"Is there some hurt in the heart space?"* If the client denies such feelings or sensations, they win, because they are the world's authority in how they feel. Often however, the client often says, "Now that you mention it, yes." and the client then is able to process.
If the therapist is intuitive	If you get pictures or words and are familiar with the appropriate, safe and ethical use of clinical intuition, and only if the processing is stuck, s/he might say, *"any idea why I might be seeing (hearing) x?"*
If the client is projecting onto the therapist	If the client says, "I can't do this, I'm failing. You're getting impatient with me, aren't you!" but the therapist is not impatient, the therapist might say, "I'm wondering if people getting impatient is part of Baby's story. Just notice that possibility."
Once processing resumes	Process enough that the client has a felt sense of their own babyhood in the time frame being processed. It may not spontaneous resolve as often as standard EMDR.
If there is no spontaneous shift	Don't wait forever. Instead ask, *"What would you have needed to have a different outcome?"* or *"What would you have needed to have this be on YOUR terms?"*
If it continues to loop	Consider that a parental introject is interfering by placing the parent's point of view above the baby's, which is what was learned. Educate that this isn't the parent's time, this is baby's time to have their story heard. Even non-dissociative clients may need orientation and appreciation of the survival function of the parental introject.
If future memories intrude	Take the theme from the later memory and see if it applies to the time period being processed, and put the later memory back into containment.

When There Are No Words - Sandra Paulsen

If the repair doesn't work	Consider that the time segment is too large and break it down further, or that some earlier disturbance wasn't fully "caught and released." Check the work repeatedly.
If the repair is rejected	If they are trying to imagine their own parents improved, suggest they use imaginary, ideal or good-enough parents instead. We aren't limited by the laws of physics.
	If they say, "but that's not what really happened," reassure them that we aren't pretending bad stuff didn't happen. But the brain has been waiting for the biochemical marinade to provide what they have longed for all these years, even imaginarily.
Dissociative Clients	Honchos/perpetrator introjects need to first give their permission for the therapist to "help the baby," be reassured they will benefit too, because they were also hurt kids, and asked to hold their later memories aside.
	It is surprising how often even hostile alters will allow the baby to be helped.
	Use small time frames. Quit while you are ahead – don't overdo.
	When it loops, ask, *"who can help me understand what's happening?"* or *"does someone have a concern? I don't want to ignore your concerns, you're had quite enough of that."*
	Often introjects that were oriented to present person, place and time LAST week are disoriented this week, so gently reorient them. Often useful to have them reach to their height on the doorframe to remind of present adulthood to maintain dual attention awareness.
Enactments	While processing very early trauma in dissociative clients, the material is under considerable pressure because it is wordless, unconscious and often horrific. That pressure causes the dynamics to manifest in the office in the relationship field. Consider that anything untoward or bewildering in the office or between sessions is part of the story, telling itself non-verbally. Puzzle gently and respectfully and be willing to be wrong. *"I see that you are angry at me, and maybe I have done something in present time to be angry about, if so, I'm sorry, please fill me in. Or, I wonder if someone being angry is part of the baby's story that we need to hear, can anyone fill me in?"*

Made in the USA
Middletown, DE
13 April 2025

When There Are No Words

Repairing Early Trauma and Neglect
From the Attachment Period with EMDR Therapy

When There Are No Words

Repairing Early Trauma and Neglect From the Attachment Period with EMDR Therapy

Written and Illustrated by Sandra Paulsen, Ph.D.

Contributing Author Katie O'Shea, M.S.

A Bainbridge Institute for Integrative Psychology Publication

Bainbridge Island, Washington

Copyright © 2017 Sandra Paulsen

All rights reserved.

No part of this publication may be reproduced, stored to a retrieval system, or transmitted in any form or by any means, electronic, mechanical, photocopying, recording, or otherwise, without the prior permission of Sandra Paulsen.

A Bainbridge Institute for Integrative Psychology Publication

9050 Battle Point Dr, NE, Bainbridge Island, WA 98110

Title ID: 5251839
ISBN-13: 978-1507507193

The author and the publisher of this work have made every effort to use sources believed to be reliable to provide information that is accurate and compatible with the standards generally accepted at the time of publication. The author and publisher shall not be liable for any special, consequential, or exemplary damages resulting, in whole or in part, from the readers' use of, or reliance on, the information contained in this book. The publisher has no responsibility for the persistence or accuracy of URLs for external or third party internet websites referred to in this publication and does not guarantee that any content on such websites is, or will remain, accurate or appropriate.

Table of Contents

	List of Illustrations	Iv
	Acknowledgements	X
1	Introduction: Why Is the Early Trauma Approach Necessary	1
2	A Few Points from the Neurobiology of Affect, Trauma and Attachment	9
3	Approaches to Integration	19
4	Introduction to the Preparation for Trauma Processing	23
5	Preparation in Complex Cases: Ego State Maneuvers and More	27
6	Technical EMDR Therapy Modifications within the Early Trauma Approach	39
7	Preparation—Containment	45
8	Preparation—Ventral Vagal Resourcing	55
9	About the Affective Circuits	67
10	The Neurobiology of Resetting Affective Circuits	85
11	Resetting the Affective Circuits - the Procedure	91
	How To: The Procedures for Resetting the Affective Circuits	99
	Troubleshooting: What to Do When Good Circuits Go Bad	106
	Case Examples: Resetting the Affective Circuits	111
12	Temporaral Integration: Introductory Concepts	117
	Recap of Preparation for Temporal Integration	117
	Basic Principles of Attachment Experience	119
	A Brief History of Approaches to Integration	121
13	Temporal Integration: Basic Procedures	135
	EMDR Therapy Phase III – Targeting	136
14	Advanced Temporal Integration for Dissociative Clients	151
	Basic Concepts re: Temporal Integration with Dissociative Client	152
	Assess the Self-System: Assessing the Degree of Dissociation, Affect and Soma Tolerance	159
	Engage the Self-System: Ego State Preparations for Temporal Integration in Dissociation	160
	Select a Target: Targeting in Temporal Integration for Dissociative and Complex Clients	164
	Desensitize the Time Frame: Desensitization in Temporal Integration with Dissociative Clients	165
	Interweave if Stuck: Ego State Interweaves in Stuck Processing in Temporal Integration for Dissociative Clients	166

	Repair: Getting to Adaptive Resolution and Repair with Dissociative Clients	172
	Close the Session: Closure Procedure for Incomplete Processing with Dissociative Clients	175
15	Final Remarks	181
	References	193
	Appendices	191
A	Working in the Intensive Format	191
B	The Mechanics	193
C	Working with Perpetrator Introjects to Reduce Loyalty to the Aggressor	197
D	Containment for Closing Sessions with Complex or Dissociative Clients	201
E	Original Worksheets by O'Shea and Paulsen	205
F	Modified Worksheets by Paulsen	213
	Step 1 – Containing Elements of the Memory	201
	Step 2 – Tuck in the Parts	201
	Step 3 – Problem Solving	202